Gales

Modern Economic and Social History Series

General Editor: Derek H. Aldcroft

Titles in this series include:

Gales

A Study in Brewing, Business and Family History

BARRY STAPLETON and
JAMES H. THOMAS

Ashgate

Aldershot • Burlington USA • Singapore • Sydney

Published by
Ashgate Publishing Limited
Gower House
Croft Road
Aldershot
Hants GU11 3HR
England

Ashgate Publishing Company
131 Main Street
Burlington
Vermont 05401–5600
USA

Ashgate website: http://www.ashgate.com

British Library Cataloguing in Publication Data

Stapleton, Barry
  Gales: A Study in Brewing, Business and Family History.
  (Modern Economic and Social History)
  1. George Gale & Co. Ltd—History. 2. Breweries—England—
  Horndean—History. 3. Brewing industry—Great Britain—
  History.
  I. Title. II. Thomas, James H. (James Harry), 1947– .
  338.4'7'66342'094227

Library of Congress Cataloging-in-Publication Data

Stapleton, Barry.
  Gales: a study in brewing, business and family history/Barry Stapleton
  and James H. Thomas.
    (Modern Economic and Social History)
  Includes bibliographical references and index.
  ISBN 0–7546–0146–3 (hb)
  1. Gales Brewery—History. 2. Gale family. 3. Bowyer family.
  4. Brewing industry—Great Britain—History. 5. Industrialists—Great
  Britain—Biography. I. Thomas, James H., 1947– . II. Title. III. Series.
  HD9397.G72G357   2000
  338.7'6633'0941—dc21
                                          99–53990
                                             CIP

ISBN 0 7546 0146 3

This book is printed on acid free paper

Typeset in Sabon by Manton Typesetters, Louth, Lincolnshire and printed in Great Britain by MPG Books Limited, Bodmin, Cornwall.

Contents

Modern Economic and Social History Series
General Editor's Preface

Economic and social history has been a flourishing subject of scholarly study during recent decades. Not only has the volume of literature increased enormously but the range of interest in time, space and subject matter has broadened considerably so that today there are many sub-branches of the subject which have developed considerable status in their own right.

One of the aims of this new series is to encourage the publication of scholarly monographs on any aspect of modern economic and social history. The geographical coverage is world-wide and contributions on non-British themes will be especially welcome. While emphasis will be placed on works embodying original research, it is also intended that the series should provide the opportunity to publish studies of a more general and thematic nature which offer a reappraisal or critical analysis of major issues of debate.

Derek H. Aldcroft

Manchester Metropolitan University

List of figures

List of tables

Foreword

Eight years after George Gale first registered his company and a century ago as I write, my grandfather brought the Bowyers into the brewery's history. Thereafter, the two families worked together to see it successfully through to our 150th Anniversary in 1997. Read on and you will see how this came about.

I first met the authors not long after becoming a full-time Director in 1980. James and Barry, with others, conducted an annual postgraduate Diploma course in English Local History at Portsmouth Polytechnic, now the University, and the student with the best overall performance received the Gale Prize, a sum of money covering the course fee. At the prize presentation in 1982, I mentioned that we were looking for someone to write our own history. As you can see they volunteered to do so in their spare time, little realising the challenge of the undertaking on top of their university duties. Work began the following year with the assembly of the company archives, a task which continued almost throughout as more and more evidence was unearthed. As a happy consequence, they have been able to bring the history right up to date and in time for the 1997 celebrations.

I am proud to introduce you to this story of the family business at a momentous time for all of us here at Horndean. My thanks to the many who have contributed, and most particularly to Barry and James for their hard work in researching and recording our progress over the years with humour, skill and precision. I am confident that this book will earn its rightful place amongst the foremost of brewery histories. I also commend it to those who will enjoy sharing our perspective of a small Hampshire village over the last 150 years.

George Bowyer
Chairman

To all who have worked for George Gale and Company,
1847–1997

Acknowledgements

In any book that has a long period of gestation it is likely that many people will have provided some assistance or information to the author. This volume is no exception. Work began on listing the known Gale archives in 1983, and since then two other sets of documents have been discovered and have consequently lengthened the process of investigation and analysis. However, hopefully, not only has this ensured a better book, but it has also allowed it to be published in celebration of the 150th anniversary of the acquisition of the *Ship and Bell* inn by Richard Gale.

Foremost in any list of acknowledgements would have to be those past and present employees of Gales who have willingly shared their knowledge and experiences with us. They remain too many to mention individually, but all are recognised in the dedication. Outside the brewery there are others who need to be acknowledged, particularly Major William Ladds and Miss Doreen Carlos Perkins, both of whom provided invaluable information about George Alexander Gale and Herbert Frederick Bowyer respectively, Paget Bowyer for the early history of the Bowyer family and Philip Eley. We have also benefited from the assistance of the following: Barclays Bank, Commercial Road, Portsmouth; Guildford Muniment Room; Guildhall Library, London, especially Stephen Freeth and Philippa White; Hampshire Record Office; Oriental and India Office Collection; Portsmouth City Records Office, especially Paul Raymond; Public Record Office, London; Portsmouth Central Library, especially Alan King and staff of the Local History Collection; Whitbread Archive, London, especially Nick Redman; Brewers and Licensed Retailers Association, especially Janet Witheridge. To all we offer our grateful thanks, as we do for assistance with typing to Paula Heiron. For any errors which may remain we alone are responsible.

For permission to reproduce illustrations we are grateful to Hampshire Record Office (Fig. 2), Ordnance Survey (Fig. 3), Major W. R. N. Ladds (Fig. 4), Group Captain R. G. Bowyer (Figs 7, 8 and 10) and George Gale and Co. Ltd for the remainder.

Abbreviations

AR	*Annual Register*
BLRA	Brewers and Licensed Retailers Association
BPP	*British Parliamentary Papers*
EN	*Evening News*
ESRO	East Sussex Record Office
GL	Guildhall Library, London
GM	*Gentleman's Magazine*
GMR	Guildford Muniment Room
HC	*Hampshire Chronicle*
HFC	*Hampshire Field Club*
HRO	Hampshire Record Office
HT	*Hampshire Telegraph*
LG	*London Gazette*
PCRO	Portsmouth City Records Office
PRO	Public Record Office
PT	*Portsmouth Times*
SRO	Surrey Record Office, Kingston upon Thames

A Note on currency

All references to money have been in pre-decimal coinage (£ s. d.). Under this arrangement, a £ contained 20 shillings and each shilling 12d. Hence 240d./£ became 100p/£ on conversion to decimal coinage.

It is expected that the Gales Archive will be transferred to Portsmouth City Records Office in early 2000.

Introduction

Much historical writing, especially mainstream political and economic history, is concerned with successes and failures. Battles, wars and revolutions – political or economic – are won or lost. Generals, politicians, diplomats and entrepreneurs succeed or fail. Nations, regions or empires rise and fall. Curiously, however, business history is different – it seldom has this balance. Businesses, of course, do succeed or fail, but failed enterprises are rarely, if ever, written about. Clearly, when a business fails it ceases to exist and in the same way that the business disappears, so usually does its records and, consequently, its history. In any case, readers are less interested in the history of companies that failed than those that are successes and continue to trade and remain a source of employment. It is good to be associated with a successful company and, similarly, nobody wishes to be identified with a failed undertaking. Thus, business history tends to be concentrated on successful enterprises, not only because they exist, but also because such companies, having been trading for several generations, have boards of directors with a desire to know about their origins and development.

This history of George Gale and Company is no exception. Gales remains one of the few family breweries still in existence in England out of the many hundreds that traded in the nineteenth century. Begun by the acquisition of the Horndean *Ship and Bell* inn in 1847, Gales is still a thriving and forward-looking business 150 years later. This book sets out to indicate how the Horndean Brewery survived the many changes and vicissitudes of the British brewing industry since 1847.

The first half-century, the era of George Alexander Gale, was the most difficult to resurrect from the past. Virtually no company records survive from this period and certainly none dealing with the output of the brewery or those who worked at it. It seems likely that when G. A. Gale sold the brewery in 1896 either he took most of the existing records with him or they were destroyed. Whatever the case, most of the nineteenth-century information about the business has had to be gleaned from a variety of other, mostly indirect, sources.

However, following the purchase of the brewery by H. F. Bowyer in 1896 the records become more prolific with statistics for output being continuous. Even so, records relating to the workforce were not retained. Thus little remains known of this important aspect of the company's structure. Only for recent years are we sure of the size of Gales' labour force.

Whilst, for the first half of the twentieth century, the British brewing industry was in decline Gales was an exception, the company's output growing steadily. However, after the Second World War, Gales was not to escape the problems of the brewing industry as a whole and began to experience the fluctuations which seemed inherent in the British economy in the second half of the twentieth century.

To many of our colleagues it would seem that writing the history of a brewery is an ideal and highly desirable occupation bringing the authors close to a favourite item of consumption. Although proximity to Gales ales may be regarded as a fringe benefit, what has been for us the most abiding memory from the long gestation period of this book is the unfailing kindness and generous assistance with personal knowledge of the past of many people at the Horndean Brewery who have waited patiently for this final product.

Foremost among those who have offered help and encouragement has been the Chairman of Gales Group, Captain George Bowyer. But we have also been the beneficiaries of assistance from: Managing Director, Nigel Atkinson; Company Secretary, Robin Heathcote; Head Brewer, Derek Lowe; Marketing Manager, Derek Beaves; and Trade Manager, George Turner. Former employees must also not be forgotten for, in our early years of research, they gave us much assistance. Notable among these were former Head Brewer, the late Ted Argyle, and the late Major Walter Gale, as well as Richard Gale, Clive Jones and Moira Chambers. Above all, we remember with gratitude the always friendly reception we received at the Horndean Brewery and the civilised research facilities provided in the board room where we spent much time working through Gales' records. There can be few places which could have made us feel so welcome a part of their business.

CHAPTER ONE

The British brewing industry over two centuries: an outline

The 150 years since the Industrial Revolution of the late eighteenth and early nineteenth centuries have seen major changes in all walks of British life – political, religious, demographic, economic and social. Transformations have occurred in agriculture, industry, finance, trade and transport, and continue at an increasingly accelerating rate. Thus, Britain's major industries both during and after the Industrial Revolution coal, iron and steel, shipbuilding and textiles are much less substantial sectors of the national economy of the late twentieth century.

Despite being subjected to significant change, the British brewing industry arguably has survived the last century and a half more successfully than most industries. Cynics might suggest that this is because it was a major source of income for the exchequers of successive governments. However, that would not explain the varied structure of the industry containing huge conglomerate multinational, national, regional and local breweries, and an explanation is necessary.

In the middle of the eighteenth century the industry consisted of some 50,000 brewing victuallers, essentially publicans who brewed their own ale for purely local consumption. During the next half century the first of the changes which were to affect the structure of the brewing industry was to result in this number being more than halved.[1] This followed from the development, in the second half of the eighteenth century, of a beer which had a longer life and became more mellow as a result of higher hop content. Bitter, dark and heavily hopped, porter was a beer that could be stored for months and improved in flavour in the process. This clearly had advantages for those who could afford to brew on a larger scale and thus store large quantities for future consumption. Those who benefited greatly were the London brewers such as Meux Reid, who opened up a gigantic container in 1799, Thrale (later Barclay Perkins), Truman and Whitbread. As London by 1750 contained more than one in ten of England's population, some three quarters of a million people,[2] there was a ready market for the larger-scale production that porter allowed and the four big brewers accounted for over 500,000 barrels between them before the end of the century.[3] Because strong porter had to be kept maturing, in order to clear and improve the beer, for up to nine months before it could be distributed for consumption, it tied up considerable amounts of capital for long periods. Thus, the lengthy process of production discriminated in favour of larger and wealthier, rather than smaller, brewers. As a result, considerable numbers of publicans lost their brewing function.

Away from the metropolitan area, however, brewers still tended to make lighter ales and in the first half of the nineteenth century the consumption of a milder, though still quite bitter and strong, paler beer began to take precedence. This development of a milder pale brew, however, was not confined to the provinces, since in 1807 the newly built Albion Brewery at Mile End Road, Bethnal Green, was advertised in search of a tenant, as 'A New compact Ale and Pale Beer Brewery', indicating that any prospective tenant would expect to have facilities for brewing pale ale.[4] This milder beer meant that the final brew could be distributed much earlier, thus brewers obtained quicker returns on invested capital.[5] As a consequence, smaller provincial and metropolitan brewers were better able to compete in this growing market, a position enhanced by the abolition of excise duty of 10s a barrel by the Beer Act of 1830, since smaller brewers were affected more seriously by excise duties than larger ones because of the capital absorbed by duty payments. As the Act also allowed any ratepayer, on payment of 2 guineas to excise officials, to obtain a licence to establish a beerhouse, a substantial increase in retail outlets was created. By 1838 almost 46,000 beerhouses had been added to the 51,000 existing licensed premises in England.[6] Generally established outside the tied house system of the large commercial brewers, the beerhouses were more likely to assist the growth of regional and provincial common brewers.

Even so, it was the development of the railway network which resulted in the real expansion of pale ale consumption in the 1840s and 1850s, with Burton upon Trent emerging as a major centre of production, its beer brewed with the local hard, gypsum flavoured water. Initially brewed for export to British settlements in India, the linking of Burton to Derby by rail in 1839 was to prove a turning-point in the demand for Burton pale ales in the home market. Bass, the prominent Burton brewer, increased output from 10,000 barrels in 1831 to 60,000 in 1847, 130,000 by 1853, 400,000 in 1863 and 900,000 in 1876. Not surprisingly, with Burton brewers growing on this scale, some of the leading London brewers established branches in Burton – Ind Coope (1858), Charrington (1871), Truman, Hanbury and Buxton (1873) and Mann, Crossman and Paulin (1875) – indicating that not only had they recognised that pale ale had replaced porter as Britain's major beer, but also that Burton had emerged as a substantial rival to London.[7] Similarly, Dublin, especially with the growth of Guinness's brewery (by 1876 it produced nearly 800,000 barrels a year and became the largest producer in the brewing industry by the 1880s), was another important rival to London. Arthur Guinness Son and Co. dominated the Irish market as well as carrying on a secondary trade to England, especially in their stout. By 1900 they sold more than any other British beer producer and had assets of more than £6 million. Even so, Guinness were unique among nineteenth-century brewers, neither producing pale ales nor owning tied public houses in England. Most other London and provincial brewers had been acquiring houses throughout much of the century and especially in its last 15 years when some £188 million public share capital was raised by 353 companies and all large companies, with the exception of Guinness, participated in the purchase of houses.[8]

The largest of these pale ale breweries were located in Burton upon Trent. Led by Bass, whose output reached 1.5 million barrels in the 1880s, Allsopp, whose output peaked at 900,000 in 1876, and Worthington, they were joined by the major London breweries in the 1870s. Below these giants of the industry came those breweries producing between 100,000 and 600,000 barrels a year. In London these were Truman, Hanbury and Buxton, Watneys, Combes, Reids and Barclay Perkins, and in the provinces William Younger of Edinburgh, Ind Coope of Romford, Walker's of Warrington and Tetley of Leeds each producing some 300,000 to 400,000 barrels a year. The majority of breweries were smaller provincial firms with less than 100,000 barrels a year output. Greene of Bury St Edmunds, Samuel Smith of Tadcaster and Greenall Whitley of St Helens were the largest of this group, but the majority were smaller like Gales of Horndean in Hampshire with an output of about 10,000 barrels a year.[9]

However, the nineteenth-century growth of large-scale brewing and its associated tied house ownership, inevitably had its effect both on the numbers of licensed victuallers who brewed their own beer and on beerhouse keepers, especially after 1870. In the 60 years between 1841 and 1900 brewing licensed victuallers declined in number by nearly 90 per cent from 27,000 to less than 3,000. Beerhouse keepers fared similarly losing just over 90 per cent of their number from over 16,000 to only 1,582. However, commercial common brewers who numbered 2,258 in 1841 had fallen only to 2,175 in 1890, less than 4 per cent (see Table 1.1). Nevertheless, the 1890s saw increasing amalgamations and take-overs; thus by 1901 their numbers had declined to 1,520, a loss of almost one third (32 per cent). Small-scale commercial brewers producing up to 10,000 barrels a year still formed the majority of producers – 911 (60 per cent). Even so, their total output was probably less than that of each of the ten largest British brewing companies.[10]

Much of the small-scale brewers output in the nineteenth century had traditionally been for the free trade, especially private customers, even

Table 1.1 Common brewers and brewing victuallers and beerhouse
keepers, 1841–1900

Year	Common brewers	Licensed victuallers	Beerhouse keepers	Total
1841	2,455	27,125	16,376	45,986
1850	2,432	26,029	13,448	41,909
1860	2,431	24,704	12,283	39,418
1870	2,591	20,216	9,735	32,542
1880	2,595	12,417	6,157	21,169
1890	2,290	6,349	3,319	11,958
1900	1,836	2,887	1,582	6,305

Source: Gourvish and Wilson (1994), p. 68. Figures are for England, Scotland and Wales.

though the brewers steadily acquired tied houses.[11] But there is little doubt that from the 1880s there was an increased development of the tied trade as brewers had to purchase properties to protect their interests, not only from rival concerns locally but also from national predators. By 1886, 75 per cent of houses were owned by breweries. This resulted in local houses becoming scarcer and breweries having to look further afield for acquisitions, invariably at higher prices. Thus most companies had property values which represented over 40 per cent of their total capital.[12]

Assisting the move towards maintaining market shares by increased property ownership were national trends in beer-drinking. Whereas from 1850 to 1880 consumption of beer per head rose from 21 to 33 gallons, in the 1880s it fell along with national output.[13] An economic depression and the growth of competing choices for consumers' expenditure such as food, clothing, furniture and leisure, coincided with the decline in beer consumption. Social and economic changes probably did more to reduce beer-drinking than the Temperance movement or the Liberal government after 1905, especially since, after a minor recovery in the 1890s, the early twentieth century saw consumption begin to fall again.[14] By the outbreak of the First World War, consumption had fallen to the levels of the 1860s (even though real wages were much higher) and brewers, not surprisingly, continued their policy of vertical integration, so that by 1913 it has been estimated that 95 per cent of licensed properties were in their hands.[15] As brewers completed this acquisitive process so, simultaneously, came the growth of bottled beer sales for home consumption, increasingly retailed through off-licences.

The popularity of public houses was beginning to decline along with brewers' profits. Their difficulties were exacerbated by the Temperance movement and the increasing refusal of licences by magistrates, without compensation. In England 240 licences were refused in 1903.

The following year a new licensing Act stated that magistrates could only close unsafe structures or houses known to be centres of undesirable conduct. Otherwise, compensation had to be paid. The Temperance movement and the Liberal party were enraged as the size of the compensation fund would limit the pace of closure. However, the arrival of a Liberal government saw licence duty raised in 1910 resulting in depressed brewery shares.[16] The process of concentration that had occurred in the late nineteenth century with the spate of amalgamations and absorptions was now felt in production, with breweries being closed and output concentrated in fewer centres.

Although the brewing industry regarded the pre-1914 period as difficult, what was to follow was much worse. War brought with it increasing government regulation. The establishment of the Central Control Board led to the imposition of a reduced gravity beer and restricted output of barley and hops to reduce the amount of land used in their cultivation. Other food crops could then be grown, so reducing imports and saving on shipping space. Shorter licensing hours were also introduced. Not surprisingly, these measures led to higher brewing costs and reinforced the trends of declining output and consumption. The latter trend was enhanced by the increased tax burden on beer – wartime duties rising by 430 per cent in real terms – ensuring that a weaker and lower-quality beer was more expensive. In 1917 further restrictions on output were introduced resulting in under 13 million barrels being produced in 1918 compared to the pre-war figure in 1913 of over 36 million barrels.[17]

There was to be no respite for the industry immediately after the war. Control over hop-growing was continued and beer duty was raised in the first two post-war budgets, being quadrupled after 1918. In 1922, beer was double the pre-war price at 7 pence per pint, almost 4 pence of this being duty. As this happened at a time when some workers' wages were cut in money terms, beer was relatively overpriced. Consumption fell and continued to do so throughout the inter-war period. Thus, by 1930–34 consumption was 52 per cent lower than it had been in 1910–14. National beer output fell by the same amount to levels which brewers would have regarded as economically unsustainable before 1914.[18]

The most important causal factor of these trends was social change. The proportion of working-class expenditure on alcohol was more than halved from about 15 per cent in the 1870s to 6.5 per cent in 1938.[19] Consumer horizons were broadening and brewers had to compete not only with increasing household expenditure, but also with widening leisure opportunities. Radios, cinemas, teashops, coffee bars, ice-cream parlours, spectator and participatory sports all increasingly consumed proportions of working-class incomes. These family-based activities meant that cinemas or football grounds were just as likely venues for working-class fathers as the pub. A secondary factor in the 1930s was the high level of unemployment which clearly exacerbated the brewing industry's position.

The fall of more than half in national demand for beer resulted in many breweries having unused capacity. Not surprisingly, therefore, the inter-war period saw an increase in mergers and acquisitions. In 1910 there were almost 4,500 breweries in Britain. A decade later there were less than 2,900 and by 1930 just over 1,400 remained. By 1939 only 840 had survived. In just 30 years 80 per cent of Britain's breweries had vanished,[20] representing a considerable concentration of resources into fewer locations. Similarly, the number of companies engaged in brewing was reduced by over half from 941 to 428 in the same 30 years, indicating the scale of merger and acquisition activity.[21] Major regional breweries such as Greene King in East Anglia, Simonds in Reading, Strongs of Romsey and Brickwoods in Portsmouth emerged.[22] Some breweries such as Barclay Perkins, Watney Combe Reid and Whitbread in London, and Peter Walker of Warrington, Greene King of Bury St Edmunds and Flowers of Stratford-upon-Avon in the provinces, responded by improving their public houses. In the eight years between 1922 and 1930 brewers spent nearly £21 million on 20,000 pubs at a time when their returns were depressed. Even so, there were five companies which spent less than £15,000 in three and a half years.[23]

Those companies which had pursued an improvement policy for their houses were to recognise the prudence of their actions with the outbreak of the Second World War in 1939. During the war period and after, building licensing regulations prevented much progress before the mid-1950s.[24] Even so, wartime controls over the industry were very different from those in the First World War. As beer consumption had declined in the inter-war period so had drunkenness and reported incidences of it during the war from 12.8 per thousand population in 1939 to 5.0 in 1946.[25] Thus, it was possible for beer-drinking to be considered beneficial to the war effort. Nevertheless, there were substantial problems for brewers. Beer duty was doubled at the outbreak of war and increased on four occasions between 1940 and 1944, when it was nearly 500 per cent above the pre-war level. Post-war austerity saw the duty rise further in 1947 and 1948 until it was 645 per cent higher than before the war (339 per cent in real terms).[26] Raw material prices also rose. The price of barley had to be fixed by the government in early

1942 at 27s. 6d. per hundredweight. Quotas were placed on malt, sugar and hops, and petrol was rationed resulting in an increased use of horse drays. In addition, landlords had to take their beers from the nearest brewery in order to save fuel and brewers thus resorted to exchanging their beers. Shortages of casks and bottles paralleled those of raw materials. Women had to be increasingly employed as male labour was disrupted by enlistment.

However, unemployment, the scourge of the inter-war period, was brought to an end by the war, resulting in both rising wages and rising demand. But rationing meant there were limitations on the opportunities for spending, thus the public house became once more a centre for leisure. As a consequence, unlike in the First World War, beer output rose by 32 per cent, despite it being weaker in strength. Output in 1945 was higher than in any year since 1914.[27]

Hence, confounding all expectations, the Second World War, unlike the First World War, witnessed a period of recovery for the British brewing industry, and in the days of victory celebrations in 1945 optimism was high. Unfortunately, it was to prove all too temporary a recovery for the industry, as two years of stagnation were followed by 13 of declining output. Demand fell year on year from 1948 to 1958, when output at only 23.8 million barrels was 17 per cent below the level it had reached at the end of the war.[28] No doubt the continuation of wartime restrictions, rationing and high beer duties were contributory factors. Even though beer duty fell from its peak in 1949, it was still three and a half times higher than its pre-war level at the new low of 1960.

Once again, however, it was mainly social change, in the form of widening personal attitudes and tastes, which caused the decline. A major growth of television viewing occurred in the post-war years, particularly in the Coronation year of 1953, reducing the popularity of the public house. At the same time as wartime restrictions were eventually eased, more was spent on food, clothing, household goods and houses, not the least in a demonstration that the years of austerity were over. Nevertheless, notwithstanding the fall in demand and output which was of concern to the more forward-looking brewers, most were not worried by the financial results. Despite the decline, average profits and dividends were increased, on the whole, by about 50 per cent between 1939–45 and 1951–55.[29]

An important cause of this profitability was the continued concentration in the industry. The 840 surviving breweries from the decimation of the inter-war years were reduced to 680 by the end of the war. No doubt some smaller companies decided to close when faced with the prospect of wartime restrictions, but by 1955 only 460 survived, the

further reduction being very much the result of acquisitions by both
national and regional brewing companies. Similarly, the number of
brewing companies fell from 428 in 1939 to 305 in 1954.[30] Yet this
decline in the number of breweries and brewing companies in the post-
war period was to be completely overshadowed by what took place in
the industry between 1955 and 1980. Described as a period of merger
mania it saw the number of breweries fall from 460 in 1955 to 358 in
1960, 220 in 1968 and 142 in 1980. Brewing companies declined from
305 in 1954 to 247 in 1960, 117 in 1968 and only 81 in 1980. The
years 1959–61 were those which saw the greatest activity with 75
mergers, some 46 per cent of the total of 164 between 1958 and 1972.[31]
Most of the mergers, being horizontal in nature, led to increasing
concentration.

In 1955 ten mergers occurred, the most significant of which was
Courage with Barclay Perkins to form Courage and Barclay. A further
19 took place in 1956 and ten more in 1957, including Watney Combe
Reid's merger with Mann, Crossman and Paulin. The following year 24
mergers included Ind Coope with Taylor Walker, before the peak of
activity was reached in 1960 with 28 acquisitions, including Courage
and Barclay with H. and G. Simonds and the merger of Hope and
Anchor, Hammonds United of Bradford and John Jeffrey of Edinburgh
to form Northern Breweries, which in the same year, significantly,
became United Breweries. Also in 1960 Scottish Breweries linked with
Newcastle Breweries to form Scottish and Newcastle. In 1961 acquisitions numbered 21, including Whitbread and Tennant Bros, Ind Coope,
Tetley Walker and Ansells to be renamed Allied Breweries in 1962, and
Bass's merger with Mitchells and Butlers. This merger activity resulted
in the emergence of the 'Big Six' – Allied Breweries, which in 1978
became Allied-Lyons on the merger with J. Lyons, a non-brewing com-
pany; Bass Charrington, the product of a merger in 1967 of Bass
Mitchells and Butlers and Charrington United; Courage, Barclay and
Simonds; Scottish and Newcastle; Watney Mann, and Whitbread. With
Guinness, these six were to dominate British brewing for 30 years,
accounting for 80 per cent of UK beer production in 1972.[32] All the Big
Six continued the process of merger throughout the 1960s and 1970s,
Whitbread, for instance, being involved in 23 between 1961 and 1971.[33]
However, along with Allied's merger with Lyons came two other signifi-
cant similar developments. In 1971 Grand Metropolitan Hotels took
over Truman Hanbury and Buxton followed by Watney Mann the next
year to create Watney Grand Met. Also in 1972 Imperial Tobacco
Group acquired Courage, Barclay and Simonds to form Courage Imperial. These were conglomerate mergers linking large brewing companies
with other sectors of the leisure industry, particularly the provision of

food, a trend which many of the smaller brewing companies would have to follow if they were to survive. They had to become more than just production companies for beer.

Since the merger and take-over activity was international as well as national, the reasons for it are varied. A rising stock market, the benefits of economies of scale, the need to retain or expand market shares – all could have played a part. However, brewing mergers began earlier than in most other industries and they may have had something to do with the traditionalist, paternalistic, yet often relaxed style of family management that many of the British brewing companies followed and that frequently resulted in their assets, particularly property, being seriously undervalued. Once the post-war building restrictions were lifted in 1954 and a property boom began, so brewing companies' properties were even more valuable. Breweries with many public houses in city centre sites became prime targets.

The two entrepreneurs central to the development of large-scale brewing were E. P. (Eddie) Taylor and Charles Clore. Taylor, a successful Canadian brewer, having turned his family's Ontario brewery into the combine Canadian Breweries and developed Carling Black Label lager, took a stake in Hope and Anchor Breweries of Sheffield, having signed a trading agreement with them in 1952. However, demand for lager in Britain was relatively small in the 1950s and, Hope and Anchor having less than 200 houses, Taylor was disappointed with lager sales. Recognising the tied house system was the block to greater sales, he realised that acquiring breweries and their houses was the key to a larger market. By 1959 Taylor was in a position to use Hope and Anchor to create a sizeable combine. In February 1960 Northern Breweries was created. During 1960 a further five Scottish brewing companies were added to the combine and in October the name was changed to United Breweries. Further acquisitions were made in Northern Ireland and Wales in the same year. In response to Taylor's activities, Scottish Breweries joined Newcastle to form one of the 'Big Six', Scottish and Newcastle. There was little doubt that Taylor caused alarm among Britain's provincial brewers, especially by his hostile bid for Bristol brewery, Georges, in 1961. This action brought a counter-bid from Courage, Barclay and Simonds, Courage being keen to keep Taylor out of the South. Georges' shareholders accepted the Courage offer. But, probably in reaction to Taylor's activities, Ind Coope, Tetley Walker and Ansells merged to form Britain's largest brewing group with 9,500 public houses, becoming Allied Breweries. However, Taylor was not to be kept out of the south for long since, in April 1962, his United Breweries merged with Charrington to create Charrington United which had national coverage. To some extent the mergers were intended to protect the lager interests of different groups. Skol was the product of the Allied group, Harp of Guinness and Carling of Charrington United.

What Taylor did in the provinces Charles Clore, head of Sears Holdings, a hosiery, shoes, shipbuilding and machinery conglomerate, attempted in London. Having made several unsuccessful approaches to Whitbread,[34] Clore offered £20.7 million for 75 per cent of Watney Mann's £9 million stock in May 1959. This hostile bid was resisted. Clore's offer was worth £3 per share but, when the shares rose to £3 17s. 0d. Clore, whose primary interest had been in the Pimlico site of the Stag Brewery, was shrewd enough not to offer an unrealistic price and took his profit instead. However, Watney Mann's reaction was to rapidly increase in size, doubling its number of tied houses through a series of acquisitions and, from a large regional brewer, became a national one within four years of Clore's bid.[35]

Behind much of the merger activity were increases in the demand for beer. The trough of national output was reached in 1958 when only 23.8 million barrels were produced. There then followed two decades of rising output so that in 1979 it had reached 41.7 million barrels, an increase of 75 per cent.[36] No doubt some of the recovery could have been the result of all the merger activity creating economies of scale, but this would not explain the improved performances of the independent brewing companies which formed the bulk of the 81 still existing in 1980. It is much more likely that rising demand was a cause rather than an effect, especially as recovery coincided with a period of increasing incomes and population, which rose by over 5 million people. There was a particular increase in the 15–24 age group which expanded by a third just when American youth culture of clothes, pop music and drink such as Coca-Cola and lager was exported to Britain, ensuring the demand for some alcoholic drinks would increase. In addition, the middle class and women increasingly became customers of the brewers. They were more likely to be found drinking in hotels and restaurants since the Licensing Acts of the early 1960s included these establishments. Between 1962 and 1989 there was a tenfold increase in licences for such outlets from around 3,000 to 31,000. Similarly, off-licences virtually doubled in number from some 26,000 in 1957 to 51,000 in 1989, by which time they included large food supermarkets which appealed more to women and stimulated more drinking at home, Thus, there were probably some 200,000 outlets for alcohol sales by 1989.[37]

As beer sales increased so the patterns of consumption changed substantially. In the 1960s and 1970s bottled beer sales fell whilst those of brewery conditioned draught beers, lager and canned beers rose. The latter was stimulated by an increasing take-home trade which, along with growing sales in clubs and off-licences, meant a considerable growth in the free trade. Nevertheless, the tied house remained the major outlet for beer sales even though the number of brands of beer fell from some 3,000 in 1966 to under 1,500 a decade later.

At the end of the 1970s economic recession returned to Britain, thus beer sales fell from 41.7 million barrels in 1979 to 36.6 millions in 1982, before levelling off some 12 per cent below the 1979 peak. This was a period of decline for Britain's manufacturing industries resulting in a fall in the numbers of semi-skilled and unskilled factory workers, especially in the North and Midlands – traditionally areas of heavy beer consumption. Between October 1979 and October 1985 unemployment rose from 1 million to 3 million, manufacturing regions being particu-larly affected. Thus many consumers had less to spend, yet the duty on beer was increased between 1978 and 1982 by 90 per cent and value added tax was raised from 8 to 15 per cent. However, in 1984, duty on wine had to be lowered to conform with European Community regula-tions whilst beer duty was raised again. To add further to brewers' problems, greater health and figure consciousness and the campaign against drink and driving also contributed to lower beer sales. That beer was becoming relatively overpriced was reflected in the increased sales of cider and wine. The former rose by some 43 per cent between 1980 and 1983 and the latter by 40 per cent between 1980 and 1986. At the same time the age structure of the population was changing with smaller numbers in the 15–24 age group and a generally ageing popula-tion resulting in more wine and less beer being consumed.[38]

For the remainder of the 1980s British beer output remained stable around the 1982 level – some 36–37 million barrels. However, this stability masked continued changes in the pattern of consumption. Whereas in 1980 lager represented only one-third of total beer sales in Britain, by 1990 it constituted half the market for beer. The Australian draught beers, Fosters and Castlemaine XXXX with the American Budweiser to a lesser extent, were instrumental in this trend. It was draught beer which suffered from lager's growth. Consumption kept on declining, although its fall was tempered to some extent by the intro-duction in 1988, by Guinness, of canned draught beer. Meanwhile, the late 1980s saw a halt to the decline in bottled beer sales.[39]

While changes occurred in the patterns of consumption in the 1980s, the structure of the brewing industry remained relatively unchanged. The Big Six breweries with tied houses, plus Guinness and, since 1973, Carlsberg without, accounted for 82 per cent of total production in 1986. However, in that year one major change occurred when Imperial Group, which owned Courage, was taken over by Hanson Trust who, later in the year, disposed of the brewing company to Elders IXL, the Australian brewers of Fosters lager. The other change to take place was the increasing rationalisation of brewing output by the closure of some breweries. Of the 142 in existence in 1980, only 117 were still producing in 1986. Diversification into other leisure and related activities began to play an increasing part in the strategies of the larger brewers.

For the smaller brewing companies in the face of growing lager and supermarket sales, holding their market share was to become increasingly problematic. For some of the regional brewers the solution was to purchase local breweries in order to acquire their tied houses. Thus, the total of 81 companies in 1980 was reduced to 68 by 1986 – eight large national, 12 regional and 48 local.[40]

Even so, it was the sale in 1986 of Courage to Elders IXL that, indirectly, was to have the greatest effect on the industry since it was to have a substantial influence on the Monopolies and Mergers Commission's enquiry into competition in brewing. The commission deliberated between 1986 and 1989 and concluded that a few large brewers producing and distributing their own beer in a tied house system led to inefficiencies being passed on to consumers and limited their choice, prevented real price competition as well as new companies entering the industry. Their first recommendation, that brewing companies should not own more than 2,000 tied houses, was aimed at the Big Six and anticipated that some 22,000 public houses would be sold.[41] Secondly, from May 1990, all tied houses should sell a 'guest' ale from another brewer. The government's response to the report was to require brewers to sell half the number of houses they owned over 2,000 or to sell their breweries, that is, they were to be retailers and not producers. The requirements had to be met by 31 October 1992.[42] The result, assisted by a downturn in economic activity and the collapse of the property market, has been the cessation of brewing at some of the regional breweries and the closure of other breweries by the Big Six.

Simultaneously, economic recession affected Britain again, but with a difference. Apart from the high level of unemployment, which was greater than at any time since 1932, there was a collapse in property prices creating the problem of negative equity. Houses were now worth less than the mortgages being repaid on them. Economic policy did not help. Aimed at keeping inflation down, it meant that house prices could not rise to reduce the negative equity and no other government assistance was forthcoming. Inevitably, both the unemployed and those caught in the negative equity trap had less to spend on alcohol. The recession was to have a serious effect on the leisure industry keeping customers at home and contributing to the continued rise in off-licence sales and a concomitant decline in the number of public houses from some 55,500 in 1988 to an estimated 45,000 in 1997.[43] There is no doubt that the Beer Orders of 1989 assisted this latter trend. An inevitable reduction in the output of beer followed so that in 1996 only 35.2 million barrels were produced.[44]

Not surprisingly, the decline in both output and outlets was accompanied by yet more changes in the structure of the industry. In 1986 the Big Six, Courage, Watney Grand Met, Whitbread, Allied Lyons, Courage Imperial and Scottish and Newcastle produced nearly 27 million barrels, some 73 per cent of total UK beer production. The two major beers without tied estate, Guinness and Carlsberg (who began in 1973 with a new lager brewery at Northampton), produced over 3 million barrels, 9 per cent of output. The 12 regional brewers had an estimated output of over 4.5 million barrels, some 12 per cent of national production. This left only 6 per cent (over 2 million barrels) for the 41 local breweries, including Gales.[45]

The early 1990s were to witness changes among the Big Six. Allied Lyons merged its brewing activities with Carlsberg to create Carlsberg-Tetley, each owning 50 per cent of the new enterprise. In 1995 Scottish and Newcastle acquired Courage from Elders IXL, becoming the UK's largest brewer with public houses spread throughout the nation by adding southern ones to those already owned in the north. A proposed merger between Bass and Allied (Carlsberg-Tetley) was opposed by the Monopolies and Mergers Commission and the failure was followed by the latter's decision to close three major breweries at Burton, Wrexham and Alloa, and concentrate production at Northampton and Leeds. Similarly, Bass decided to centralise its output in Burton at the cost of breweries in Cardiff and Sheffield.[46] Even so, a year later in 1996 Allied sold its 50 per cent stake in Carlsberg-Tetley to Bass and ceased brewing. In October 1997 came a further change with the merger of Guinness and Grand Met to form the rather curiously named Diageo. Thus both the non-pub owning big brewers had joined forces with tied house brewers and the Big Six had become the Big Five – Bass, Scottish Courage, Carlsberg-Tetley, Whitbread and Diageo. Not to be outdone, Whitbread did not remain completely inactive, for in 1996 they acquired the UK arm of the Canadian Labatt brewing empire from its owners, the Belgian company Interbrew, producers of Stella Artois.

Like all the Big Five, Whitbread had also diversified strongly into wines and spirits, acquiring Langenbach and Stowells wines and Beefeater gin in the 1980s. Guinness, the world's largest producer of scotch whisky, having purchased Bells Whisky and Distillers in 1985–86, acquired a large stake in Moet-Hennessy the champagne and cognac producers, while their partners in Diageo, Grand Met, acquired the wine and spirits merchants Saccone and Speed in 1987, Cinzano in January 1992 and a 30 per cent stake in Gonzalez Byass in November of the same year. But diversification went wider than other alcoholic drinks. Whitbread and Courage both moved strongly into food. The former developed Beefeater Steak Houses, Pizza Hut – a joint venture with PepsiCo – and TGI Friday in the 1980s, while the latter built up the Harvester, Happy Eater and Welcome Break restaurants. Courage also bought the newsagents, Finlays, demonstrating a move into the wider leisure industry, one which their new partners, Scottish and Newcastle, had shown by acquiring both the holiday company Pontins and Center Parcs. Guinness expanded into retailing and newspapers, and Bass into hotels. Clearly with a sluggish market for beer, diversification into other sectors of the leisure industry was economically sensible.

In the light of all these developments it comes as no surprise to discover that the number of breweries and brewing companies continued to decline. In 1996 only 62 companies survived and 89 breweries out of nearly 6,500 some 96 years earlier (see Table 1.2). It cannot be assumed that no further merger activity will take place, it being more likely that the next decade will see more amalgamations and, therefore, even fewer breweries and companies.

Of the larger brewers in 1997, Whitbread owned 4,100 public houses and Bass 4,000. The next three sizeable pub owners were all non-brewers. Allied Domecq had 3,800 and Phoenix Inns and Inntrepreneur Estates Ltd (50 per cent owned by Grand Met) had some 2,900 sites each. Scottish Courage came next with 2,500 followed by Greenalls,

Table 1.2   Breweries and brewing companies in the UK, 1900–96

Year	Breweries	Brewing companies
1900[1]	6,447	1,466
1910[1]	4,512	1,284
1920[1]	2,914	941
1930	1,418	559
1940	840	428
1950	567	362
1960	358	247
1970	177	96
1980	142	81
1985	121	73
1990	99	65
1996	89	62

Note: [1] Includes the Republic of Ireland.

Source: BLRA Statistical Handbook (1997), p. 85.

who also gave up brewing in 1991, with 1,900. Thus four out of the seven largest pub-owning companies were non-brewers, indicating the substantial change which had occurred in the industry following the Beer Orders of 1989. Regional brewers still successfully competed, since Greene King had 1,147 houses, Wolverhampton and Dudley 1,000, Vaux 950 and Marston, Thompson and Evershed 900.[47] All, no doubt, were assisted by the requirement that the big brewers had to divest themselves of large numbers of their houses.

However, public houses can no longer be seen as places for men to drink draught beer or lager. Women, families and the over 50s are likely to be the important consumer groups of the late 1990s.[48] To some extent, demographic trends will drive this change in consumers, since the 18–24 age group, traditionally seen as the most important customers of pubs, is declining in number as births between 1963 and 1976 fell by approaching one-third. By comparison, changes in age structure between 1993 and the year 2000 mean that there will be over 2 million more consumers in age groups between 35 and 64. Many of these see the public house as a place of leisure and eating out, not drinking. As more public houses provide food, a growing trend, increasing proportions of their turnover come from catering while that from alcoholic drinks falls to about half. As more customers find greater value for money in meals sold in public houses,[49] so more pubs will have to introduce or extend their catering and family facilities. Already pub catering in 1997 is estimated to have a market value of over £5.1 million, almost twice that of restaurant meals.[50]

Undoubtedly brewers have risen to the challenges presented to them in the 1990s. Thus in place of the traditional pub are many themed as well as restaurant pubs. The large brewers have the resources to undertake the changes while the major problems have fallen both on the smaller brewer and the small independent public house. With the likelihood that there will be fewer brewers in the UK by the year 2000,[51] brewers like Gales will need to continue to develop their retailing activities, particularly since the trend of declining on-trade in pubs and rising off-trade is likely to continue. Already a quarter of the beer market is in the off-trade and is likely to rise to over 30 per cent by the year 2000.[52] This process is aggravated by the increased cross-Channel imports of beers which in 1997 represented 5 per cent of UK consumption, approximately equal to the total production of the 45 smaller brewing members of the Brewers and Licensed Retailers Association (BLRA). The cause of this growth is the differential between UK and French beer duty at 32p and 5p respectively. Between 1992 and 1996 there was a 250 per cent increase in day-trips to France,[53] and British retailers are now investing in the Calais area to sell alcohol to the

British. This is a serious problem for small breweries and especially ones like Gales whose trading area lies adjacent to the cross-Channel ferries, and emphasises the need to be constantly on the alert for new approaches to retailing in the leisure industry in order to survive into the twenty-first century.

Notes

1. P. Mathias, *The Brewing Industry in England, 1700–1830* (Cambridge, 1959), p. 343.
2. For estimates of the national population and London's contribution see E. A. Wrigley and R. S. Schofield, *The Population History of England, 1541–1871: A Reconstruction* (London, 1981) pp. 208–9 and 531–5.
3. O. Macdonagh, 'The Origins of Porter', *Economic History Review*, 2nd series, **16**, no. 3 (1964), pp. 530–35.
4. H. Janes, *Albion Brewery, 1808–1958, The Story of Mann, Crossman and Paulin Ltd.*, (London, 1958), p. 13. The brewery was to become the home of Mann, Crossman and Paulin from the 1820s although Crossman and Paulin did not join until 1846: ibid., pp. 27–38.
5. Mathias, *Brewing Industry*, pp. 76–7.
6. T. R. Gourvish and R. G. Wilson, *The British Brewing Industry 1830–1980* (Cambridge, 1994), p. 3.
7. E. M. Sigsworth, 'Science and the Brewing Industry, 1850–1900', *Economic History Review*, 2nd series, **17**, no. 3 (1965), pp. 536–50.
8. Gourvish and Wilson, *British Brewing*, pp. 102–3.
9. D. W. Gutzke, *Protecting the Pub, Brewers and Publicans against Temperance* (Woodbridge, 1989), pp. 12–13.
10. Gourvish and Wilson, *British Brewing*, pp. 67–9, 111. The figures for 1841 exclude 30,499 non-brewing licensed victuallers and 26,327 non-brewing beerhouse keepers.
11. Gutzke, *Protecting the Pub*, pp. 17–19.
12. K. H. Hawkins and C. L. Pass, *The Brewing Industry: A Study in Industrial Organisation and Public Policy* (London, 1979), p. 31.
13. B. R. Mitchell and P. Deane, *Abstract of British Historical Statistics* (Cambridge, 1962), pp. 343–45 and G. B. Wilson, *Alcohol and the Nation: A Contribution to the Study of the Liquor Problem in the United Kingdom from 1800 to 1935* (London, 1940), p. 335.
14. Ibid.
15. J. Vaizey, *The Brewing Industry 1886–1951: An Economic Study* (London, 1960), p. 16.
16. Ibid., p. 17.
17 Gourvish and Wilson, *British Brewing*, p. 320.
18. Ibid., p. 618.
19. A. R. Dingle, 'Drink and Working-Class Living Standards in Britain, 1870–1914', *Economic History Review*, **25**, no. 4 (1972), pp. 608–22; Hawkins and Pass, *Brewing Industry*, p. 153.
20. Hawkins and Pass, *Brewing Industry*, p. 48.
21. Gourvish and Wilson, *British Brewing*, p. 346.

22. Ibid., p. 349.
23. Ibid., pp. 425–30.
24. Ibid., p. 365. Building restrictions were removed in 1954.
25. Ibid., p. 358.
26. Ibid., p. 356.
27. Ibid., p. 359.
28. Ibid., pp. 367, 630.
29. Ibid., pp. 368–70.
30. Ibid., pp. 370–71, 448.
31. Ibid., pp. 447–97.
32. Ibid., pp. 449–50, 623–9.
33. B. Ritchie, *An Uncommon Brewer: The Story of Whitbread 1742–1992* (London, 1992), p. 115.
34. Ibid., p. 113.
35. Much of the information on merger activity has been obtained from Gourvish and Wilson, *British Brewing*, pp. 447–97, a valuable survey of 'merger mania'.
36. Ibid., p. 630.
37. Ibid., pp. 456–7.
38. Ibid., pp. 581–4.
39. Ibid., pp. 585–6.
40. Ibid., p. 490.
41. Monopolies and Mergers Commission, *Supply of Beer*, Cmnd. 651 (1989).
42. The Supply of Beer (Tied Estate) Order 1989, S.I. 1989 No. 2390, 19 December 1989.
43. The Leisure Industry Report, *Leisure Week* (September 1997), p. 47.
44. BLRA, *Statistical Handbook* (London, 1997), p. 7 (year ending 31 March 1997).
45. Gourvish and Wilson, *British Brewing*, pp. 588–9.
46. *Brewery History* (88), Summer (1997), p. 3; (89), Autumn (1997), p. 3; (90), Winter (1997), p. 3.
47. The Leisure Industry Report, *Leisure Week* (September 1997), p. 47.
48. Ibid., p. 48.
49. A *Daily Mail* reporter, 'Pubs Find More Pulling Power by Winning the Big Price War on Meals', *Daily Mail*, 15 November 1993, p. 24, showed more people (52 per cent) thought meals sold in pubs represented value for money.
50. The Leisure Industry Report, *Leisure Week* (September 1997), p. 51.
51. John Spicer, *Brewing and Pub Retailing: Towards 2000*, SBC Warburg, October 1995, p. 5.
52. Ibid., p. 6.
53. 'Turning the Tide, the Case for a Lower Beer Duty', Brewing and Pub Industry submission to HM Treasury, January 1998.

CHAPTER TWO

Horndean and the Gale family, 1700–1847

England in the eighteenth century was a nation undergoing a transformation. Much of its agriculture continued to be changed from open-field farming to enclosures, major innovations altered manufacturing industry especially in textiles and iron and steel, turnpike roads and canals improved the speed and quality of travel, technological inventions saw the application of steam power in industry, the growth of insurance companies and banks in the provinces enhanced the mobility of capital and the numbers of people in the country began to increase at an unprecedented rate in the second half of the century, from 5 million in 1700 to approximately 5.75 million in 1750 and nearly 9 million in 1800.[1]

Not surprisingly the brewing industry was not only affected by some of these changes but was also part of the transformation. In 1700 there were considered to be almost 40,000 brewing victuallers, publicans brewing their own ale. By 1750 this number had risen to 50,000 but by 1800 only about 24,000 are thought to have survived.[2] This change in the second half of the eighteenth century was mainly owing to the emergence of large-scale porter brewers in London such as Thrale (later Barclay Perkins), Truman, Whitbread and Meux Reid, as well as the growth of common brewers serving a number of inns in the provinces. Even so, in the pre-railway age, the most dynamic brewer was governed by high transport costs, which effectively limited the market area for the brewery drays to within a radius of a few miles. Since much of the rural population lay thinly scattered through the countryside eighteenth-century publicans generally brewed their own beer.

At Horndean, which had three inns the *Anchor* at the Petersfield end of the village, the *Ship and Bell* towards the centre and the *Red Lion* in the square, the publicans were no exception for much of the eighteenth century. In the early nineteenth century a fourth inn appeared, either in the 1820s or early 1830s. Originally called the *Woodman*,[3] it was soon to become the *Good Intent*. The existence of four inns, however, testified to the importance of the Portsmouth–London road which carried many travellers.

Nevertheless, Horndean was ignored by Celia Fiennes, Daniel Defoe and George Pinckcard, the better known travellers of the late seventeenth and early eighteenth centuries. However, by the late eighteenth and early nineteenth centuries the village began to be commented upon.

> From hence we approach the forest of Bear, a large tract of wood-land. Pass through the village of Hamden, beyond which the country changes to extensive downs, the road widening through a deep vale, surrounded with noble hills of verdure, heaped in various forms; while the fleecy flocks, that strayed along their sides, with each a shepherd, with his crook and dog, made the same truly Arcadian.

So wrote the Reverend S. Shaw, Fellow of Queen's College, Cambridge, in 1788 of the countryside around Horndean. This view was shared, and to some extent echoed, some 14 years later by Mrs Montefiore, *en route* for her Portsmouth honeymoon, who described Horndean as a 'pretty little village'.[4] Located in south-east Hampshire, ten miles north of Portsmouth and seven south of Petersfield, Horndean developed as a ribbon community. Astride the busy road linking the capital with the country's premier military and naval town, Horndean had grown in a hollow surrounded by partially wooded downland. It was a typical eighteenth-century rural community, large estates, farms and smaller holdings providing employment for many in what was still a predomi-nantly agricultural age. Most of Horndean lay in the parish of Catherington, brought to national prominence by the creation of naval hero Admiral Samuel Hood as Baron of Catherington in 1782. The population of the parish, standing at roughly 322 in 1725, rose to 559 in 1801 and then virtually doubled, in line with national trends, to 1,094 in 1851. The remainder of Horndean lay in Blendworth parish, where the community was much smaller. From about 120 persons in 1725 Blendworth's population rose to 174 in 1801 and to 280 in 1841, before falling to 236 in 1851.[5] This parochial imbalance was further reflected in eighteenth-century poll books, in which Catherington's vot-ers outnumbered Blendworth's by nearly four to one and only one man – William Carter – was shown as a voter actually residing in Horndean.[6]

With their idyllic rural charm and peacefulness along with good communications the two parishes had, by the late eighteenth century, become a magnet for service personnel, especially officers, wishing to exchange Portsmouth's increasingly crowded and fetid confines for the fresh downland air. At Catherington, in 1764, Lieutenant Samuel Hood leased an existing farmhouse on the corner of Five Heads Road leading to Horndean and enlarged it into Catherington House. While residing there Hood became an Admiral, entertaining the great and famous, including George IV's wife Queen Caroline as well as the Younger Pitt, Nelson and Earl Howe. In 1820 the house was bought by Francis Morgan a retired Indian civil judge.[7]

Until June 1820, Horndean was the home of Vice-Admiral Edward Osborne, descended from a reputable naval family.[8] Cadlington House, on the road between Horndean and Blendworth, was long the Seymour family home. With a strong tradition of naval service, they were to lose two family members and acquire one in the 1830s.[9] Less well-known naval personnel were equally attracted to Horndean, since naval purser Thomas Giles lived at Castway (Causeway), while neighbouring Merchiston Hall became the home of Admiral Sir Charles Napier until his death in 1860.[10] The concepts of comfort and rural charm were exemplified in the 1805 advertisement for a house and 77 acres in 'the delightful Village of Horndean'. Features included a hunting box, garden, orchard, stables, carriage, dove, cow and cart houses, with the added attraction that a 'pack of harriers have been kept on the spot upwards of 48 years, and it is presumed as a scenting and sporting country to be surpassed by very few'.[11] Most of these large and impressive houses in their own grounds were on the outskirts of the villages in which, as well as on the farms, most of the agricultural labourers lived.

Horndean's economy during the years between 1700 and 1847 was heavily dependent on agriculture. Blendworth's farmers concentrated increasingly on grain production with some sheep and other livestock being raised. Manorial copyholders in 1710, for example, had 720 sheep, George Foster's 320-strong flock being the largest. During the century after 1750, however, sheep lost ground steadily to cereal production, the 1801 crop returns revealing that of Blendworth's 378 acres under cultivation some 314 (83 per cent) were growing grain with a further 55 (14.6 per cent) being devoted to turnips. Similarly of Catherington's 1,346 acres under cultivation, some 1,070 (79.5 per cent) were accounted for by cereals and 213 (15.8 per cent) by turnips. This trend was to be accompanied during the first half of the nineteenth century, especially in the economic depression following the Napoleonic Wars, by a substantial drop in the number of both landowners and tenants, as estates and farms were amalgamated. Additionally, the advance of mechanisation, demonstrated in the steam-powered corn mill installed at nearby Purbrook in 1801, incendiarism on farms in and near Horndean[12] and post-war depression, brought both gloom and tension to the area. Jervoise Clarke-Jervoise, of Idsworth House, as local manorial lord, was so unnerved by the 1830 agricultural labourers' disturbances that he sought permission from the Lord Lieutenant, the Duke of Wellington, to raise a yeomanry troop. The report of November 1830, which described how a 1,000–strong mob passed through Chichester and Emsworth destroying all the machinery it could find and heading for Horndean and then Petersfield, had clearly alarmed him. Seeking to preserve the peace in 'the towns of Horndean, Havant and Emsworth', Clarke-Jervoise lamented the 'absence of any available force in the part of the country to which I refer'. While permission was granted his fears, fortunately, proved to be largely unfounded, and farming in the local communities remained largely unaffected by the disturbances.[13]

While Horndean relied mainly on agriculture for its economic sustenance, the community's spiritual needs were met by the churches both at Blendworth and Catherington. Despite attempts to keep Blendworth church, dedicated to St Giles, in reasonable repair, expenses in 1708–09 including 8s. 1d. 'to Miles for Glasing the Church' and 4s. 6d. 'Layd out for foxes', the church had to be substantially rebuilt in 1759, an operation necessitating the fetching of 2,000 tiles from Stockheath in Havant and lime from nearby Bedhampton. John Marman and William Minchin (jun.) were paid £132 17s. 5d. for building and carpentry work, leaving churchwarden Christopher Lockyer with £5 'to Beautifie the said Church'.[14] As in the early eighteenth century, churchwardens' expenses for the rebuilt structure were to show much variety, ranging from the 2s. paid to 'Master Lover for Hops ... by order of the Parish' (were they brewing parish beer?) to the binding of the church Bible and Common Prayer Book in 1809–10 which necessitated an outlay of £3.[15] Yet by 1847 the church was both insufficient to accommodate the local population and in a dilapidated condition, necessitating the erection of a new structure on a different site and St Giles was allowed to moulder until demolition in 1960. By contrast, Catherington's larger All Saints Church, basically a Norman building, seems to have been well maintained and in 1750 had an additional red-brick storey added to its tower in order to accommodate a peal of five bells.

Educational needs from 1702 onwards were met by Blendworth Free School set up under the terms of Winchester College porter William Appleford's will of 1696. Books, materials and teaching occasioned expenditure, as did the apprenticing of children such as John Barnard with Petersfield shoemaker Thomas Page in 1708 and James Rennet with Arundel shoemaker Jeremiah Scawel in October 1772. Income for the charity was derived from a house and 17 acres at nearby Lovedean, churchwardens reserving the right to cut all timber on the land and add the proceeds to the charity land account. For the poorer children in both Blendworth and Catherington parishes the Appleford charity at least provided some semblance of a rudimentary education as well as a reasonable start in life, a start which they probably would not otherwise have received.[16] According to the 1725 Visitation Return the school catered for both sexes, was located in Catherington parish, and had a woman teacher.[17]

For the disposal of surplus produce and acquisition of goods, materials and services not available in the community, Horndean residents resorted to a number of nearby markets and fairs, each of which was within a day's travelling time. Petersfield supported a regular market, where a Richard Gale, probably of Froxfield, was selling sheep in 1796. The town also hosted two annual fairs, each three days long. Primarily for buying and selling cattle and sheep, the fairs subsequently widened in scope.[18] Portsmouth's economic attractions included the High Street market held each Tuesday, Thursday and Saturday offering a wide range of foodstuffs, a separate fish market, an impressive array of shops selling exotic products, and Free Mart Fair. Held each July until 1847, the fair offered items as disparate as stays, thread and books, the opportunity of a lottery win and a wide range of side-shows, human freaks and entertainment.[19] Portsdown fair, located between Portsmouth and Horndean and taking place in the immediate aftermath of Free Mart Fair, offered commodities as diverse as cheese, horses and pearl brooches.[20] Nearer to Horndean were Havant market and the stock fairs staged at Rowland's Castle each May and November, as well as that at Southwick in April.[21]

Horndean's location in terms of communications was, however, to be the key to its eventual economic prosperity. The London to Portsmouth road, turnpiked between Sheet, north of Petersfield, and Portsmouth in 1711, was in constant and sustained use. Repairs were carried out regularly. In June 1711, for example, it was estimated that £2,816 was needed to repair the road between Horndean and Wait Lane End (later Waterlooville)[22] to the south. In the 1720s and 1730s highway surveyor Michael Atkins was to repair the 'most Broken and Dangerous parts of the High way leading through the Forest from Wait Lane end to Hordeane'. The flints for such work came from Horndean. While regular coach, carrier and wagon services, tramping troops, mail carriers and others placed the road under constant strain, Horndean residents could see a great diversity of people passing through while some would benefit commercially at the same time, for Horndean importantly was invariably the village where the final change of horses was made before completion of the London to Portsmouth run, hence the existence of four inns.[23] Indeed, it could be said that in the eighteenth and early nineteenth centuries all human life passed through the community. For example in July 1706 some 400 Swiss and Walloon troops passed through, destined for the Isle of Wight. Wagons with wounded Highlanders from the action at Ticonderoga lumbered through in 1759; in January 1807 part of the 91st Highland regiment marched through *en route* from Hilsea Barracks to Edinburgh.[24] An expedition planned for late 1760 led to 900 men marching from London through Horndean to Portsmouth, only for the expeditionary orders to be countermanded at the last moment. In the following May upwards of 50 wagons, laden

with ordnance stores, passed through Horndean in readiness for another expedition. In 1787 some 1,000 dreaded Hessian troops marched
through the village bound for Portsmouth and their eventual destina-
tion of India. Soldiers were also to be found in the community for other
reasons, as mariner William Richardson, who had sailed to Portsmouth,
explained in 1790:

> I had three of my messmates with me, all bound for London, so we
> agreed to walk it at our leisure and have a good view of the
> country; so after dinner we set off, and in the evening we got to
> Horndean, where we stopped for the night. Here we found several
> people in smock frocks at the inn, whom we took for farmers' men
> until a weary soldier came in and called for a pint of beer. One of
> the smock-frock gentlemen soon began to ask him questions, some
> of which he answered and some he would not, when to our sur-
> prise the smock-frocker pulled off his frock and discovered himself
> to be a serjeant, and the others that were with him were of his
> party. Fortunately the poor soldier had a furlough, which cleared
> him, but we could not help thinking how easy a poor fellow might
> get trepanned when he was least expecting it: these soldiers had
> been stationed here to take deserters either from the army or
> navy.[25]

Wagon-loads of money, whether going towards London as captured
booty for safe lodging in the Bank of England, or towards Portsmouth
as pay for dockyard workers, obviously attracted both curiosity and
attention.[26] Besides service personnel, Australia-bound convicts, pimps,
errant apprentices, prostitutes and ambassadors also journeyed to and
from London via Horndean. Thus Hamed Aga, ambassador from the
Bey of Tripoli, was a visitor in October 1765, while outgoing ambassadors from Morocco and Tripoli passed through in July 1774, as did the
two-coach retinue of Mirza Abul Hassan Khan, the outgoing Persian
ambassador in July 1810.[27] Periods of war increased substantially the
volume of traffic and the pressures of the French Revolutionary and
Napoleonic wars resulted in local militia units, such as the East Kent
militia bound from the Isle of Wight to Lewes via Petersfield, passing
through Horndean. When the Finchdean Volunteers were dismissed in
June 1802, they were given a farewell dinner at Horndean 'where they
spent the evening in social enjoyment'.[28]

These were some of the recorded travellers upon the road, but with
eighteenth-century growth of the Empire and the increasing importance
of the navy, Portsea Island expanded from a population of about some
6,000 or 7,000 at the beginning of the century to over 33,000 by 1801.
Many must have been the unrecorded and anonymous travellers along
the road from the capital to England's premier naval port. However,
although the road brought economic prosperity to Horndean, it also

brought problems. Adverse weather, such as the snow and ice which occasioned William Hickey and his travelling companion Mordaunt to take four hours for the stage-coach journey from Petersfield to Portsmouth or the snow which 'drifted ten feet deep' on Horndean Down in January 1786,[29] clearly made for difficulties. So, too, did the wealth and other attractions of some of the road's users for in November 1802 two gentlemen travelling to Petersfield by post-chaise 'were robbed on Horndean-down, by three fellows in sailors habilments'. Four years later an armed gipsy gang was apprehended in the Forest of Bere where, from a tent, they had ranged forth and terrorised local travellers. A sad case demonstrating some of the undoubted hardships of life for those less well off was reported from Portsmouth on 28 April 1810:

> On Thursday evening an unfortunate girl, of the name of Neale, who had followed some soldiers that were going to London, in a fish-cart, was abandoned by them at Horndean. Being intoxicated, and without any money, she wandered about the lanes till daylight, when she went into a farmer's out-house, and attempted to hang herself, with the strings of her pocket. Early in the morning a labourer discovered her, in a senseless state, hanging with her feet upon the ground. After several hours process the functions of life were restored, and she was taken to the Poor House.[30]

On the benefit side, however, was the fact that the road and its users brought additional wealth to Horndean, a community which had clearly prospered since along the road could be found in the early 1830s at least three baker's shops, two grocers and general shops, two boot and shoemakers, a butcher, wheelwright, carpenter, tailor, painter, plumber and glazier, as well as a corn dealer, land surveyor and two surgeons. Of the shopkeepers one was Anne Gale listed as shopkeeper and dealer in sundries and another was her son Richard who was stated to be baker and shopkeeper.[31] Not surprisingly the village inns were particular beneficiaries having four guest beds and stabling for six horses between them in 1686, the largest of these establishments being the *Ship and Bell*. Originally known as the *Plough*, it had become the *Ship* by May 1699 when held by Petersfield cordwainer Robert Brett, with a house and ten acres, from Chalton's manorial lord.[32] Like so many other inns in seventeenth- and eighteenth-century England the *Ship and Bell*, as it had become known by at least 1710, offered a variety of services beyond the obvious ones of providing drink, food and shelter to weary travellers. Auction sales of timber, hurdles, property and other items were frequently held there.[33] It was also a suitable location for official meetings. In December 1711, for instance, it was used for a bankruptcy hearing, suggesting that the bankrupt had no funds to be able to undertake the journey to London, whilst in 1754 and again in

1812 it was used for Turnpike Commission meetings, and in 1824 the inquest upon servant Amelia Hoare who, 'without any apparent cause', drowned herself in a large water tank,[34] was held there. It was also an important information centre. The Hampshire wagon, patented by Robert Mason of St Thomas's Street, Portsmouth, in June 1803 and remarkable for the fact that it could be broken and used as two carts, could be viewed at the inn. In late October 1810 the *Ship and Bell* was the collecting point for a 20s. reward offered for a red pocket book lost between Petersfield and Portsmouth 'containing Writings and Memorandums of different kinds'.[35] Earlier that year, in April, when the services of 'two sober young men' were sought to 'superintend a farm or two near Spanish Town, Jamaica', details could be obtained from landlord Daniel Wise. Correspondent and agent for the *Hampshire Telegraph*, Wise, who passed the tenancy temporarily in March 1802 to William Collins, also offered a service of 'Neat Post Chaises to every part of the Kingdom'.[36] Wise, however, was to be just one of an assortment of landlords who ran the *Ship and Bell*, but one of the more prominent.

In November 1725 the premises belonging to Horndean victualler William Basing, and then known as the *Bell*, were conveyed to Catherington gentleman John Brett who, in July 1746, sold them to Horndean victualler Richard Harrad, then the tenant, for £290. Eight years later Harrad and his wife Mary sold the inn at a loss, to Havant grocer and tallow chandler John Wackett. In January 1760 Wackett assigned the mortgage term in trust for Henry Budd, a Hayling Island yeoman, to Havant saddler Thomas Witcombe, the property being mortgaged to Budd for £500. In June 1767 the inn was sold by Harrad and Gosport cooper William Harrad, presumably his brother, to Hambledon brewer Henry Coles. Coles was undoubtedly something of an eighteenth-century entrepreneur being styled a common brewer. Apart from his Hambledon Brewery he had at least 16 inns in his possession, scattered between Compton in West Sussex to the west and Bishops Waltham to the east and including both the *Anchor* and the *Ship and Bell* in Horndean. It would seem then that these inns were not brewing all, if any, of their own beer after 1767 but being supplied from Coles's Hambledon Brewery. However, he probably overstretched himself because in 1792 he conveyed all his properties to Henry Mullens, yeoman of Hambledon, subject to the payment of all debts and mortgages on the premises.[37] It may well be that Coles was in debt to Mullens, but in any case it seems unlikely that the yeoman farmer would have taken up brewing and presumably sold off the properties making a substantial profit.

Before 1811 the *Ship and Bell* had passed into the ownership of another common brewer – Joseph Eyles of Petersfield – who sold it in

February of that year, to Horndean victualler Daniel Wise and Finchdean yeoman David Padwick for £1,500. Ten years later, in August 1821, Wise and Eyles's brother leased the building to Portsmouth innholder John Billett but by 1842 the premises were owned and occupied by Hannah Wise. In June of that year, she advertised the *Ship and Bell* inn and posting house in a wealthy and popular neighbourhood for sale or to let, stating that she had 'carried on the business for 50 years'.[38] This suggests that Daniel Wise had been a tenant possibly of Mullens and then Eyles, before purchasing the inn in 1811. No sale was achieved so that in mid-January 1842, the *Hampshire Telegraph* was again advertising the *Ship and Bell*, 'an old-established inn and posting house with a 259 foot frontage and stabling for 28 horses' for sale.[39] Again it remained unsold until, on 7 May 1847, Daniel Wise's son, also called Daniel, a Singleton gentleman, Portsmouth merchant Joseph Cave and Billett who had clearly prospered as he now styled himself as gentleman 'of Highfield Lodge, Waterloo', conveyed the property, for an undisclosed sum, to Richard Gale of Horndean, merchant, and his eldest son Henry Giles Gale of Horndean, grocer.

The legal side of the purchase cost Richard Gale £22 3s. 4d. which he duly paid his attorney Henry George Way by cheque.[40] By then Richard Gale had been involved in commercial activity in Horndean for at least 23 years for he was stated to be a shopkeeper at the baptism of his first child, Henry Giles, at Catherington church on 7 November 1824 following his marriage earlier that year to Eliza Hoare at Blendworth.[41] His occupation as shopkeeper continued throughout the baptism of his four sons and at least until 1838 when the tithe map shows him to have his business located opposite the Square, on the crown of the bend, in the road at Horndean.[42] However, by 1841 Richard was being described as a corn merchant.[43] He was then a respected member of the community, being involved in the vestry business of St Giles Church, Blendworth and Surveyor of the Highways in 1847.[44] At the same time, his shop had clearly prospered and he had expanded his activities, perhaps helped by inheritance on his mother's death in 1838. He had been no older than 22 when he began keeping his shop and it would seem that he had seen his eldest son Henry Giles also established as a shopkeeper at an early age since he was described as a grocer on the deeds of purchase of the *Ship and Bell* when he was only 23 years of age. However, although shopkeeping on the Portsmouth–London road was clearly a profitable business Richard Gale could see that commercial inns benefited greatly from the passing traffic and thus acquired the largest one only a little way along the opposite side of the road from his shop. By then he was 45 years old having been baptised at Chalton in 1802 the son of Richard and Anne Gale.[45] He was never to know his father who had died and was buried at Catherington before Richard was even two years old. He was raised entirely by his mother who had property on the southern side of the junction of Five Heads Road with the Portsmouth Road.[46] Since the first that is known of Anne Gale is that she was a shopkeeper, it seems more than likely that her shop was located at the Five Heads Road junction and that her husband had also kept the shop before his untimely death, probably in his early forties in 1804. So far her husband Richard's marriage and baptism dates have not been traced but it seems certain that he was the son of Richard Gale who married Hannah Brown on 12 May 1759 in Catherington church.[47]

Notes

1. E. A. Wrigley and R. S. Schofield, *The Population History of England, 1541–1871: A Reconstruction* (London, 1981), pp. 528–9.
2. P. Mathias, *The Brewing Industry in England, 1700–1830* (Cambridge, 1959), p. 343.
3. See Hampshire Record Office (HRO) 21M65/F7/43/1 and 2 Catherington Tithe Map (1838) and Award (1843) for reference to the *Woodman* public house. The site was a house and garden on the Catherington Enclosure Map of 1816.
4. Reverend S. Shaw, 'A Tour to the West of England, in 1788', in J. Pinkerton (ed.) *A General Collection of the Best and Most Interesting Voyages and Travels in all Parts of the World* (17 vols, London, 1808–14), vol. 2, p. 312; L. Wolf (ed.), *Essays in Jewish History* (London, 1934), pp. 251–2. See also HRO Catherington Tithe Map, 1838.
5. B. Stapleton and J. H. Thomas (eds), *The Portsmouth Region* (Gloucester, 1989), pp. 91, 102.
6. *Poll Books for Hampshire: A true copy of the Poll for the electing of Knights of the Shire ...* (1705), p. 16. *An Exact List of the Names ... that voted for Knights of the Shire ... 1734* (1736). *A True Copy of the Poll Book for the Election of one Knight* (1780), pp. 69, 77; *The Poll for the Election of Two Knights* (1790), pp. 4, 5.
7. R. J. Parsons, *Catherington: The Church and Village* (Catherington, 1986), p. 3.
8. *Annual Register (AR) for 1820*, pt I (1822), p. 577.
9. Sir Michael Seymour died in July 1834. Captain Michael Seymour's wife gave birth to a daughter in September 1836, while in the following June his brother, Captain Edward Seymour 'in the prime of life, sincerely regretted', passed away: *Nautical Magazine*, 3 (1834), p. 639; 5 (1836), p. 574; 2nd series, no. 1, 6 (1837) p. 495.
10. *Nautical Magazine*, 2nd Series, 2 (1838), p. 287. For Admiral Napier see HRO Catherington Tithe Map (1838) and Award (1843) for his residence. His tomb is in Catherington churchyard.
11. *Hampshire Telegraph (HT)*, 298, 24 June 1805.
12. R. A. Pelham, 'The Agricultural Revolution in Hampshire, with special reference to the Acreage Returns of 1801', *Proceedings of the Hampshire Field Club (HFC)*, **18** (1951–53), pp. 150–51. The Purbrook Mill,

'intended to grind corn at a cheap rate for accommodating the neighbouring poor', used half a bushel of coal to grind seven bushels of wheat in an hour: *HT*, 109, 9 November 1801. In mid-August 1800 it was reported that farms near Horndean 'have had several valuable stacks of corn burnt' (ibid., 45, 18 August 1800).

13. Material drawn from B. Worton, 'The Parish of Blendworth, Hampshire, 1700 to 1851' (unpublished dissertation for Portsmouth Polytechnic, 1982), pp. 21–33.

14. The strength of Anglican belief in Blendworth and Catherington was such that the former contained only one papist and no dissenters and the latter only two or three families and 'Only 1 old woman Anabaptist' in 1725: HRO B/2/A, Visitation Return, vol. 2. Sadly the returns of the 1788 Visitation Return for the two parishes do not survive. Portsmouth City Records Office (PCRO) CHU 40/2/2 Blendworth Churchwardens' Account and Vestry Book 1706–83, n.p., *passim*.

15. PCRO CHU 40/2/2, Blendworth Churchwardens' Account and Vestry Minute Book 1785–1862, n.p., *passim*.

16. Ibid., CHU 40/3/1, Blendworth Free School Account Book 1702–1827, n.p., *passim*. For further details see Worton, pp. 45–9. Papers *re* Appleford's Charity are contained in PCRO CHU 40/40/4.

17. HRO B/2/A Visitation Return, vol. 2.

18. *The Hampshire Repository*, **1** (1799), p. 86. J. Potter, *The Traveller's Pocket-Book* (17th edn, London, 1775), p. 155, lists fairs on 10 July and 11 December for sheep and horses. S. Lewis, *A Topographical Dictionary of England* (4 vols, London, 1842 edn.), vol. 3, p. 361, gives 10 July for toys, 6 October for lean cattle and 11 December for sheep. The summer fair ceased in 1902.

19. PCRO Borough Sessions Papers S3/56, deposition dated 13 July 1711; S3/98, depositions dated 6, 14 July 1732; S3/114, deposition dated 7 July 1741; J. Webb, *Portsmouth Free Mart Fair: The Last Phase 1800–1847* (The Portsmouth Papers, no. 35, 1982), *passim*.

20. *HT*, 616, 29 July 1811; 617, 5 August 1811.

21. Ibid., 129, 29 March 1802; 133, 26 April 1802. The Rowland's Castle fairs were 12 May for horned cattle and 12 November for horned cattle and pigs. Attended by cattle dealers from Hampshire, Sussex and Surrey, both fairs were described as 'obsolete' in 1859: J. McIntyre, 'Rowland's Castle Hampshire, 1790s to 1860s' (unpublished dissertation, Portsmouth Polytechnic, 1986), pp. 16–17.

22. B. Stapleton, *Waterlooville: a Pictorial History* (Chichester, 1996), n.p.

23. W. Albert and P. D. A. Harvey (eds), *Portsmouth and Sheet Turnpike Commissioners' Minute Book 1711–54* (Portsmouth Record Series, **2**, 1973), pp. 97, 2, 65, 89; C. Aldin *The Romance of the Road* (1986 edn), p. 111.

24. N. Luttrell, *A Brief Historical Relation of State Affairs from September 1678 to April 1714* (6 vols, Oxford, 1857), vol. 6, pp. 53, 66; *AR for 1759* (8th edn 1802), p. 77; *HT*, 380, 19 January 1807.

25. *Gentleman's Magazine* (*GM*), **30** (1760), pp. 485, 486, 592; **31** (1761), p. 236; *Hampshire Chronicle* (*HC*), 759, 9 April 1787; S. Childers (ed.), *A Mariner of England* (London, 1970 edn), pp. 70–71.

26. On 9 August 1762 historian Edward Gibbon travelled from his Buriton home to Petersfield 'to see the prize money of the Hermione go thro'. The booty captured amounted to 'about £616,000 as one of the officers

informed us; but the idea of the treasure was all. The procession was only twenty Waggons without the least ornament whatsoever and guarded by forty Marines': D. M. Low (ed.), *Gibbon's Journal to January 28th, 1763* (London, 1929), pp. 110–11.

27. *Calendar of Home Office Papers 1760–1765*, pp. 607, 611–2; *1773–1775*, p. 301; M. M. Cloake (ed.), *A Persian at the Court of King George 1809–10* (London, 1988), p. 292.

28. *HT*, 107, 26 October 1801; 139, 7 June 1802.

29. P. Quennell (ed.), *Memoirs of William Hickey* (London, 1960), p. 313; *GM*, **56**, pt 1 (1786), p. 72. Hickey's problems had been compounded by the fact that the 42nd Regiment bound for Petersfield and thence Portsmouth and India, 'had engaged almost all the horses in the place'.

30. *HT*, 163, 22 November 1802; 551, 30 April 1810.

31. *Pigot and Co. Directory* (1831–32), pp. 422–3.

32. Public Record Office (PRO) WO 30/48, Survey of 1686; Anon., 'Records of the Manor of Chalton' (typescript study, 1959), p. 15. (Copy in Portsmouth Central Library.)

33. *HT*, 515, 21 August 1809; 1069, 3 April 1820; 1071, 17 April 1820; 1353, 12 September 1825.

34. *London Gazette* (*LG*), 4939, 13–15 December 1711; Albert and Harvey, *Portsmouth and Sheet Turnpike* p. 166; *HT*, 666, 13 July 1812; 1277, 29 March 1824.

35. *HT*, 187, 9 May 1803; 577, 29 October 1810. For further details of the Hampshire Patent Wagon see S. L. Thomas, 'Living off the Land: A Study of Portsea Island Agriculture, 1793–1851' (unpublished dissertation, Portsmouth Polytechnic, 1985), pp. 89–90.

36. *HT*, 547, 2 April 1810; 126, 8 March 1802; 129, 29 March 1802. Collins had formerly run the *Nelson's Arms* in Winchester.

37. HRO 50M82/1 Clerke-Jervoise Estate Papers.

38. *HT*, 2228, 20 June 1842.

39. *HT*, 2467, 16 January 1847.

40. Deeds *re Ship and Bell*, 1725–1847. Way may perhaps be identified with George Henry Way, solicitor of Cosham, who had left there by 1852 (*Post Office Directory of Hampshire* (1847), pt 2, pp. 1116, 1344; *Hunt and Co.'s Directory of Hampshire and Dorsetshire* (1852) does not mention Way).

41. PCRO CHU 41/1B/1 Catherington Parish Baptism Register 1813–42; CHU 40/1C/1 Blendworth Parish Baptism Register 1813–36.

42. PCRO CHU 41/1B/1 Three other sons were born in 1826, 1827 and 1829; HRO Catherington Tithe Map 1838. The building occupied by Richard Gale's shop is now Horndean Post Office.

43. PRO HO 107/396, 1841 Census. Richard Gale was also registrar for the census in Horndean.

44. PCRO CHU 40/2/2, Blendworth Churchwardens' Accounts and Vestry Minute Book 1785–1862, n.p., *passim* from 1843.

45. PCRO CHU 39/1A/3 Chalton Parish Register of Baptisms, Marriages and Burials 1747–1807.

46. PCRO CHU 41/1A/7 Catherington Parish Register of Baptisms and Burials 1763–1812; HRO Q23/2/21 Catherington Enclosure Map 1816.

47. PCRO CHU 41/1A/6 Catherington Parish Register of Marriages and Burials 1754–1812.

CHAPTER THREE

Sorrow and success: the era of George Alexander Gale, 1847–96

When Richard Gale, along with his son Henry, acquired the *Ship and Bell* he was a family man having been married by licence at Blendworth church at the age of 21 to 24-year-old Eliza Hoare of Blendworth on 29 January 1824. Unlike many of their contemporaries both were educated and literate enough to be able to sign their names in the parish register. Nearly ten months after their marriage their eldest son was born and in the next four years another three sons completed their family. Following Henry Giles came Richard Rogers Gale in February 1826, William Simpson in June 1827 and, finally, George Alexander born on 17 December 1828 and baptised on 26 March 1829 at Catherington church, where in fact all four Gale boys had received their baptisms.[1] At all these ceremonies their father had been described as a shopkeeper. The shop was a grocery and bakery combined and belonged to Richard's mother Anne, with whom he worked until shortly before her death and burial at Catherington in May 1838.[2]

Anne Gale deserves rather more than a footnote in the pages of history. At her death she was stated to be 77 years old. Nothing has been discovered about her early life but she must have been a remarkable woman since she was widowed 22 months after the birth of her only child and remained a widow for more than 34 years. In the male-dominated age of the early nineteenth century she managed, nevertheless, to be a successful businesswoman and to raise her son into accomplishing even more. When she died as an elderly lady in the first year of Queen Victoria's reign she had reason to feel content not only at her own achievements but also at those of her son Richard.

After more than a decade of working as a shopkeeper, Richard had clearly prospered and decided to develop his own shop. Thus, on 25 March 1836, he leased from Sir William Knighton of Horndean a piece of ground of 28 roods in size adjoining the London Turnpike Road with the tailor's shop on its Portsmouth side and the stables opposite the *Ship and Bell* on the London side. The lease was for 999 years and the rent £8 13s. 4d. per annum. Richard had to pay all taxes and rates and was to spend £500 on erecting a house with the best materials and to maintain it for the same term. This was a prime central site in Horndean and Richard built his house, including shop with bakery ovens behind, and began in business on his own account.[3] Not surprisingly, in view of it's location, the shop did so well that, by 1841, Richard had become financially able to link himself more closely with the major sector of the local economy, agriculture, by combining his grocery business with that of corn merchant.[4] By the end of that year, with four teenage boys between the ages of 13 and 17, he could have been expecting some filial assistance in his commercial activities. The 1840s seem to have been profitable for Richard, allowing him both sufficient funds to buy the *Ship and Bell* as well as to concentrate on corn merchanting, since the deeds of conveyance clearly show that his eldest son Henry was at least managing the grocer's shop, being described as a grocer at 22, the same age as when his father was first identified as a shopkeeper.[5]

What Richard Gale's motives were for acquiring the *Ship and Bell* remain unknown, but it was not an inauspicious time to buy and perhaps the purchase reflects his commercial acumen. First, changing tastes in beer-drinking had seen the decline in the primacy of porter and a swing to the consumption of mild beer in the early nineteenth century. This was fortunate for any intending or existing brewer since the strong porter had to be kept maturing for nine months before being distributed to public houses. This long maturing time was essential to clear and improve the beer, but it also tied up considerable quantities of capital for long periods thus discriminating in favour of large, rather than small, brewers. The swing to mild beer meant that the final brew could be sent out much earlier and thus the brewer obtained quicker returns on his capital investment.[6] Secondly, allied to the technical improvements in brewing, especially controlled fermentation, and to the increasing efficiency in the use of malt by brewers as well as the rising quantity of barley used for malting, brewers were able to draw an increasing volume of beer from the same quality of raw malt.[7] Thirdly, clearly indicating the era of Free Trade, in 1830 Parliament, through the Beer Act, had repealed all duties on beer and brought to an end the restrictive licensing of public houses. By 1838, some 46,000 beerhouses had been added to the existing 51,000 licensed premises[8] ensuring increased consumption as prices fell. Public finance had been heavily dependent on the malt and beer duties, the brewing industry providing nearly one-fifth (£9.8 million) of all national taxation in 1805 and this proportion was to rise further as the Napoleonic Wars continued.[9] Smaller breweries were affected more seriously by these excise duties than the larger ones because of the capital that was absorbed by duty payments, so their abolition was particularly advantageous to local brewers. A fourth factor was the rapid rise in population. Nationally, the first half of the nineteenth century saw England's population rise faster than it had ever done before or ever has since. The population doubled from over 8 million people to over 16 million people. However, this growth was not accompanied by an equivalent rise in beer consumption, partly because of fluctuations in living standards that for many clearly fell between 1800 and 1820 in the years of the Napoleonic Wars and the post-war depression, and partly because of the rise in coffee and, especially, tea-drinking. Thus in 1722 some 5.5 million people consumed over 6 million barrels of beer – more than one barrel per person – whereas in 1833 some 13.5 million people consumed less than 7.5 million barrels, just over half a barrel per head. In the same period tea-drinking had risen from approximately 1oz per person per year to 2lb 5oz (i.e. 0.37 million lb to 31.83 million lb).[10]

Counterbalancing these factors from the 1840s was the more certain upward trend in living standards as average wages were beginning to rise generally.[11] Fifthly, the year 1847 was the one in which the major building of England's railway network was to take place, thus a cheaper form of transport was to be made available for the supply of raw materials to brewers as well as to convey their finished product to the market. This latter factor would clearly not have been prominent in Richard Gale's mind since brewing at the *Ship and Bell* could have been only for a local market and Horndean had no railway, the nearest being at Rowland's Castle.

There were also personal factors which could have influenced Richard's decision apart from the greater economic safety in diversification. His movement into the corn merchant's business brought him much closer to the major raw material of brewers – barley. The most usual origin of new entrants into the brewing profession was from those trading in brewers' raw materials, although it was primarily maltsters rather than corn merchants and, secondly, farmers who formed the major sources of external entrants.[12] In many cases the motive behind such entry into brewing was a father who had more than one son but whose own business was too small to absorb them all. Richard Gale had four sons aged between 18 and 23 when he and his eldest son Henry bought the *Ship and Bell* and its associated brewing facilities. He had already established Henry in the grocer's shop. His second son, Richard, was aged 21 and William, his third son, just 20, so it seems likely the public house and posting station was intended for one of them. As it happens, fate was shortly to intervene in Richard Gale's family intentions. On 9 December 1847, only seven months after Richard and Henry Gale had purchased the *Ship and Bell*, Richard's third son, William Simpson, died at the age of 20 and was buried in Catherington churchyard.[13]

By 1851, however, Richard's merchanting activities had clearly thrived since in the census of that year he is not only described as a corn merchant but also a coal merchant employing three men. He still lived and worked at the house and shop which had been built to his instructions in 1836 but, by then, his second son Richard had taken over the grocer's shop and was living as a single man with his parents who had a living-in house servant, Jane Silvester. Richard employed a 14-year-old Catherington-born boy, Henry Glasse, also living in, as an apprentice.[14] Both the shop and the merchanting activities seem to have been prospering. However, it was noticeable that the eldest son Henry was no longer managing the grocery business. He had become a married man, his wife being Sarah Bilton who was baptised at St Mary's Church, Portsea on 21 December 1827, her father William being a chemist.[15] Henry and Sarah's first child Eliza Jeanette was baptised at Blendworth church on 12 July 1850 when Henry was described as a yeoman.[16] He had moved to become the tenant of Pyle Farm in Blendworth parish, not far along the eastern side of the road from Horndean to Havant. Being already joint owner of the *Ship and Bell* with his father, the move to Pyle Farm could be regarded as eminently sensible since Henry would produce the barley and his father in his capacity as a corn merchant, could trade in the commodity required for the malting process. Since Hampshire was among the eight counties noted as providing quality barley for malting in the London market and a ubiquitous local trade in barley and malt flourished throughout England,[17] the decision for Henry to take on Pyle Farm can only have been part of a deliberate plan rather than accidental.

Just over two years after the birth of their first child, Henry and Sarah had a second daughter, Frances Emma, baptised at Blendworth Church on 10 October 1852.[18] Earlier that same year on 6 March, Richard's fourth and youngest son George Alexander, aged 23, had married Hester Ross at St Thomas's church, Portsmouth.[19] Hester had been baptised at St Mary's Church, Portsea on 4 April 1828, the daughter of Thomas Ross described as a draper and his wife Ann,[20] although by the time of Hester's marriage Thomas was described as a shoemaker of Landport Road, Portsmouth, a description which somewhat understated his occupation since, in 1851, he employed 22 men and 28 women as a boot and shoe manufacturer in Russell Street, Landport.[21] George Gale had clearly left home before his marriage since, in April 1850, he was described as a grocer of Portsea[22] and at his marriage his address was given as High Street, Portsmouth, and his occupation that of a commercial traveller. Whether he was acting for his father's corn merchanting business or attempting to sell the products of the *Ship and Bell* to a wider clientele is unknown.

By the end of 1852 Richard Gale could thus have been forgiven for feeling a degree of contentment with his life. His three surviving sons were all established in business, two of them were married, he had two grandchildren and a third expected, and his own business ventures were successful. However, within the first month of 1853 tragedy was to strike again as a death notice in the *Hampshire Telegraph* on Saturday, 29 January revealed.

> On the 19th inst. at Pyle Farm, Blendworth in the 28th year of his age, of consumption, Mr. Henry Giles Gale, yeoman, eldest son of Mr. Richard Gale, Horndean, and son-in-law of Mr. William Bilton, Chamberlain of the Borough of Portsmouth, leaving a young widow and two infant children to mourn their loss.[23]

Henry was buried in Catherington churchyard on 25 January. This grievous event was to alter radically the lives of both Richard and his youngest son George. The remarkable and resourceful Richard having already had two successful careers, first running a grocer's and baker's shop, secondly as a corn and coal merchant now, at the age of 51, took up a third. He and his wife Eliza moved to Pyle Farm to take over his deceased son's tenancy of the farm and help the young widow in the upbringing of their two small granddaughters. It would not be every man's choice in his early fifties to move into the world of sleepless nights and interrupted days that would be occasioned by the presence of a $2^1/_2$-year-old girl and a 3-month-old baby.

For George Alexander his eldest brother's death was to bring to an end his brief career as a commercial traveller and to ensure his return to Horndean along with his pregnant wife Hester. George came home to begin what was to become probably the most significant career move in Horndean's history, the master of the *Ship and Bell* inn. When his first child George William, was baptised at Catherington on 10 July 1853, George's occupation was given as 'Innkeeper, *Ship and Bell Inn*'.[24] By then instead of having three older brothers George had only one, Richard Rogers who, after Henry's death, remained as keeper of the grocer's shop; a position that it seems he had taken over in 1851, since in that year the bills from the shop began to be made out as from Richard Gale and Son instead of R. Gale only. Surviving bills for the years 1847 to 1852 show the shop had the custom of both the Reverend S. C. Jervoise and the Lord of the Manor, Sir J. C. Jervoise, supplying them at Idsworth House with a wide range of groceries such as currants, raisins, sugar, salt, bread, cheese, eggs and flour, and spices including nutmeg, cloves, pepper, mixed spice and lemon peel as well as lemons, vinegar and mustard. Tobacco and pipes along with cigars were also provided. William Wise, Richard's tenant at the *Ship and Bell*, also supplied spirits to the Jervoises.[25] Despite the untimely death of his older brother in January, Richard junior was soon to bring some happiness back to the Gale family for, on 31 March that same year, he married at Chalton

Parish Church Susan Boys, the 23-year-old daughter of Thomas Boys, a Chalton farmer, and his wife Ann.[26] He was the last of Richard and Eliza's sons to marry and the marriage register gave his occupation as grocer.

His marriage, however, was to be tragically short for just over 13 months later Richard Rogers, Richard Gale's second son, died aged 28 on 5 May 1854 and was buried three days later with his older and younger brothers in Catherington churchyard.[27] From being the youngest of four sons, fate had now ensured that George Alexander was the only survivor, but not the only male member of the Gale family to survive, for when Richard junior died, his wife was already in an advanced state of pregnancy, and only a month later Susan gave birth to a baby boy and, not surprisingly, called him Richard Rogers after the young husband she had so recently lost and still mourned. The baptism of baby Richard was, however, to prove a double Gale celebration for on the same day, 4 June, at Catherington church, the young Richard Rogers was joined by George Alexander and Hester Gale's second child and son Herbert Ross in the baptism ceremony.[28] Once again, some light had come to brighten the darkness for the ageing Richard and Eliza and their widowed daughter-in-law Susan.

In the summer of 1854, George Alexander was still stated to be of the *Ship and Bell*, but 'Master' not 'Innkeeper'. The following year, however, when his first daughter Julia Ann was baptised at Catherington, he was described as a merchant[29] and the *Post Office Directory of Hampshire* (1855) clarifies what type of merchant since he is there described as brewer and wine and spirit merchant of Horndean,[30] this being the first reference to G. A. Gale as a brewer and suggests some expansion of the brewing facilities at the *Ship and Bell* had occurred. In the same commercial directory, his father Richard is named both as a farmer of Pyle Farm, Blendworth, but also appears as Richard Gale and Son, coal and corn merchants and farmers of Horndean.[31] Clearly Richard had continued his merchanting activities after taking over Pyle Farm and, as his sole surviving son, it would seem George Alexander was assisting his father in these aspects of his business.

With his three older brothers all having died, it was George Alexander's life, both family and business, which was to dominate the late 1850s. Then a young man in his late twenties, George was to demonstrate that he could be no less successful in business than his father had been and still was. There is no doubt that he substantially expanded brewing facilities at Horndean, for, by 1861, then aged 32, he was described as a brewer, wine, spirit, coal and corn merchant employing nine men and two boys.[32] In the process of growth he had also acquired, in April 1859, a dwelling-house in South Street, Emsworth, with garden, orchard, stable and outhouses for £475 from Robert Stafford, grocer of Emsworth, which he was to convert into the *Coal Exchange* public house. In March of the following year, *The Heroes of Waterloo* was purchased from Messrs. John and William Rudge. The inn had been built on a piece of land of 'over three acres of the Forest of Bere on the turnpike road from London to Portsmouth and north east of the Hambledon Road', which had been bought in 1814 by Charles Matthew from Thomas Fitzherbert Esq. This was to be the north quadrant of the crossroads in the centre of Waterlooville. The following month, in partnership with his father Richard, described as a merchant of Pyle Farm, George bought, for £240, the two dwelling-houses on the west side of the London road at Cowplain Bottom, then used as a beerhouse called the *Spotted Cow*.[33] These are the tangible indications of expansion, but it is quite possible that other properties were acquired, having since been disposed of and, hence, no trace of them as assets of Gales Brewery remains.

Nevertheless, it is clear that, at least from the late 1850s, George Alexander was successfully expanding his brewery business, aided by the growing consumption of beer per head in England from 29.2 gallons in the late 1850s to 40.5 gallons in the late 1870s.[34] In addition, water was regarded as potentially injurious to health before the public health improvements of the 1870s and work practices for many were laborious and believed to be helped by nutritious beer consumption. Urban growth contributed to increased beer-drinking. Often bad housing, overcrowded with children meant that the pub provided more warmth and companionship than the home. In Gales' case, Portsmouth was the growing town and seaports had the highest levels of drunkenness.[35] Thus the 1860s and 1870s were good decades for brewers.

George Gale's success, however, was not enjoyed without interruption, for considerable personal adversity and sorrow was to fall heavily upon the young couple. The year 1857 was to be a particularly devastating one both for George, but especially for his wife Hester, for within the space of five months, they were to gain one child but lose three. Late in July, their second son 3-year-old Herbert Ross died and was buried on the 27 July. Only five days later, their first-born, and only surviving son, George William, was to follow his younger brother into the grave at Catherington churchyard.[36] At the time of this double tragedy, the 29-year-old Hester was between four and five months pregnant with her fourth child who was born in mid-December. Baptised Alice Helena on 16 December, the tiny girl had only a brief and tragic stay on earth, being buried with the brothers she never knew just three days later.[37] What this final fatality of 1857 must have done to Hester can only be guessed at, but the couple were left with their single surviving daughter, almost 2 years old Julia Ann, that Christmas time, whereas the previous summer they could have expected to spend it happily with the lively and noisy sounds of four delighted children ringing in their ears.

Little Julia would at least have been able to enjoy the company of her 7- and 5-year-old cousins Jeannette and Frances, her Aunt Sarah's daughters, and no doubt the family spent some of their Christmas at Pyle farmhouse, their cousins' home, where grandparents Richard and Eliza would have been able to help care for the three girls. For Hester, however, it must have been a particularly sorrowful and joyless Christmas during which she would have had much time to dwell on her year of terrible misfortune, since her household consisted of two single teenage girl servants and probably a nurse to care for Julia. Certainly in 1861 after she had given birth to her fifth child and third baby boy, baptised Richard Lewis on 29 January, a 57-year-old married nurse Jane Lock was also living in.[38] These assistants would have eased the workload for Hester but in so doing gave her time to spend brooding heart-brokenly over her lost children, as well as her father, who died in 1860.[39] And, as if life had not dealt Hester enough blows, tragedy was once again to stalk the young Gale couple, for within four months of his birth, the young baby Richard was to join his brothers and sister in the family grave in Catherington churchyard, a victim of bronchitis. Even the most stone-hearted of Horndean residents could not help but have felt some sympathy for the quadruple loss, including all their three sons, which the couple had suffered.

No business success could substitute for such real and human despair. Yet George Alexander at least had his commercial activities in which he could immerse himself to reduce the pain and his father Richard was still available to assist, as was seen in the purchase of the *Spotted Cow*. George also had responsibilities to a growing workforce. His clerk and assistant, 16-year-old Portsmouth-born Edward Ozborn, lived in with George's wife, family and servants, and along the Havant Road lived 36-year-old brewer's labourer Henry Grafham with his wife and 1-year-old daughter, as did brewery cellarman, 32-year-old widowed John Munday and his three daughters and housekeeper.[40] With these and other family men, some of whom would have been working in his other diverse merchanting activities, dependent on his business skills and decisions, George would have had little time for long-term mourning.

In addition to the brewery, he maintained a lucrative sideline in the expanding local coal trade. Hampshire, with defence, industrial and demographic expansion in the first half of the nineteenth century, needed growing amounts of coal. Increasingly larger volumes were shipped in from north-east England, especially Sunderland, and from various Welsh ports to a number of Hampshire ports, the most significant of which were Southampton and Portsmouth. Coal was needed by a variety of enterprises and customers, ranging from educational institutions, learned groups and public utilities, to industrial concerns such as salt processing, paper manufacture and brewing, from private consumers to the ubiquitous armed forces. Coals were available in great quantities and qualities and between 1784 and 1830, the number of south Hampshire coal merchants had risen dramatically from 24 in 1784 to 118 in 1830.[41] From at least 1851, and doubtless before, Richard Gale had been actively working as a coal merchant in Horndean. While the records of coal landed at Portsmouth for 1837–41 show no direct purchases by him, he probably bought from one of the town's many coal merchants. He certainly had trading links with 'vile dirty' Portsmouth in the early 1840s, wharfage accounts revealing the unloading of starch, vinegar, sugar, paper, a hamper and pails for him between August 1840 and April 1841, materials that were doubtless disposed of during the course of his general trading activities at Horndean.[42] From March 1853 Richard's customers for coal included Blendworth vestry and churchwardens. From 1854 onwards, he supplied them with wine as well. In March 1859 his account for 'Wine, Coals and Straw' amounted to £2 4s. 6d. *Circa* 1860 he appears to have made this part of the business over to George who, from March 1861, was supplying the Blendworth authorities with coal and continued to do so throughout the ensuing decade, albeit in small quantities only. In March 1874, some £1 0s. 4d. worth were supplied; two years later the bill amounted to £1 17s. 8d.[43] But such amounts were hardly destined to make him a fortune. Other customers would have been the brewery, following the adoption of steam technology, the local workhouse and private residences, both grand and small, in Horndean's immediate neighbourhood.

Though never a farmer himself, his father Richard having gone into that line of business following his eldest son's death, George nevertheless retained links with that sphere of economic activity. Some links came, quite naturally, through the family concern of corn merchanting, in which George appears to have been directly involved from at least 1859 onwards.[44] Even so, later in 1861, George was to take Hester and the household away from the sad and debilitating memories of Horndean to live in the fashionable and growing middle-class resort area of Southsea. He bought Osborne Lodge, 53 Osborne Road,[45] and set up house some distance from his growing brewery but near his expanding business interests in Portsmouth, although, more importantly, where the sea air could help to restore Hester's spirits from the melancholy depths into which they must have sunk following the repeated tragic loss of so many of her babies during the first ten years of their marriage.

Brewing was perhaps the one industry in which the entrepreneur did not constantly need to be in attendance at his plant. Most of the expense was tied up in the circulating capital stocks of malt, hops and brewed beer. Considerable skill was required in buying malt and hops, and in taking the decisions in the actual processes of the brewing. Once the processes were commenced, however, only general supervision was necessary and could be delegated to a brewery manager, as could the more routine tasks of distribution, collecting cash and accounting. Once the business had been developed then the skills of buying and brewing could be carried out by the able men trained in the relevant skills.[46]

There is little doubt that George Gale continued to develop his brewery despite his move to Southsea. The tangible evidence of growth was the acquisition of at least three more public houses, the *Fifth Hants Volunteer Arms*, Southsea, in February 1864, and *Uncle Tom's Cabin*, Cosham, in September 1865 and the *Dolphin Tavern*, Landport, in June 1866. The addition of the *Golden Lion*, Fareham, in February 1869, gave a total of nine houses known to have been acquired by then[47] and, assuming a horse dray travelled at no more than 4 miles per hour, a considerable extension to Gales trading area. But since, at some time in the early 1860s, a steam-engine was installed in the brewery, the implication of this technological improvement is that the brewery must have been supplying rather more than the half a dozen or so inns for which evidence still survives. The costs of buying, installing and operating a steam-engine would make no sort of economic sense if output to supply a handful of public houses was all that was required.[48] Additionally, it is clear that the brewery itself was extended, since in March 1863 'The Horndean Steam Brewery having been considerably enlarged by adding extensive cellars, etc., the proprietor Mr. G.A. Gale gave a supper on the 20th inst. to the workmen and his staff'.[49] Even so, perhaps demand for George Gale's ale was growing faster than he could supply it for, in late 1867 or early 1868, he was to lease, from J. L. Anderson, the Newtown Brewery at 259 Commercial Road, Portsmouth, for £41 per annum.[50] The taking on of this lease also suggests that George must have acquired some licensed houses in Portsmouth as supplying them from a local brewery would be economically justified by reduced transport costs. It was also conveniently located on the main road out of Portsmouth for George to be able to call on his way from Southsea to his larger operations at Horndean.

For Hester the move to Southsea would have provided her with the temporary diverting mental activity of arranging and organising the establishment of a new home. But, even so, in these years of turmoil, yet another shadow was to fall across the couple, for in early June 1862, George's mother Eliza was to die at the age of 63 at Pyle Farm and to be buried on 7 June with her three sons as well as George and Hester's children in the family tomb in Catherington churchyard. Old wounds were not being allowed to heal too easily. Fortunately, happier events were not too far away. George and Hester produced the ideal solution to combat the young wife's sorrow – children. In 1864 Hester gave birth to another daughter, Agnes, to whom, no doubt, the now eight-year-old Julia would have been delighted to act as a little mother. Then, in 1869, at the age of 41, Hester had a third surviving daughter and final child, Beatrice Ada.[51] From this time on George would have been the only male in the Victorian household containing six females – his wife, three daughters and two servants!

However, although 1869 was to see the end of George and Hester's family building, it was also to see the end of most of the Horndean Brewery, for on a still March day:

> A serious fire broke out on Saturday morning [6 March] at Mr. G. A. Gale's steam brewery and spirit stores, Horndean. A plentiful supply of water being at hand, the fire had considerably abated before the arrival of the fire engine from Havant. The office, engine room, grinding room and a considerable portion of the brewery, however, were destroyed. Fortunately the fire was discovered in time to save the stock of ale and beer, as well as the spirit store and a very large quantity of malt and barley. The malt-house, through the exertions of the workmen, was not much damaged. Providentially there was very little wind, or the whole of the buildings and the stock must have been destroyed. Great sympathy is felt for Mr. Gale, who is generally respected by the neighbouring gentry and inhabitants. It is satisfactory, however, to know that as Mr. Gale has a brewery in Landport, he will not be considerably inconvenienced by the occurrence. The property is insured in the Royal Farmers' Insurance Company and the fire is supposed to have broken out in the engine room.[52]

Steam-engines could clearly have disadvantages as well as advantages. Installed in breweries to provide power for grinding the malt and raising the water, in Horndean's case from a well of considerable depth, they were also employed for driving machines and using surplus steam to heat the copper. Thus, not only were various economies achieved in the use of horses and labour, but also engines provided uninterrupted and constant work adding efficiency and greater convenience to the operation of the brewery. The cost in coal to feed the engine was much less than that in horses and horse feed which it replaced.[53]

Since a substantial portion of the brewery was destroyed yet the spirit store, malt house and the stocks of ale and beer were saved, it would seem that the brewery was of considerable size before 1869, thus confirming the view that a steam-engine would not have been installed simply for supplying a few inns. In addition, references to the malthouse and large quantities of malt and barley suggest that, like most brewers in southern England, George Gale made his own malt. However, traditional floor-malting took up much space, thus his scope for expansion in this activity on the Horndean site would have been limited. Of the part that remained undamaged, the cool cellars were probably the largest area. Built of thick solid flint walls, they were used for fermenting the beer in an age before refrigeration and no doubt it was in these that the stocks of ale and beer were preserved. They are still to be seen at the Horndean Brewery along with a flint-walled building, adjacent to the north-east rear corner of the *Ship and Bell*, and the well-head which was probably part of the undamaged malt-house. The size of these surviving parts confirms the considerable scale of the brewery which pre-dated the fire.

It did not take George Gale long to repair the damage, since rebuilding on an even larger scale was shortly commenced with an imposing new tower carrying the date of its erection as 1869. No doubt the insurance payout assisted the speed of the building, since only ten days after the fire, the Royal Farmers Insurance Company paid out £424 4s. 0d. to Richard Gale and £508 12. 0d. to George Alexander Gale – a total of £932 16s. 0d.[54] If the date of 1869 on the brewery tower represents the year in which rebuilding was completed, then a prodigious amount of work was carried out within eight and a half months at most, by what must have been an extensive workforce.

Again, the scale of redevelopment testifies to the substantial growth of George Gale's brewing enterprise and reflects his optimistic view of the future despite the reintroduction of licensing for public houses that same year as a result of the activities of the growing Temperance movement. Even so, following the fire there must have been at least several months in which brewing could not have been undertaken at Horndean, so it was indeed most fortunate that George had rented the Newtown Brewery only the year previously, thus allowing him to continue to supply his customers. He had also diversified within the industry since he was obviously buying in wholesale stocks of spirits to sell on to the landlords of his houses, as the spirits supplied to the *Golden Lion*, Fareham, testify (see Table 3.1). Clearly the inn was a regular and reliable customer with a steady spirits intake averaging 148 gallons per year, with some exceptions, such as 1871 when the figure just topped 200 and 1875 when supplies only went in for the first half of the year, probably because of overstocking between 1870 and 1874.

That his business activities at Horndean had flourished can be seen by the fact that his workforce had more than doubled in the space of ten years, for in 1871 the 42-year-old brewer and wine merchant was employing 20 men and two boys.[55] Assisting the growth of the brewery

Table 3.1   Spirits supplied to *Golden Lion*, Fareham, 1868–89

Year	Amount in gallons
1868 (March–December)	111.75
1869	155.00
1870	139.75
1871	200.50
1872	162.13
1873	202.00
1874	170.00
1875 (January–June)	88.00
1882	134.00
1883	130.00
1884	130.00
1885	139.00
1886	147.50
1887	136.00
1888	91.50
1889	133.00
Total	2,270.13

Source: Gales Archive, Spirits Ledger for *Golden Lion*, Fareham, 1854–1950, n.p.

was the continued rise in the population both of Horndean and south-east Hampshire as well as the increasing standard of living in the 1860s.[56] Both Blendworth and Catherington's population rose by nearly 20 per cent between 1851 and 1871 whilst that of south-east Hampshire rose by 44 per cent to over 52,000 people. However, the greatest increase was on Portsea Island since over 44,600 additional inhabitants were recorded in the 20-year period when population grew by 65 per cent.[57] Clearly, the acquisition of a brewery and public houses on the island was an astute move by George Gale and the growing population at Horndean would not only have ensured local labour for rebuilding after the fire, but also a workforce for the brewery.

The most important member of his workforce was 51-year-old Cosham-born family man, Edward Windebank, who was the only brewer and had been so at Horndean for most of the 1860s at least, having previously been in London. With his wife and three school-age children, the youngest of whom, Matilda, was baptised in Catherington church on 4 February 1865 when her father was described as a brewer,[58] Windebank lived only three doors north of the *Ship and Bell* along the

London Road so was in close proximity should he be needed, and from where he could keep a close eye on the brewing operations. On Horndean Hill lived 38-year-old George Holmes, also with a wife and three children, and described as an 'assistant in brewery'. It seems that the brewery was already large enough to employ an assistant to the brewer. Holmes had come from Hambledon and had not been in Horndean for more than four years at most and it seems more than likely that he had been hired as a result of the expansion after rebuilding.

Despite the fire caused by the steam-engine, George Gale was not put off modern technology and his rebuilt brewery also contained a new steam-engine which was under the supervision of Derbyshire man Stephen Farnsworth, the 49-year-old engineer in the brewery. He had come to live in Portsmouth Road, Horndean from Portsea with his wife and two children, both of school age. Indicating the rise in administration costs as the brewery grew was the employment of three clerks. Chief of these was 30-year-old married man Jeremiah Stubington and under him were two young single men, 22-year-old Henry Feltham and Richard Gale, aged 17. The latter was the young Richard Rogers born in 1854 shortly after his father's death at the grocer's shop built by his grandfather. Richard was starting out on his career in the brewery, a career which was to lead to a succession of later Richard Gales being involved. Both he and his fellow clerk Henry Feltham were lodgers with Edwin and Sophia Martin, who it seems had leased the grocer's shop from Richard Gale, now 69, still farming at Pyle Farm but on a prodigious scale, especially in view of his age, since the farm was then of 600 acres and employed 11 men and four boys. His younger granddaughter, Frances, aged 18, still lived with the widowed Richard, but his elder one, Jeanette, had married the previous year at the age of 20 another farmer, Soberton-born James Goldsmith, who held the 596-acre Blendworth Farm, employing 11 men and six boys. No doubt both farms were able to supply the increasing quantities of barley which George Gale's expanding brewery required.

The brewery also employed a cooper, 34-year-old Odiham-born Thomas Freeman, indicating the growing need for more wooden casks and barrels to be made or kept in good order. In addition, three cellarmen, all living in Horndean, were on the brewery payroll. Swanmore-born David Burgess, a 30-year-old married man with a 1-year-old son, and 24-year-old Edwin Westbrook from Southwick, who was also married, were the general cellarmen, whilst 48-year-old Edward Lawrence from Southsea was the wine cellarman living with his wife and 19-year-old daughter in Horndean. Two draymen were James Smith from Bishops Waltham, aged 30, married with four children, living along the Portsmouth Road, and single man Harry Wyatt living with his parents, and one of only two of the brewery staff who was born in Catherington parish. The other was one of the four identifiable labourers, Albert Shawyer, also a single man living with his parents. The remaining three labourers were 53-year-old Charles Brice from East Stratton, who had a wife and three children, 24-year-old single man William Jackson who lodged with Edward Lawrence the wine cellarman and, finally, William Drewatt born in Kingsclere but living with his parents at Waterloo, making him the one worker who had a considerable walk to work each day. None of these brewery staff is named among the six who were identified in the census ten years earlier, although Henry Grafham, who was named as brewer in 1861, was only a labourer in 1871.[59]

By 1871, Horndean also boasted a maltster in residence, 37-year-old Richard Payne who lived with his wife and six children in the Blendworth parish part of Horndean. He was from Christchurch and had a maltster lodging with him, 22-year-old Henry Stubington from Hambledon. It seems an inescapable conclusion that a maltster's presence in Horndean could only be connected with the growth of the brewery and its consequent increasing demands for malt.[60]

After the turbulent years of the late 1850s and 1860s, the 1870s were for the Gale household at Osborne Lodge a quiet decade, in so far as any family with a teenage daughter and two small ones growing up could ever be regarded as quiet! The end of the decade was marked by grandfather Richard, at the age of 77, at last ceasing his agricultural activities at Pyle Farm and retiring honourably to live at Crookley, where he had built a large and imposing house in its own spacious grounds, close to the rear of the brewery at Horndean.[61] Almost simultaneously, George's eldest daughter, Julia, married at St Judes Church, Southsea, on 23 October 1879, Edwin Marvin an upholsterer from a long-established family firm in Portsea.[62] A further happy event of the 1870s was the marriage of George's nephew, young Richard Rogers Gale, to Brighton-born Elizabeth Newman, daughter of an ironmonger from Ardingly, Sussex, in 1879.[63]

Although family life may have been more tranquil for George Gale, the same cannot be said about his business activities. There is little doubt, though equally little firm evidence, that the number of outlets for the brewery's output grew, as did the volume of work at the brewery itself. Certainly, the tangible evidence is that George acquired a beerhouse in Lake Road and another in Oxford Street, both in Landport,[64] as well as an outlet in Little Southsea Street, Southsea, in 1877.[65] Even more indicative of growth was the increase in the number of employees at the Brewery. By 1881 at least 24 workers were employed and probably considerably more since, of the 22 employees in 1871 only 17 were traced, and only six of the 11 in 1861, it seems that the known 24 in

1881, must understate the real figure, especially since three other cellarmen were known to be in Horndean in the early 1880s.[66] Nevertheless, the indications of an expanding brewery are inescapable. Only one cooper was known to be employed in 1871 whereas there were three in 1881 plus four hoop-makers, indicating a large expansion in the provision and maintenance of barrels. Similarly, the five known labourers in 1871 had become eight in 1881. Conversely, the two draymen had become only one, Catherington-born George Martin. It is in this transport section of the brewery that more staff must have been employed in delivering the barrels to the expanding number of public houses and off-licences in south-east Hampshire that Gales supplied.

However, continuity in employment at the brewery was limited, being provided by only three members of staff. Edward Windebank, now a 61-year-old widower, continued as the brewer but his assistant was Richard Rogers Gale who had exchanged the administrative side of the brewery as clerk, for the production side. By now a married man with a 1-year-old son, Richard Newman, he had worked in the brewery for something like 12 years. The third long-serving employee was former chief clerk, Jeremiah Stubington, who had been elevated to brewery manager, again an indication of growth that such managerial posts were required. One other new post which had been created was that of fireman in the brewery, held by 36-year-old Charles Hall, a married man from Midhurst who had five children, all born in Blendworth, suggesting he had been employed by George Gale for at least eight years whilst raising his family.[67]

Despite the fact that when the fire at the brewery occurred in 1869, 'great sympathy was felt for Mr. Gale, who was generally respected by the neighbouring gentry and inhabitants',[68] perhaps much of that sympathy was related to the harrowing events through which his family had recently gone, for there are two intriguing features of his workforce. First, that very few of his staff, the only exceptions being in senior positions, continued for any length of time in the brewery, and none looked upon it as a place of work for life, and secondly, that increasingly smaller proportions of those traced were local Horndean residents born and bred. For example, in 1861 half of the six known members of the workforce were born in the Catherington parish. By 1871 that proportion had fallen to less than a quarter and in 1881 it was only one-sixth.[69] In an age of population growth and the lack of trade unions it was clearly a buyer's market for labour, but the lack of traditional loyalties known to exist in brewing[70] suggests that George Gale left something to be desired as an employer. It also implies that he had not developed tied private houses for brewery labourers since such ties would have more firmly fixed his workforce into his brewery. No doubt, his continued residence in Southsea would mean no close or paternalistic relationship was developed with his men.

George's empire was growing in other directions as well. Between at least 1878 and 'registration' as an incorporated company in 1888, he supplied nearly 200 customers privately.[71] That neither address nor occupation is given in all cases, precludes a full analysis. It is, however, possible to draw out some conclusions about his clientele during these ten years. Geographically they were divided between four counties, with a heavy concentration in Sussex. In Hampshire there were two communities served – Petersfield, where William Chase purchased small amounts of beer in September 1880 and February 1881, and Southsea, where Kings Road wine merchant George Peters was a customer in July 1880. A Mr Atkinson from Blandford Road, Ealing, was the one customer from the metropolis, while Surrey produced four, two from Chiddingfold and two from Haslemere. It was Sussex that provided the bulk of the customers, some 142 distributed between 29 communities (see Table 3.2). What the table shows quite clearly is the overwhelming preponderance of customers in the Sussex market town of Midhurst, while the geographical proximity of many of these communities to one another should be noted.

Where social and/or occupational details are given, this permits further analysis as shown in Table 3.3. George Wild from Stedham was the solitary beerhouse keeper who made one purchase from George in

Table 3.2   George Gale's Sussex customers, 1878–88

Ambersham	2	Lurgashall	3
Bepton	1	Midhurst	63
Chichester	6	Milland	1
Chithurst	1	Northchapel	2
Cocking	3	Petworth	4
Cowdray	5	Pulborough	1
Didling	1	Rogate	2
Easebourne	8	Selham	2
Elsted	1	Stedham	5
Fernhurst	5	Sutton	1
Graffham	2	Terwick	1
Heyshott	2	Tillington	6
Iping	3	Trotton	2
Lavington	1	Wisborough Green	3
Lodsworth	5		

Source: Gales Archive, Supply Ledger 1878–89.

Table 3.3 Social/occupational status of
George Gale's customers, 1878–88

Beerhouse keeper	1
Clergy	4
Earls	1
Esquires	6
Farmers	9
Innkeepers	20
Ladies	5
Officers	5
Professionals	4
Servants	6
Tradesmen	17
Total	78

Source: Gales Archive, Supply Ledger 1878–89.

mid-June 1881. Four customers were clergymen and while three made only modest purchases, Reverend Noakes of North Street, Midhurst, clearly worked up an insatiable clerical thirst purchasing, between January and September 1880, supplies of ale, medoc, claret, tarragona and whisky. Socially, the most important of George's customers, was the Earl of Egmont at Cowdray Park, while there were also a liberal sprinkling of esquires, four of whom resided in Midhurst. Nine customers were farmers, ranging from James Allen of Trotton who made only one purchase in late May 1882, to the unnamed farmer at Selham near Midhurst who regularly purchased beer supplies between October 1878 and June 1880. Richard Bridger at Iping bought 63 gallons of beer between January and May 1880, possibly laying in supplies ready for the thirsty work of sheep-shearing and hay-harvesting. Easebourne farmer Thomas Winter bought beer from George in September 1878 and also sold him 5 tons of mangold-wurzels for £5. Farmer William Richardson of Lurgashall purchased beer, rum, brandy, ale, gin, whisky, sherry and stout in early July 1879, either to slake his own thirst or in preparation for Harvest Home. Some 20 of the customers were innkeepers such as Mr Webb at the *New Inn*, Chiddingfold, Rueben Rollett at the *Railway Tavern*, Haslemere, both in Surrey, Sidney Callingham who ran the *Noah's Ark* at Lurgashall and made one purchase on 30 July 1878, and Mr Willison who kept the delightfully named *Three Moles* at Lodsworth. Some of the establishments served, such as the *Railway Inn* at Elsted, the *Angel* at Midhurst and the *Greyhound* at Cocking, were eventually to become company houses. Such an arrangement would, therefore, have clearly provided George and subsequent members of the family with useful local knowledge and insights into the relative economic viability of houses with a view to purchase. Equally, it is not impossible that some of the houses served may have actually been owned or leased and then disposed of by George prior to company formation in 1888. In this context, Midhurst was to be particularly important, George serving six innkeepers there. Of the five ladies, four came from Midhurst, where North Street resident Mrs Goodner was a particularly ardent tippler, purchasing sherry, claret, whisky, rum and brandy in mid-February 1880. Five were service officers, though whether retired or still on the active list is unclear. Their custom spanned from 19 July 1879 when Captain Gilpin of Tillington near Petworth purchased spirits from George, to 14 October 1881 when Captain Barnett of Midhurst did likewise. The most senior was General Paxton, a customer in late March 1880, who resided at St Anne's Hill, Midhurst.

Of identifiable professional customers there were just five – a veterinary surgeon, two doctors, an excise officer and a superintendent, all but one of whom came from Midhurst. The group categorised as servants included Charles Goble, 'Mr. Gosden's Bailiff' from Midhurst and a gardener from the town who purchased in January 1880. The foreman, butler, coachman and gamekeeper at Cowdray Park followed their employer's example and did business with George. Christmas 1878 was clearly convivial for Mr Norman the gamekeeper and his family, with supplies of whisky, cider, brandy, stout, gin, soda water and beer being laid in. Finally, there were 17 customers who were identified as tradesman, the bulk being, yet again, Midhurst residents. Grocer Henry Pescod bought stout, while Graffham grocer Frederick Pescod, possibly a relative, was a customer between June and September 1879. Andrew Fish, whose name belied his calling, for he was a butcher, bought gin and brandy. Chichester cooper W. H. Grover had a penchant for beer, while builder George Miles's favourite tipple was gin for he purchased 2 gallons early in July 1879. Midhurst coach-builder William Newman bought 477 gallons of beer between January 1880 and late April 1881, while Wisborough Green grocer A. W. Upfield made only one purchase in August 1881.

Throughout this period, since 1868, George had maintained his lease on the Newtown Brewery in Commercial Road, Landport, and from the beginning it is noticeable that William Wise, probably the son of the former innkeeper and brewer of the *Ship and Bell* in 1851, had been living next door to the Landport brewery presumably to act as brewer, where he remained until 1880, when he would have been in his seventieth year. By 1879 his home had been converted into a public house, the *Newtown Tavern*, which had a new landlord, John James Field, in 1881.

The following year Gales bought the brewery and public house from J. L. Anderson and sometime in the late 1880s the brewery was discontinued and the public house upgraded to incorporate the brewery site.[72] It would seem that growth at the Horndean Brewery had rendered the Landport Brewery redundant and George Gale had decided to concentrate his activities on a single site. Even so, he still continued to reside in Southsea. In fact he decided to change his residence from Osborne Road to a new and more imposing house, a further sign of business success. 'Elmsleigh' was on the corner of Yarborough Road, Southsea, a newly developing area of sizeable houses and gardens, to which he moved in 1883 and remained until the early 1890s when, while retaining ownership, he leased out the property.[73]

In the same year that he moved to Yarborough Road, he also became a grandfather, for his daughter Julia gave birth to a girl, Faith Evelyn, baptised at Catherington on 6 July. This was Richard Gale's third great-grandchild, for Richard Rogers had produced a second son, Herbert Reginald, in 1881, and was to complete his family the following year when daughter Kathleen Winifred was born.[74] She was the last great-grandchild Richard was to see, for having shared Christmas 1885 with George and Hester at Southsea and leaving 'in his usual health and spirits' he was taken ill on reaching Horndean and 'confined to his room which he did not again leave alive'.[75] On 16 January 1886 he died at 'Crookley' after some seven years or so of richly deserved retirement, still living with his 34-year-old granddaughter Frances Emma, whom he had gone to help raise from infancy at Pyle Farm in 1853. On a bleak, snow-swept day, the funeral cortege wound its mournful way to Catherington, family and private mourners being followed by the workhouse inhabitants who, 'dressed in their Sunday best', brought up the rear of the procession. The cortege was joined 'by the whole of the men employed in the brewery', the oldest hands carrying the coffin into church ready for the service. Afterwards it was taken to the south-east side of the church where in his eighty-fourth year, Richard joined his beloved wife Eliza and his three sons in their grave in Catherington churchyard,[76] having left his imprint on Horndean for generations to come.

The loss to George not only of a father but also of a mentor in both business and life could only have been tempered by Richard's age. When, early in April 1886, Richard's will was proved by George and James Goldsmith (jun.) as executors, the value of the personal estate exceeded £36,000. Three bequests, each of £7,000, were left to his grandson, Richard Rogers Gale, his granddaughter Jeannette Eliza Goldsmith, and in trust for his granddaughter Frances Emma Gale. To his great-grandson, Mortimer Gale Goldsmith, he left £1,600, his real estate and the remainder of his personal estate going to George,[77] as his only surviving son. Richard had already transferred the lease of the grocer's shop and house to his son 20 years earlier in 1866 and George had been receiving rent from whichever tenant ran the shop. In August 1887 George purchased the freehold of the house, shop, premises and several other lands for £2,905 19s. 0d.[78] Along with his business interests George was now comfortably off since his father's estate included 'Crookley' and its surrounding acres.

His brewing business, despite the changing climate of opinion, continued to expand. From the 1870s came the growth of the evangelical temperance movement, increasingly hostile to brewers and drinking. Even so, sales of beer do not seem to have been affected. In 1830 some 14 million standard barrels of beer were consumed in England and Wales. In 1860 that figure had risen to 20 million barrels, a rise of 43 per cent, and by 1890 to 32 million barrels, an increase of 60 per cent, although population growth meant consumption per head remained much the same, declining before the First World War from the 1870 peak to its 1840s level.[79] However, following the 1830 Beer Act, private brewing declined, more people turning to common brewers who could produce a consistent and, probably, no more expensive beer. Many country brewers were, therefore, engaged in a substantial private trade, as were Pike Spicers in Portsmouth and Gales in Horndean. Even so, licensed victuallers brewing on their own premises and beerhouse keepers doing the same far outweighed in number, although not in output, the number of common brewers. In 1841 there were nearly 28,000 brewing licensed victuallers, over 16,000 brewing beerhouse keepers and 2,258 common brewers. In 1870 over 20,000 victuallers and nearly 10,000 beerhouse keepers were still operating. However, in the two decades after 1870 substantial changes occurred with common brewers acquiring increasing tied estate and closing down associated brewing activities. Thus, by 1890, brewing victuallers numbered over 6,000 and beerhouse keepers over 3,000, whereas common brewers had only marginally shrunk in number to 2,175. The 1890s saw a large decline to 1,711 with amalgamations and take-overs, but the number of victuallers fell to under 3,000 and the beerhouse keepers to 1,582.

Publican brewers found it difficult to compete with the new pale and bitter ales that common brewers produced in the second half of the nineteenth century.[80] Small-scale brewers, like Gales, producing between 1,000 and 10,000 barrels per year increased in number from 1,300 in 1834 to about 1,800 in 1870. Then, in the period of increasing concentration, declined to just over 900 by 1900. Even so, they formed 70 per cent of the producers in 1891.[81] Gale, a newcomer in this trend, clearly realised the opportunity which accelerating demand and technological change provided, and consequently prospered, although it is unknown what proportion of the prosperity was due to the brewery's tied trade and how much to the free trade or private customers. Meanwhile, the big breweries, especially in London and Burton, grew faster and by 1880 the brewing industry was undergoing concentration into larger units, a trend which was to continue to the end of the century.[82] By the 1880s the temperance pressure groups began to be politically identified with the Liberals and the brewing interests with the Conservatives. Temperance groups certainly became active in Portsmouth[83] and in 1883 Hampshire brewers found it necessary to take concerted defensive action when in May at a meeting in the *Pier Hotel*, Southsea, they formed the Hampshire Brewer's Union 'for watching proposed legislation and defending the rights and interests of their trade'. Among their number was George Alexander Gale who was elected to the committee that had to at once 'select a deputation to call on the County and Borough Members [of Parliament] of Hampshire with a view to securing their opposition to the Local Option resolution down on the papers of the House'.[84] The local option was the proposal for local polls to determine whether any particular locality should have prohibition and, clearly, brewers were becoming concerned at the growing volume of temperance views.

Nevertheless, it is perhaps easy to exaggerate the strength of these views for it is clear that for some sections of society brewing was regarded as an attractive investment . The first public issue of brewery shares was the very successful Guinness £6 million float of 1886, heavily oversubscribed by £124 million. By 1890, only four years later, 200 brewery companies had share issues and this Stock Exchange boom brought a scramble for licensed properties as the fear grew that rival breweries would buy up all the tied houses. Limited liability and public ownership of shares meant breweries could raise capital and buy public houses on a scale far greater than previously. Thus, between 1888 and 1900, all the larger brewing partnerships became limited liability companies – 353 firms had raised £188 million in share issues by 1905.[85] The price of many licensed premises thus doubled and their number declined either through brewery amalgamation or the unwillingness of some local magistrates to renew licences. The number of licences fell from 104,792 in 1886 to 88,445 in 1914, whilst population in England and Wales rose between 1881 and 1911 by 44 per cent. Small brewery companies became the prey of larger ones and were bought out in order to gain control of their tied trade, some 125 companies at least being absorbed between 1888 and 1902.[86]

Remarkably, Gales survived this process of concentration even though it occurred locally. For example, Portsmouth United Breweries Ltd, having itself resulted from an amalgamation, centralised output at their Southsea Brewery and, in order to achieve economies of scale, closed those at Cosham and Portsmouth.[87] Although there is no evidence of Gales ever being involved in discussions concerning a take-over, it would seem that George Gale was personally uninterested in any such possibility, since on 13 April 1888 he had the brewery business registered as an incorporated company but retained control, in effect a private limited company. Three days later, at four in the afternoon on Monday, 16 April, George Gale and Company Limited held the first meeting of its board of three directors who were entered in the articles of association, namely George Alexander Gale, Richard Rogers Gale and William Smeed. Not surprisingly, George Gale who chaired the meeting was made managing director and Mr J. S. Stubington accepted the appointment of company secretary and brewery manager at a salary of £300 per annum. Forty-five-year-old Jeremiah Stubington had done well, rising from brewery clerk to manager during the 1870s. At the next meeting of the board on 21 April the directors reached agreement on the sale of the brewery and its associated properties from themselves to the company. George Gale's share was valued at £98,500 and William Smeed's at £1,500. Smeed joined Gales in 1884 having been involved in brewing at the Eagle Brewery, Spring Street, Landport in Portsmouth. However, the brewery was closed and Smeed's connection was through the operation of the Southsea branch which Gales ran as a separate account from Horndean. It was basically a wine and spirit merchants at 16 Osborne Road, which had also provided an outlet for Gales beers, supplying the well-to-do of the growing middle-class holiday resort of Southsea from at least 1857.

The valuation of the company at £100,000 represented the ownership of 18 public houses, one leasehold house, four off-licences, 18 brewery cottages, some small holding of land, as well as the brewery,[88] all of which admirably indicated the success of George Gale's business. After 1830 successful brewers had usually inherited or expanded a family enterprise or, alternatively, invested considerable sums in the purchase of a brewery. More rarely did they come from publican-cum-smaller common brewers.[89] George Gale was clearly one of these rarities, rather like John Smith, son of a Leeds tanner, who bought a Tadcaster coaching inn with its associated brewing facilities in the very same year – 1847 – that Richard Gale bought the *Ship and Bell* and developed one of Britain's largest breweries.[90] Gales, however, remained a single owner brewery – a rarity. Most were brewing partnerships, usually restricted to families.[91]

Meanwhile George Gale was not getting any younger, celebrating his sixtieth birthday in 1888. Perhaps by then the travelling back and forth from Southsea to Horndean was becoming more onerous for, in the early 1890s, he and Hester decided to return to Horndean to settle at his father's former house, 'Crookley', from where he could easily oversee operations at the brewery. Since their youngest daughter Beatrice, aged 21, married on 20 June 1891 at Blendworth church, it is clear they had already moved to 'Crookley' by that date.[92] Beatrice's husband was 29-year-old Edward Charles Jewell stated to be a brewer of Crookley, probably a member of the family which operated Jewell and Sons' Catherine Brewery in Catherine Row, Portsea, although on 5 April 1891, he was listed as a visitor to Crookley where George Alexander was in residence with his wife, two daughters, two sisters-in-law and five servants.[93]

Now back in Horndean George Gale began to take an increasing part in the affairs of the local community. He had previously been a member of the St Catherine's Lodge of Oddfellows (Manchester Unity) attending their annual dinner at the *Ship and Bell* on Tuesday 14 December 1869. Then the health of the army, navy and volunteers, including the names of 'Lieut G.A. Gale of the 2nd Hants Artillery' and 'Mr Richard Gale', was proposed. At the first meeting of Catherington Parish Council on 18 December 1894 G. A. Gale was unanimously elected chairman, a post he was to hold until his death in 1914.[94] In addition, he became chairman of the Catherington Board of Poor Law Guardians and was a magistrate for the Petersfield Division. He had also served as a member of the Portsmouth Hospital Committee and was a Master of the Carnarvon Lodge of Freemasons. He clearly had strong religious principles being for many years churchwarden at Blendworth church and worked to enlarge the Mission Hall at Lovedean,[95] as was later recalled: 'In religious circles he was prominent as the Churchwarden of Blendworth, and his work in connection with the Mission at Lovedean, where he, some time ago, had the Mission Hall enlarged, and where services are held each Sunday evening, is well-known.'[96]

Along with his increasing involvement in local affairs and the marriage of his last single daughter Agnes to Arthur Charles Harris Esquire, of Hayling Island, at Blendworth church on 5 September 1895,[97] George's life had come to a crossroads where he had to stop and review the future. He and Hester could look back not only on much sadness but also much success. Their three daughters were married well. Indeed Julia's husband, Edwin Marvin, was described as a gentleman at the baptism of both their second child George in 1888 and their third and final child, Dorothy, in 1890,[98] and they had a governess to look after the three children.

George was approaching his sixty-fifth birthday having built up the major business enterprise in the locality, owning the brewery, at least 30 public houses, leasing another six, possessing four off-licences and other small holdings in an area stretching from Chichester to Southampton and the Isle of Wight,[99] as well as supplying a long list of private customers. Running this scale of business at his age with a wife who was not always well were influences that must have caused George to ponder on his future. Fate had decreed that he had no surviving son to inherit his creation and he finally took the decision in 1896 to sell his brewery. At the height of the movement towards amalgamation and take-over by large breweries it was remarkable that his company did not suffer the same fate as many others. It can only be assumed that, with his nephew, Richard Rogers Gale, firmly established as brewer and with all the effort he had put into his creation he did not wish to see it disappear. Thus, following an interview between the two men, George Gale offered to sell on 30 July 1896 his entire interest in the company to Herbert Frederick Bowyer of Stoke Mill, Guildford for £97,240. Bowyer was given until 6 August, one week, to reply. Later the same day George remembered he had not stated in his letter to Herbert Bowyer that he reserved the right of supply of water and electric light to 'Crookley' which he had mentioned in discussion. He thus dashed off that same day another letter stating that he included the electric plant and water tunnel in his offer so long as the conditions of supply were met.

There is little doubt therefore that George had kept his business up to date with the installation of electricity long before its general application and it could be noted that electrification at the progressive brewery Bass at Burton was not undertaken until the 1920s.[100] That his business was successful can be seen by a reply Herbert Bowyer received from W. Laban, an auditor and accountant from London, whom he sent to Horndean to check Gales' company accounts. The result was that on 5 August Bowyer heard that for each of the three years 1893 to 1895 Gale and Co. had made over £8,000 profit averaging nearly £8,300 per annum. Laban said: 'There is no doubt that the business is a good and genuine one and I consider that the terms on which Mr G. Gale has offered to sell you his interest therein are very reasonable.' Laban was to write further about Herbert Bowyer finding the capital to purchase George Gale's interest but hoped he now had sufficient information, along with the 1895 balance sheet he sent, for H. F. Bowyer to lay before his friends. Clearly Bowyer did have enough information for the contract of sale drawn up by T. Blanco White was dated 10 August 1896.[101] An era had ended; another was about to begin.

Notes

1. PCRO CHU 41/1B/1 Catherington Parish Baptism Register 1813–42.
2. PCRO CHU 41/1D/1 Catherington Parish Burial Register 1813–56.
3. George Gale and Co. Collection of Property Deeds. Richard Gale's building is now Horndean Post Office.
4. PCRO HO 107/396 Census of Great Britain 1841.
5. George Gale and Co. Collection of Property Deeds.
6. P. Mathias, *The Brewing Industry in England, 1700–1830* (Cambridge, 1959), pp. 76–7.
7. Ibid., p. 373.
8. T. R. Gourvish and R. G. Wilson, *The British Brewing Industry 1830–1980* (Cambridge, 1994), p. 3.
9. Mathias, *Brewing Industry*, p. 356.
10. See E. A. Wrigley and R. S. Schofield, *The Population History of England, 1541–1871: A Reconstruction* (London, 1981), pp. 208–9 for population figures and Mathias, *Brewing Industry*, p. 375 for beer and tea consumption statistics.
11. P. Mathias, *The First Industrial Nation*, (2nd edn, London, 1983), pp. 191–202.
12. Mathias, *Brewing Industry*, pp. 255–7.
13. PCRO CHU 41/1D/1 Catherington Parish Burial Register 1813–56.
14. HO 107/1677 Census of Great Britain 1851.
15. PCRO CHU 3/1B/14 St Mary's Portsea Parish Baptism Register 1 January–21 December 1827.
16. PCRO CHU 40/1B/1 Blendworth Parish Baptism Register 1813–1914.
17. Mathias, *Brewing Industry*, pp. 435–6.
18. PCRO CHU 40/1B/1.
19. PCRO CHU 2/1/C/16 St Thomas Portsmouth Parish Marriage Register 31 May 1851–12 August 1855.
20. PCRO CHU 3/1B/15 St Mary's Portsea Parish Baptism Register 13 January–28 December 1828.
21. PRO HO 103/1677 Census of Great Britain 1851.
22. Guildhall Library (GL), MS 14989/11 Royal Farmers Insurance Company Minute Book 1848–50, n.p. , Transfer 16 April 1850.
23. *HT*, 2783, 29 January 1853.
24. PCRO CHU 41/1B/2 Catherington Parish Baptism Register 1842–68.
25. HRO 43M75/E/B2/1 Clarke-Jervoise Estate Papers.
26. PCRO CHU 39/1B/2 Chalton Parish Marriage Register 1838–1938; CHU 39/1A/5 1813–82 Chalton Parish Register including baptisms 1813–52. Susan was baptised on 6 December 1829.
27. PCRO CHU 41/1D/1 Catherington Parish Burial Register 1813–56.
28. PCRO CHU 41/1B/2 Catherington Parish Baptism Register 1842–68.
29. Ibid.
30. *Post Office Directory of Hampshire* (1855), p. 31.
31. Ibid., pp. 24, 31.
32. PRO RG9/699 Census of Great Britain 1861.
33. George Gale and Co. Collection of Property Deeds.
34. Gourvish and Wilson, *British Brewing*, pp. 30–32.
35. Ibid., pp. 437–8.
36. PCRO CHU 41/1D/2 Catherington Parish Burial Register 1856–1900.

37. PCRO CHU 41/1B/2 Catherington Parish Baptism Register 1842–68 and CHU 41/1D/2 Catherington Parish Burial Register 1856–1900.

38. CHU 41/1B/2 Catherington Parish Baptism Register 1842–68 and PRO RG9/699 Census of Great Britain 1861.

39. Thomas Ross appeared in the *Post Office Directory of Hampshire* (1859), p. 121, but not in any subsequent issue.

40. PRO RG9/699 Census of Great Britain 1861.

41. Material drawn from J. H. Thomas, 'Dirty but Necessary: The Coal Trade of Portsmouth and the Solent Ports 1700–1830' (unpublished paper, 1988).

42. PRO HO 107/1677 Census of Great Britain 1851; PCRO CF21/2, Day Book for Coals 1837–41; CF13/23, Wharfage Dues July 1840–April 1841, ff. 34, 99, 106, 190, 232, 243; E. C. Curwen, *The Journal of Gideon Mantell* (Oxford, 1940), p. 186.

43. PCRO CHU 40/2/2, Blendworth Churchwardens' Accounts and Vestry Minute Book 1785–1862, n.p., *passim*; CHU 40/2/3, Blendworth Church-wardens' Accounts and Vestry Minute Book 1865–96, *passim*. When, in the late1840s, Blendworth church was rebuilt, Richard Gale is shown as having contributed 100 tons of flints valued at £10, shown in another copy of the subscription list as 100 tons of coals to the same value: PCRO CHU 40/4/3, papers *re* building of Blendworth Church 1849–52.

44. *White's Directory of Hampshire* (1859), p. 576.

45. PCRO Parish of Portsea Rate Book 1861.

46. Mathias, *Brewing Industry*, p. 320.

47. George Gale and Co. Collection of Property Deeds.

48. For evidence of the existence of the steam-engine see reference in note 52.

49. *HT*, 3312, 28 March 1863. We are grateful to Philip Eley for drawing our attention to this entry.

50. PCRO Parish of Portsea Rate Book 1868, p. 36. 259 Commercial Road was in a row of buildings on the west side of the street between Thomas Street and Fitzherbert Street approximately where Sainsbury's car park and the adjacent filling station are now located.

51. Exact dates of birth have not been discovered and are calculated from ages given at death.

52. *HT*, 3815, 10 March 1869.

53. Mathias, *Brewing Industry*, pp. 89–98. In 1905 the well was 150 feet deep, with water at a depth of 82 feet: HRO 57M92/4, Clarke-Jervoise Estate papers.

54. GL MS 14989/17, Royal Farmers Insurance Company Minute Book 1864–69, Policy Nos 92919 and 92921, 16 March 1869.

55. PRO RG10/1145/89, Census of Great Britain 1871.

56. E. H. Phelps Brown and S. V. Hopkins 'Seven Centuries of the Prices of Consumables Compared with Builders' Wage Rates', *Economica* (1956), reprinted in E. M. Carus-Wilson (ed.), *Essays in Economic History*, vol. 2 (London, 1962), pp. 179–96.

57. B. Stapleton and J. H. Thomas (eds), *The Portsmouth Region* (Gloucester, 1989), p. 102.

58. PCRO CHU 41/1B/2 Catherington Parish Baptism Register 1842–68.

59. The details of the workforce in 1871 are taken from the census, PRO RG 10/219 Census of Great Britain 1871. Four other members of staff

have not been identified nor the two boys. Probably they were labourers and not specifically identified as associated with the brewery in the census schedules.

60. PRO RG10/1219.
61. *White's Directory of Hampshire* (1878), p. 151 gives Richard Gale as a farmer at Pyle Farm, Blendworth, whereas *Kelly's Directory of Portsmouth* (1880), p. 45 states Richard Gale senior was of Crookley, Blendworth.
62. PCRO CHU 36/1B/2 St Jude's Southsea Marriage Register 1870–89, Edwin Marvin's marriage to Julia Gale 23 October 1879.
63. East Sussex Record Office (ESRO). Richard Rogers Gale to Elizabeth Newman Ardingly May 1879.
64. *White's Directory of Hampshire* (1878), p. 420 and *Kelly's Directory of Portsmouth* (1880), p. 182 for Lake Road and Oxford Street beer outlets respectively.
65. George Gale and Co. Collection of Property Deeds.
66. The 1881 census does not state how many men and boys were employed by George Gale. Additional cellarmen were found in PCRO CHU 41/1A/7 Catherington Parish Register of Baptisms 1868–94.
67. PRO RG 11/1239 Census of Great Britain 1881 provides details of the staff employed at the brewery.
68. *HT*, 3815, 10 March 1869.
69. PRO RG 9/699; RG 10/1219; RG 11/1239 respectively Censuses of Great Britain 1861, 1871 and 1881.
70. Gourvish and Wilson, *British Brewing*, p. 198 when discussing the industry before the First World War, state 'All breweries could cite remarkable instances of the longevity of individuals' service and the attachments of families'. Gales Brewery, however, did not conform to this national characteristic.
71. Unless otherwise stated, what follows is based upon an analysis of a Supply Ledger for 1878–89, located in the Gales Archive. That a number of 1878 entries included sums of money brought forward suggests that there was an earlier ledger, the whereabouts of which is unknown, and possibly another covering west of Horndean.
72. The information about the Newtown Brewery and inn is obtained from PCRO Parish of Portsea Rate Books 1868–85 and 1891.
73. PCRO Parish of Portsea Rate Books 1883–85, 1891 and 1896. 'Elmsleigh' is now 31 St Edward's Road.
74. PCRO CHU 41/1B/3 Catherington Parish Baptism Register 1868–94.
75. *Portsmouth Times* (PT), 2401, 23 January 1886.
76. PCRO CHU 41/1D/2 Catherington Parish Burial Register 1856–1900. Richard Gale died 16 January 1886.
77. *Hampshire County Times*, 2422, 7 April 1886. Frances Emma Gale died shortly before her ninetieth birthday on 9 June 1942. She spent much of her time in travelling both at home and abroad: *HT*, 8315, 8316, 12, 19 June 1942. Mortimer Gale Goldsmith died on 12 September 1934, aged 62: PCRO CHU 40/3/7, Blendworth Transcripts and Monumental Inscriptions.
78. George Gale and Co. Collection of Property Deeds.
79. Gourvish and Wilson, *British Brewing*, p. 30.
80. Ibid., pp. 67–9.

81. Ibid., p. 111.
82. J. Vaizey, *The Brewing Industry 1886–1951: An Economic Study*, (London, 1960), pp. 3–4, 12.
83. For evidence of temperance movements in Portsmouth see J. M. Griffiths, 'The Rev. Charles Joseph, Leader of the Portsmouth Social Purity Organisation', (unpublished dissertation, Portsmouth Polytechnic, 1984).
84. *HT*, 5302, 26 May 1883.
85. Gourvish and Wilson, *British Brewing*, p. 262.
86. Vaizey, *Brewing*, pp. 8–12.
87. Ibid., p. 17.
88. H. F. Bowyer's Pocket Book 1896–1935, list of properties 1896.
89. Gourvish and Wilson, *British Brewing*, p. 226.
90. Ibid., p. 238.
91. Ibid., p. 239.
92. PCRO CHU 40/1C/2 Blendworth Parish Marriage Register 1837–1929.
93. PRO RG12/944 Census of Great Britain 1891.
94. HRO 20M81/A/PX1 Horndean Parish Council Minutes 1894–1944.
95. *PT* 4111, 6 November 1914.
96. *HT*, 6935, 6 November 1914.
97. PCRO CHU 40/1C/2 Blendworth Parish Marriage Register 1837–1929.
98. PCRO CHU 41/1B/3 Catherington Parish Baptism Register 1868–94.
99. Gales' Archive, Schedule of Properties 26 September 1898.
100. Gourvish and Wilson, *British Brewing*, p. 403.
101. The documents and letters referring to the sale are in the Gales Archive.

CHAPTER FOUR

The early years of H. F. Bowyer to the First World War

The Bowyer family had long been established in that part of southern England where the counties of Sussex, Kent and Surrey become contiguous. From at least the early sixteenth century they had been domiciled at Hartfield, Sussex where, apart from having sufficient land for farming, they were involved in the expanding and important sixteenth-century Wealden iron industry in which many of the armaments for contemporary warfare were produced.[1] As the century progressed, however, one branch of the family migrated westwards, first to East Grinstead and secondly to Charlwood on the Sussex–Surrey border north-west of Crawley.

This area was to be the Bowyer home for the seventeenth century when their fortunes were in the descendent, along with those of the Wealden iron industry. This branch of the family appeared to be in some financial difficulties and, although involved in farming, financial problems saw their farm at Worth, just east of Crawley, being sold. As a result, by the early eighteenth century their descendant John, was occupied as a carpenter and living at Newdigate, north-west of Charlwood.

However, by the end of the eighteenth century the family fortunes had been restored and they were again involved in farming, this time further north at Betchworth between Dorking and Reigate. With grain prices rising in England from the 1760s along with increasing population and especially the growth of London, it was an auspicious time for successful farmers and James Bowyer, who died in 1803, had clearly done exceedingly well since he was able to leave a farm in Leigh parish, south of Betchworth, to his eldest son James, a copyhold and black-smith's shop, also in Leigh, plus £500 to his second son John, and to his third son, Michael, a copyhold with windmill at Shellwood Common in Leigh plus his copyhold at Gadbrooke Common in Betchworth and £400. (See Appendix 1 for the Bowyer family tree.)

James had married three times and these three were sons by his first marriage. There were no children from his second marriage but his third produced a fourth son, Joseph, who inherited a house in Leigh. Moreover, if James's widow was to remarry, then Joseph was to receive all the contents of James's own house which he had bequeathed to his third wife Hannah. Out of the money in his Bank of England account

£1,000 was to be set aside to provide an annuity of £30 for his widow. James had clearly amassed a considerable fortune and left his children comfortably provided for.[2]

Michael, his third son born in 1770, was the first known Bowyer to be directly involved in milling, having inherited the windmill on Shellwood Common. He married Mary Ede, a farmer's daughter from Leigh, in 1793 and had one surviving son Michael and seven daughters. He evidently prospered for, when he died in February 1823, he left property in Betchworth, Charlwood and Reigate Heath to Michael, £14,000 to be shared equally between his daughters and an annuity of £100 per year from principal in the Bank of England plus all his household goods, together with a residence for life at Wonham Mill, to his 'loving wife Mary'. Wonham Mill was also to be a home for all his children until they reached the age of 21.

The mill and the miller's business was to become Michael's, but he had to pay a fair valuation on the land, stock, tackle, hay and corn pertaining to 'the farming business'. Even so, he also inherited two copyholds plus four acres of adjoining land and a 3.5 acre enclosure all in the manor of Brockham in Betchworth parish, in addition to almost 1.5 acres of land on Gadbrooke Common, also in Betchworth, a 17–acre freehold in Charlwood and a windmill with house and buildings on Reigate Heath. The rest of Michael senior's lands were to be sold and the money invested in government securities to pay his daughters' legacies. Clearly Michael Bowyer senior had been very successful both as a farmer and a miller, having acquired substantial landholdings and two mills.[3]

Michael junior, had been the second son of four when he was born in 1795, but his three brothers had all died in childhood, while his seven sisters had all survived. Being the only surviving son meant, first, that his inheritance was much larger than it would have been had his brothers been alive and, secondly, that at the age of 27 he was a wealthy young man. Just over a year after coming into his inheritance, in April 1824, he married Sarah Till, at St Mary's, Battersea. They were to have five sons and a daughter all surviving to adult life, although the eldest son Michael was accidentally killed at the age of 22. Their next three sons – William, Frederick Joseph and Henry Downs – were all to become established as millers. William remained at Wonham Mill, being buried in Betchworth in 1899, while the third son, Frederick Joseph, and the fourth, Henry Downs, moved westward jointly leasing Stoke Mill at Guildford in 1855 before Henry went on to Ockham Mill at Ripley, probably in 1866 when his brother Frederick Joseph leased Stoke Mill on his own for 14 years at a rent of £140 per annum. The mill had two wheels, three pairs of stones and came with 8 acres of land.[4]

The brothers' arrival at Guildford may not have been accidental since their Aunt Harriet, youngest sister of their father Michael, had married Thomas Bowyer, a grandson of John Bowyer, brother to the James who had established the family fortunes before his death in 1803.[5] Harriet's husband was a brewer and at least from the early 1850s, had been pursuing his craft at the Stoke Brewery, Chertsey Street, Guildford.[6]

Thus the brothers, Frederick and Henry, could have known of the lease of Stoke Mill becoming available from their family connections in the parish. Frederick Joseph was to stay at Stoke Mill until his early death at the age of 47 in 1877.[7] Even so, he had done well enough to take out a further lease on a recently erected neighbouring water mill, built as a paper mill, on the site of a previous one destroyed by fire in 1863.[8] This, along with Swan island, was leased for three years at a rent also of £140 per annum.

However, the year before he went to Stoke, Frederick Joseph had married Mary Bull and their union produced two sons and two daughters the last three surviving whereas the first born, a daughter Alice Mary, died aged only 2. Two surviving sons meant only one could inherit the family milling business. At the time of Frederick's death his elder son, Walter Paget, was only 18 and thus the estate was left in trust. The trustees, including his wife, had the choice of continuing the business or selling and investing the proceeds in securities with the dividends being used for the maintenance of the widow and children as well as for the latter's education. In the event, the 47-year-old Mary decided to continue in business until her elder son was old enough to take over, Walter remaining at Stoke for the whole of his life until his death in 1931.

Meanwhile, his younger brother Herbert Frederick, born in 1860, went to work for Lord William (Bill) Beresford as his factor, managing his estate near Dorking. He became an excellent horseman and, whilst working for Beresford, rode Lord Lonsdale's horse in a race against Beresford, the two Lords having bet on their respective horses. Bowyer won and may have been well paid for his victory.

In his estate manager's job Herbert Bowyer became acquainted with the Barclay Perkins brewing family, Augustus Frederick Perkins and his wife living at Holmwood just south of Dorking and being friendly with Lord Beresford.[9] They had three children, a son and two daughters. The younger, Elsie, who was also an able and enthusiastic horsewoman, clearly formed an attachment with the 36-year-old Herbert Frederick which became permanent on 22 April 1897, when the 23-year-old girl became his wife. The marriage took place at Southwark cathedral – Southwark being the home of the Barclay Perkins Anchor Brewery. However, the young couple were to make their home in Horndean and when their only child, Frederick Hugh, was born on 5 July 1898, his baptism took place at the ancient church of Catherington,[10] the Horndean Brewery lying just within the boundary of Catherington parish. Bowyer's residence at Westfield in Horndean, within a stone's throw of the brewery where he could keep in touch with the daily developments, was to prove of crucial importance in a period when the brewing industry generally was to pass through difficult times prior to the First World War.

The years between company formation and the outbreak of the Great War were to be remarkable for Gales in various ways. First, the period was hallmarked by general expansion of the business, exemplified in the take-over of local brewing concerns, in a run of healthy balance sheets and the acquisition of increased numbers of licensed premises. Secondly, there was the changing role and importance of the Gale family within the business. Thirdly, the brewery demonstrated an ability to keep abreast of technological developments and introduced modern sophisticated business aids. Finally, there was the effect these factors had on the brewery's output.

In the years before 1914 burgeoning company strength was amply demonstrated in a series of take-overs in 1903, 1907 and 1912 of rival brewing concerns, representing a steady accumulation of tied property. The first, in July 1903, was of Clarke's Homewell brewery situated in the nearby market town of Havant. Gales purchased the premises of this local rival for £15,000,[11] acquiring at the same time eight additional inns.[12] Havant merchants William and Harry Clarke, the vendors, also included in the deal some land contiguous to North Street in Havant. Of the eight houses purchased[13] five, the *Star Hotel, Robin Hood, Old House at Home, Brown Jug* and the *Dolphin*, were in the town itself. Also included were the *Ship Inn* at Langstone, the *Maypole Inn* on Hayling Island and the *Milkman's Arms* at Emsworth. The Clarke family connection went back about 50 years and each of the Havant premises was of considerable age. The *Star Hotel* site had been occupied by a cottage in 1703, of which brewer Samuel Clarke was a tenant from October 1850. The *Old House at Home* in South Street, originally called the *Laurel*, had been purchased by Clarke for £360 at a sale of premises in the *Dolphin*, Havant, on 13 August 1850, and the *Brown Jug* had been acquired by him in late September 1878. The *Robin Hood*, a cottage in 1802, had come into Clarke's possession in October 1857 whilst the *Dolphin*, an inn since at least 1846, had been acquired by him in May 1872. The *Ship Inn* at Langstone consisted of premises and a store, while the *Maypole Inn* at South Hayling had a rather different history. A messuage with garden and orchards and known from at least April 1735 as 'Biskins', the property had become the *Maypole* by July 1823 and been acquired by Samuel Clarke in September 1862. By contrast, the *Milkman's Arms* at Emsworth had not been acquired by him until 6 December 1884. Collectively, these inns were to provide Gales with a considerable proportion of the market for beer in the Havant area.

In 1907 came a further foray into rivals' territory, with the acquisition of the *Square Brewery*, the last of the combined breweries and alehouses in Petersfield, the market town with which George Alexander Gale already had links. Five years later, at least one public house was bought when the Wickham Brewery ceased operations. On 25 June 1912 the *Kings' Head* in Wickham Square passed into Company possession. Since at least mid-July 1909 John Smith had been the publican at a rent of £40 per annum. The formal owner was Mrs Frances E. Baxter of Blundellsands near Liverpool and she it was who sold the premises to Gales for £1,900.[14]

Much of the output of country brewers was traditionally supplied to the free trade, but from the 1880s there was an increased development of the tied trade as they followed in the footsteps of the larger provincial brewers. No self-respecting brewer could afford to ignore this process since if he did not purchase properties other rival concerns would undoubtedly do so. Generally, strengthening the local market base was the imperative behind the increasing scramble for licensed properties, but as local free houses became scarcer then firms not only had to look further afield for their acquisitions but also to pay higher prices. Thus, most brewery companies found that their property values represented over 40 per cent of their total capital and some even as much as 90 per cent.[15]

However, despite the acquisition of other breweries the company's asset value remained remarkably unchanging until the First World War (see Table 4.1). It would seem that either new acquisitions were offset by sales of other houses or, more likely, that no revaluation of properties was made since, even when asset value rose by more than £30,000 during the First World War, it was not as a result of increasing property values but because of an accumulation of stocks and growing debts and investments. Consequently, whereas Gales' property values represented some 76 per cent of their total capital before the First World War, they only accounted for 65 per cent at the end of it.

The need to maintain market shares was emphasized by national trends in beer-drinking. Whereas from the late 1840s up to the mid-1870s consumption of beer per head in England had risen consistently, during the 1880s it declined, as did national output (see Table 4.2).

This decline in consumption coincided with a national economic depression as well as alternative attractions for the beer-drinking public

Table 4.1 Total company assets, 1903–19
(year to 31 December)

1903	£155,273
1904	£155,438
1905	£155,427
1906	£156,226
1907	£157,634
1908	£156,802
1909	£156,046
1912	£159,116
1913	£161,129
1914	£164,347
1915	£169,924
1916	£174,965
1917	£177,976
1918	£191,709
1919	£197,235

Source: G. A. Gale and Co. Balance Sheets
1903–19, *passim*.

Table 4.2 UK beer output, consumption and real wages, 1850–1914

Years	Beer output (million barrels)	Consumption per head (gallons)	Average real wages (1850 = 100)
1850–54	16.1	21.1	101.2
1855–59	17.2	22.0	96.2
1860–64	19.9	24.6	105.8
1865–69	24.3	28.8	111.6
1870–74	27.6	31.1	127.4
1875–79	31.0	33.2	132.0
1880–84	28.5	29.2	137.2
1885–89	28.7	28.4	149.4
1890–94	31.5	29.8	164.0
1895–99	34.6	31.2	176.4
1900–04	35.2	30.2	175.2
1905–09	33.2	27.3	173.0
1910–14	34.1	27.0	171.2

Source: Mitchell and Deane (1962), pp. 343–5; Wilson (1940), p. 335.

in music halls and sporting occasions, plus the rise of mass markets in clothes and shoes, and the appearance of packaged foods such as tea and condensed milk as well as the increasing volume of imports of grain, meat, fruit and dairy produce. These, together with machine-produced furniture and cheap rail excursions, assisted by rising real wages, widened consumers' choices. It seems likely, therefore, that such social and economic changes did more to reduce beer consumption than the temperance movement, or the opposition of the Liberal government from 1905.

Perhaps such trends provided another reason for George Gale's decision to sell the brewery. Although in the 1890s there was some recovery in beer consumption, the early twentieth century saw the amounts consumed per head begin to decline yet again until a new low was reached in the years preceding the First World War, the like of which had not been seen since the early 1860s (see Table 4.2). In such circumstances, brewers who had expanded in the boom years up to the 1870s had to protect their market shares and did so by forward integration, leading to the rapid spread of tied house acquisitions after 1880, resulting in the powerful presence of brewers in the retail trade. Thus, from 75 per cent of licensed properties being in brewers hands in 1886, the proportion had risen to 95 per cent by 1913.[16] Gales, not surprisingly, participated in this process. Even so, as brewers completed this exercise, so the popularity of public houses began to decline with a shift to bottled beers retailed increasingly through off-licences.

However, by the end of the nineteenth century the brewing industry, like others, was to be affected by the downward drift in real wages and, although the population continued to increase by almost 13 per cent between the beginning of the twentieth century and the First World War, beer consumption per head in England and Wales fell by 18.5 per cent. Thus brewers generally, with surplus productive capacity and falling demand for their product, experienced declining profits.

Their difficulties were not helped by other developments. Beer duty had been raised in 1880, 1889, 1894 and 1900, although these increases were somewhat offset by the falling price of barley in the agricultural depression. Whereas before 1900 licensing restrictions, as imposed by the 1872 Act, had been applied in a somewhat leisurely fashion, particularly whilst Conservative governments were in office, the position was becoming increasingly difficult to maintain, not the least because of the growing propaganda of the Temperance movement. In 1899, the report of the Royal Commission on Licensing favoured further restriction. If it remained of a limited nature, however, and compensation was offered for lost licences, brewers would hardly object, since it allowed them to suggest uneconomic tied houses for closure which would maintain high property prices. But in 1902 the Farnham magistrates at the brewster sessions in Surrey decided to impose the full restrictions of the 1872 Act and faced with 45 renewals, refused nine licences without compensation. This was on the very edge of Gales' territory, particularly as they had acquired one property, the *Queen's Head* in Farnham, in late June 1888. The following year (1903) 240 licences were refused in England and brewers everywhere seemed threatened.

The Conservative government promised action and in 1904 passed a new licensing Act which ensured that Justices of the Peace (JPs) had to have valid reasons for closure, such as unsafe structures or houses habitually involved in undesirable conduct. Otherwise, compensation had to be paid on closure from a fund levied on all licensed premises. The size of this fund would clearly limit the pace of closure, consequently the Liberal Party's temperance element and the temperance movement generally was outraged.

The following year saw the arrival of a Liberal government and conflict with the brewing trade seemed inevitable since brewers had consistently donated to Conservative Party funds. The budget of 1909 contained proposals to raise licence duty on public houses, but was defeated in the House of Lords. The general election which followed brought yet another Liberal government into power and in 1910 its budget raised the licence duty with depressing effects on brewery shares.[17] The process of concentration, which had been so noticeable in the industry from the 1880s with at least 125 companies being absorbed between 1888 and 1902, was now to be felt in production. Thus Portsmouth United Breweries closed both their Cosham and Portsmouth breweries in an attempt to ensure the company's survival.[18]

The achievements of Gales throughout these difficult pre-war years when the brewing industry had such problems is undoubtedly remarkable. From Herbert Bowyer's acquisition of the brewery, records of performance become more readily available. Fortunately, Bowyer kept his own personal pocket-book which indicated monthly output figures for the brewery beginning in 1897.[19] From this it is clear that the Horndean Brewery's performance went completely against the trend of declining national consumption by producing a remarkable 48 per cent increase in output between 1897 and 1914 (see Tables 4.3 and 4.4).

However, this increase was not the result of growth in the production of draught beer, since its output in 1911 was virtually the same as that in 1897. Only in the last two years before the war did the output of barrels rise significantly, when production increased by more than one-fifth. Over the whole period, however, the rise was under 17 per cent. It was in the production of bottled beers that astonishing growth was

Table 4.3 Annual beer output: Gales Brewery, 1897–1914

Date	Barrels	Bottles (doz.)	Bottles as equivalent no. of barrels	Total (barrels)
1897	10,239	5,481	228	10,467
1898	10,081	7,463	325	10,406
1899	9,934	9,062	378	10,312
1900	995	15,811	718	10,713
1901	10,824	19,793	890	11,714
1902	10,869	30,566	1,329	12,198
1903	11,304	38,530	1,675	12,979
1904	12,039	34,162	1,552	13,591
1905	11,687	36,280	1,649	13,336
1906	11,042	33,921	1,541	12,583
1907	11,028	39,082	1,776	12,804
1908	10,955	43,239	1,965	12,920
1909	10,282	42,591	1,936	12,218
1910	9,943	52,960	2,407	12,350
1911	10,474	73,119	3,323	13,797
1912	11,316	81,966	3,725	15,041
1913	13,446	91,888	4,176	17,638
1914	13,688	96,867	4,403	18,091

Source: H. F. Bowyer's Pocket Book 1896–1935.

Table 4.4 Beer output: Gales Brewery, 1897–1914 (five-year averages)

Date	Barrels	Bottles (doz.)	Bottles as equivalent no. of barrels	Total (barrels)
1897–99	10,085	7,335	310	10,395
1900–04	11,006	27,772	1,233	12,239
1905–09	10,999	39,023	1,773	12,772
1910–14	11,773	79,360	3,607	15,383

Source: H. F. Bowyer's Pocket Book 1896–1935.

achieved. Year on year from 1897 to 1903 growth was virtually exponential, followed by a lull to 1907 after which, especially from 1909,
new growth, in absolute terms, was even faster. By 1914 bottled beer
output had grown by over 1,000 per cent and represented nearly a
quarter of total output accounting for most of Gales' ability to outper-
form its more famous and long-established competitors in the brewing
industry. In England as a whole, bottled beer production had not risen
to 25 per cent of output by the outbreak of the Second World War.[20]
Underpinning the growth was considerable expenditure on new bottling
plant, nearly £2,300 being spent between 1903 and 1912, new plant
being paid for in 1904 and an extension in 1911.[21]

A change in the system of wage payments may well have provided an
incentive for growth at the Horndean Brewery. In the last nine years of
George Gales's control combined annual wages and salaries had averaged just over £1,600. The young Herbert Bowyer, however, showed an
innovative approach to workers' payments from his first year, introducing in 1897 a commission system. The result was that annual wage
payments immediately rose to over £2,000 and Bowyer's first nine
years' wage bill averaged over £2,300. But with rising production for
the eight years from 1907 to 1914 inclusive, the wage costs rose to an
average of over £3,000. Thus, wages and salaries had more than kept
pace with the increase in output, partly explaining Gales' excellent
growth. At the same time it is noticeable that while directors' fees had
been regularly £200 per annum under Gale's leadership, when Bowyer
took over these fell to £75 and remained without change to 1909, the
last year they were entered.[22] Similarly, whereas between 1888 and
1896 George Gale paid dividends of between 7 and 10 per cent to
shareholders, in Herbert Bowyer's first year no dividends were paid and
then, from 1897, between only 3 and 5 per cent were issued until 1909,
after when dividends remained as low as 2 per cent until 1916. Thus,
Bowyer clearly adopted a policy of paying the workforce more, whilst
the directors' and shareholders' remuneration was more than halved. It
can hardly be doubted that such a policy must have contributed to the
brewery's performance against the national trend in a period of difficult
economic circumstances.

Other factors would have made some contribution to the company's
gratifying performance. The opening of the Portsdown and Horndean
Light Railway in March 1903 brought many visitors from urban Portsmouth to rural Horndean,[23] which with its woods and ponds gave
fresh air and pleasant walks and, no doubt, a thirst to those who
ventured to the light railway's terminus within easy walking distance of
the brewery. Four years later Gales won the contract for supplying beer
to Haslar Hospital in competition with its Portsmouth rival Brickwoods.[24]

No doubt this success was influenced by the company's growing reputation for the excellence of its beers, for it had already won prizes at the Brewers' Exhibitions in 1902, 1904 and 1906, and was to repeat these successes in 1908, under the guidance of its accomplished brewer Sydney Steel. Perhaps these attainments, along with the demand for Gales bottled beer, were causing problems in supply to their growing number of public houses since, in November 1910, an offer by Gales to sell 11 licensed premises was reported to Brickwoods' board as having been made on 22 September[25] but does not seem to have been followed up. Perhaps the brewery had reached a peak in its capacity to supply its tied houses with cask beers or was short of funds? Indeed, balance sheet evidence demonstrated, perhaps, an ability to overcome a number of setbacks. At the first annual meeting, on 25 May 1889, George Gale presented and explained the balance sheet for the previous year. After paying interest on debentures and preference shares, the accounts showed £4,401 17s. 0d. available for distribution. Of this, the directors recommended that £4,000 be paid out to ordinary shareholders and that the balance be carried forward.[26] Performance during the ensuing year showed a slight improvement with a profit of £4,827 2s. 4d.[27] Net profits were to remain at or near £4,000 until the brewery was sold in 1896 following which, the costs of reconstructing the brewery's finances eroded the level of profit for several years, perhaps affecting the ability to continue increasing the number of houses after 1903. Before that date, the acquisition of licensed premises continued, the purchase of the Havant-based Homewell Brewery and its eight houses forming only part of the story. Within three months of the board's first meeting, the Secretary could report that: 'the purchases had been completed of the Queens Head Coffee House at Farnham for £1,300 and that of the *Bevois Castle Hotel*, Bevois Street, Southampton for £2,000'.[28] In 1899 houses such as the *Shakespeare's Head Hotel* in Landport, Portsmouth and the *Wheatsheaf Inn* at Liphook were added, as was the *Bugle Inn* at Ryde in 1902 reflecting growing involvement in the tied trade.

Some houses were leased while others were held for a short period only and then conveyed away. Such was the *Angel Inn* at Salisbury. Licence to assign the lease was granted on 18 August 1903 and the company sold the lease in December.[29] Perhaps Gales were endeavouring to reduce their Wiltshire interest and operations, the distance being regarded as uneconomic. Since at least 1875, as brewers and wine and spirit merchants, they had maintained an outlet at Fisherton Anger in the cathedral city,[30] having disposed of it by 1895.[31]

Seven houses were located within the confines of Portsmouth, while two were in Ryde and Cowes, doubtless a reflection of the company's short-term hold on an Isle of Wight base. Between at least 1895 and

1898 Gales operated as wine, spirit and ale merchants from 13 St James Street, Newport, disposing of these loss-making premises by 1903.[32] Some of the acquired inns were not to remain long in the company's possession. The *Forester's Arms* in Havant, acquired before 1888, was rented out to tenant Josiah Carter at £15 per annum and then closed. The contents, including a 'Mahogany 4–post Bedstead', were sold in August 1910 and, taking advantage of the compensation scheme, the premises in 1920.[33] The *Wheatsheaf* at Liphook was also rented out from 10 October 1899, as was the *Shakespeare's Head Hotel* in Landport, Portsmouth, but this latter house was to embroil the company in serious legal difficulties. In August 1906 Portsmouth builder William Beaton took the company to court, claiming £50 for damages arising from an alleged breach of contract. That March, he maintained, the company had entered into a contract to accept him as tenant of the *Shakespeare's Head Hotel* in Charles Street, Portsmouth. He was to pay £350 in respect of the house's goodwill and purchase the stock at valuation. The arrangement would be subject, he stated, to receipt of satisfactory references. His £25 deposit was returned to him, however, when Gales wrote before the April Brewster Session, declining to accept him. Beaton maintained that this was despite considerable additional expense which he had undertaken in arrangements to protect his building business. A protracted legal wrangle followed, from which it emerged that what had been entered into was only a *provisional* agreement. Judge Gye gave judgement to the company without costs.[34]

Following the pre-1903 acquisitions, however, there came a quieter period with only the *Square Brewery* in Petersfield bought before 1912. Despite rising output profits remained modest reflecting not only the restructuring costs, but also the necessity of installing new boilers in 1907, the rising cost of materials, especially coal, and the rising duty levels.

One very clear hallmark of the 20 years before the First World War was the way in which the company endeavoured to keep abreast of technological change. Thus, the latest methods of transport were introduced. While horse-drawn drays were still being used in Horndean by the company until 1928, the last horse being sold in 1929 for £20,[35] some considerable changes had been made. By 1895, for example, a traction-engine and trucks had been acquired for delivering brewery products. Within four years, a second engine was purchased. There were also short-lived attractions to steam motor wagons and steam lorries in 1903 and 1905. However, from 1908 petrol-engined motor lorries began to replace traction engines and trucks, with three in operation by 1913. In 1912 the company acquired its first car, adding a second in 1917.[36]

Even so, the value of horses, their harness and drays was always greater than that of traction-engines and trucks, and was to remain so until 1903 when £629 was paid almost certainly for a steam wagon. From 1905, when it seems likely a steam lorry was added to the emerging vehicle transport fleet, the value of horses and drays declined dramatically. In 1903 they had been valued at £670 but clearly some stock had been sold, for in 1906 they were valued at only £300, and for the rest of the period before the First World War their value declined steadily until in 1914 it was only £100, whilst the motor lorries and car were valued at over £1,000 in 1913.[37]

Such acquisitions, however, were not always problem-free. There was at least one legal entanglement and one accident involving early company vehicles. No sooner had the company acquired their first traction-engine than they were in trouble with the law. A few days after Christmas 1895 driver George Rogers was summoned before Havant magistrates under the Locomotive Act. Early on the morning of 6 December PC Pope had observed Rogers stop his traction-engine within five yards of Purbrook Bridge to replenish the boiler with water. George Gale was personally summonsed 'for permitting on the highway a traction engine which did not consume its own smoke'. Ever-vigilant PC Pope had seen the same offending machine on the road between Purbrook and Waterlooville, observing 'smoke and fire issue from it'. The charge hung on the semantics of a plate fixed to the engine which simply read 'George Gale, Horndean'. Defence council stated that the engine was actually company property. If anybody should be prosecuted, it should, he maintained, be the Company Secretary! A one shilling fine and costs were imposed, the bench Chairman remarking that the company was liable to a heavy penalty for not having its name demonstrated properly on the engine.[38]

Some years later, in May 1907, the dangers inherent in the new transport technology tragically cost the company a member of the workforce. Labourer Edward Sheppard, 42 years of age, left home for work at the brewery between three and four in the morning. With traction-engine driver Charles Hall, he went to Portsmouth on a regular run, presumably for delivery and collection purposes, returning to Horndean between five and six in the afternoon. That day at the top of Horndean Hill he stepped from the truck on to the towing bar between it and the traction-engine, slipped and was run over. Taken home unconscious, he died soon afterwards. Though the traction-engine was running at only 2 miles per hour, the Coroner observed that 'the practice of men jumping off and on moving vehicles was a very dangerous one' and a verdict of accidental death was recorded.[39] That year's wages account shows that the dependants of workers at Gales were not forgotten since a payment of £31 0s. 6d. was made to 'Sheppard's widow'.[40]

The accounts reveal quite clearly how the company's attitude towards methods of transport changed over time. In 1903, for example, both horse and steam transport were being used, with a preponderance towards the former. Between then and 1908 the preference was very much towards traction-engines, despite the attendant risks. It is by no means impossible that the fatal accident of 1907, may have persuaded the company to change its mind. Quite clearly, the preference from 1908 onwards was towards the use of petrol-engined motor lorries, expenditure on which almost doubled between then and 1914.

For transport further afield, recourse was made to the London and South Western Railway, the nearest station being at Rowland's Castle. They had certainly been doing considerable trade with James Budden of Chatham since his account in 1896 stood at nearly £3,500. After that it dropped away sharply being less than a tenth of that figure by 1899 and the trade terminated in September 1901.[41] No doubt the rising costs of transport were partially responsible but the major contributing factor to the decline was the fact that in 1897 Budden merged with the Strood brewery of Biggs and hence would have increasingly had access to supplies from the newly formed Budden and Biggs.[42]

The desire to keep abreast of technological change was not limited to the transport department but seen elsewhere inside the brewery premises. Gas, electricity and telephones were all used by Gales from an early date. At least by 1898, for example, the company had acquired a telephone with the imposing number of 10, at a time when the nearby market town of Petersfield could not boast of a single telephonic installation, as indicated in reports from the Parliamentary Select Committees on the telephone service between 1895 and 1898 that stated that the market town did not have an exchange of the National Telephone Company, adding 'Active canvas proceeding; results not at present encouraging'.[43] The first mention of a typewriter at Gales was in 1909,[44] shortly after improvements in the performance of these machines had been introduced in America and two years before the first Italian typewriter was produced by Olivetti!

Many of the innovations ushered in at the brewery appear to have been implemented as a result of the change in the company's ownership during the 1890s and reflect the philosophy of the younger man who had now assumed control. It was perhaps, therefore, an auspicious moment for H. F. Bowyer to take over the reins of leadership. He had moved to Horndean in the month after his marriage in April 1887 and was to live at 'Westfield' for the rest of his life with his wife Elsie who, it is thought, had a reasonable dowry settled upon her which was used in part for developing the brewery. 'Westfield', the Bowyer family home, lay on the opposite side of the Portsmouth road at Horndean and further south on the rise of Horndean Hill. It was a spacious house which, in the early-1890s when owned by George Gale, had been occupied by the brewer who became brewery manager, Jeremiah Stubington. The ground floor consisted of a small morning room, a medium-sized drawing-room with a sizeable antique table, dining-room, butler's pantry, kitchen with large cooking table, scullery, toilet, store cupboard and stairs down to the cellar which was used for storing wine, apples and bottled fruit. On the first floor was a master bedroom with washbasin, H. F. Bowyer's dressing-room, a double bedroom, a small bedroom, bath-room and separate toilet. The second floor contained servants' rooms, day nursery and night nursery. The house had no central heating, hav-ing open coal fires, there being a coal-house at the rear.

Life at 'Westfield' was certainly comfortable, the household having a living-in cook and parlourmaid, as well as a daily maid who regularly cleaned and additionally so when visitors were expected. There was an extensive garden with a tennis court and a paddock. A gardener was employed as was a cowman since both cows and pigs were kept. Until the late 1920s the house was lit by candles and oil lamps, but then electricity was installed. Elsie refused to have gas laid on as she was certain her husband would not allow electricity if he already had gas! This indicates, as did his management of the brewery, the financially cautious side of his nature, which was also demonstrated by H. F. Bowyer regularly chiding people on saving their pennies, as well as the fact that the house had a commercial refrigerator because it could be acquired more cheaply through the company. It also suggests that he was very much in charge in his household, as in the brewery, and opposition to his views was not acceptable.

Bowyer was a physically active man and his daily exercise was to roll the grass tennis court. Unfortunately, a riding accident left him with a badly fractured leg and ankle reducing his mobility and preventing him from riding again. He thus sold not only his own horses, but also those of his wife. Although he knew she loved riding and visiting friends on horseback, she was not to ride either. Despite the difficulties that such a decision must have created, Elsie remained unresentful and a loyal wife, her attitude perhaps ameliorated by the fact that they became a two-car household. Hence, Elsie could visit friends on four wheels instead of four hooves.

Herbert Bowyer's main interest in life, however, was the brewery. He lived for it except for visits to the races. He always went to Goodwood, Salisbury and Newbury, but rarely to the theatre or concerts except for an occasional performance of Gilbert and Sullivan. His wife, who had much wider interests, thus often found herself attending the theatre in London or Southsea with friends. She, therefore, in the early years would have liked to move away from Horndean but her husband had no intention of so doing since his major interest lay there.

Even so, the Bowyers seem to have been integrated with some of the figures of local society, being friendly with the Wilders at Stansted House near Rowland's Castle, the Joddrells at Merchistoun Hall, Horndean, and the Learmonths at Cadlington House, Blendworth. Elsie was involved with the Horndean Women's Institute and also regularly drove to Winchester to visit friends. However, her husband played no part in local politics and little in local societies, having no interest in positions of importance.

His narrowness of interests – the brewery and horses – suggests almost a tunnel vision and he cannot be remembered as having ever taken a holiday, although his wife did so separately, going off with female friends in her car to Cornwall. However, he was not a 'workaholic' as his regular visits to the races testify but he did wish to keep a close eye on all aspects of work at the brewery, being meticulous in ensuring that everything was accounted for. After his riding accident he bought a cycle and obtained his exercise cycling almost everywhere in the locality, especially after tea at 5.00 p.m. and after dinner. This allowed him to arrive quietly and unexpectedly at the brewery to ensure that everything was in good order! It also meant that the Managing Director could be seen arriving at work in no greater splendour than his workforce whilst giving him the opportunity of communicating with his men more easily.[45] On the surface there seems little doubt that from his arrival in Horndean he had a major objective – to operate a successful business.

However, only four months after acquiring the Horndean Brewery, Herbert Bowyer was negotiating to sell it to the Portsmouth brewery, Brickwoods. Their major interest would have been in the tied houses which Gales possessed, rather than the brewery in Horndean. Through William Smeed, who it seems had retained his £1,500 share of the brewery and who also would have been known to the Brickwoods board, Bowyer offered to sell the Horndean business for £125,000. Such a sale would have resulted in a substantial profit of £27,760. It seems that Bowyer wanted Brickwoods shares in part payment but, on 21 December 1896 at an extraordinary directors' meeting, the Brickwoods board decided not to purchase on the terms offered, but would be 'prepared to buy at a fair price for a Cash transaction not issuing any Shares in part payment'.[46] The following February the Brickwoods board were informed that their offer of £95,000 cash for the Horndean business had been refused[47] – not surprisingly, since this would have left Bowyer with a loss of £2,240, excluding any other costs his purchase would have incurred. Only two years later, on 28 February

1899, Herbert Bowyer personally attended at Brickwoods and proposed an amalgamation of the two businesses should Brickwoods purchase Jewell's Brewery. The terms were to be arranged. However, Brickwoods' directors declined to entertain the proposition.[48]

Once these early attempt to dispose of the business had failed Herbert Bowyer and his associates seem to have decided to work to ensure the success of the Horndean venture. For example, from spring 1899 Frederick Riddell and Leonard McMullen, both of whom came from brewing backgrounds, seem to have taken their responsibilities as directors of the brewery seriously. Riddell, by March 1899, had moved to Waterlooville. Subsequently he may well have moved to Ryde in the Isle of Wight,[49] continuing to serve as a director until September 1902.[50] In December of that year his 1,500 shares were transferred to Frederick William Riddell who replaced him as a director and continued to attend meetings until 1927.[51] McMullen came from P. McMullen and Sons who brewed at Mill-bridge, Hertford[52] and joined the Gales board, having acquired 500 shares from G. A. and R. R. Gale.[53] His attendance at meetings appears to have been good and he took a prominent part on a number of occasions. It was McMullen, for example, who moved at the 1 June 1897 meeting that Gale's resignation be accepted. He it was who seconded the move, on 4 November 1897, that the new Secretary, Ernest H. Taylor, receive a salary of £115. At the meeting on 31 May 1898, it was moved by Riddell and seconded by McMullen that an issue of £60,000 debentures be offered to the public[54] and at the annual meeting in March 1899 his proposition that a more thorough audit be carried out by Masons before the auditors were reappointed was carried.[55] Like Riddell, he had moved locally to attend to his duties, being described as of 'Downend', Horndean between March 1899 and late September 1900. On 28 September notice of his resignation was accepted, having sold his shareholding to Mr F. J. Douglas of Catherington House, Horndean. He returned to the McMullen Brewery, for on 10 December 1901 he was described as 'brewer of Hertford'.[56]

Meanwhile, George Gale continued to live at Crookley just by the east side of the brewery and although no longer personally involved, he maintained a financial stake. A sum of £9,420, however, was paid by the company in June 1898 for George Gale's debentures and in March of the following year he lent £5,240 to Bowyer, Riddell, Smeed and McMullen on which they paid £262 interest per annum, a rate of 5 per cent, until 1905.[57] This was a personal loan to the four directors and it seems it was to allow them to purchase from Washington Single his 525 ordinary shares since these were transferred to them the same month, except for one share which went to Herbert Bowyer's wife, Elsie.[58] This would seem to indicate that the negotiations between Gale and Bowyer had been transparently amicable, and further evidence of a good relationship between the two men is that Bowyer's early years at Westfield were as a tenant of George Gale, paying him a yearly rent of £85.[59]

With his brewery sold, his three daughters married well and Julia presenting him with three grandchildren George Gale could perhaps have been expected to take life in a more leisurely fashion. However, he became a substantial landowner in Catherington and Blendworth parishes acquiring three farms – Parsonage, Causeway and Myrtle – plus many other acres of land and a number of villas and cottages, as well as the shop his father had built. In addition, he became the owner of another estate in Southsea including the Osborne Road shops where Gales' Southsea branch was located, 12 flats in South Parade and other properties in Castle Road, Pelham Road, Fawcett Road and elsewhere, a major estate at Donnington near Chichester and property in 14 streets in Manchester. He also acted as a provider of mortgages and loans, and had a substantial portfolio of shares both in England and abroad. From all these activities he had a considerable annual income.[60]

It could be that the major motivation behind these real estate and financial dealings was the changes which had occurred in his personal life. Less than two years after the sale of the brewery on 5 February 1898, George's wife Hester died at their home 'Crookley'.[61] His loss, after almost 46 years together with their shared sorrows and successes, must have been deeply felt. Their first ten years of married life were undoubtedly ones which contained bitter disappointment and severely tested their love, as they lost four of their five children, including all their three sons. It cannot be doubted that both must have felt a deep and lasting disillusionment.

Following Hester's death, after so many years of companionship his large house must have seemed particularly empty, especially since George Gale was then in his seventieth year. He had his five grandchildren and his daughter Julia with her husband Edwin Marvin to visit – they lived in comfort at Parsonage Farm House in Catherington, which George owned. Julia employed a daily governess, Miriam Stares, daughter of Samuel Stares, Relieving Officer, Rate Collector and Registrar for Horndean,[62] to assist her with the children, and it seems clear that George and the much younger governess formed a close attachment, for on 7 February 1900, when he was 71 and just after the second anniversary of Hester's death, George married the 33-year-old Miriam. This, however, was not a marriage for companionship alone, for just over a year later the marriage was blessed with a daughter, Marjorie Doudney, christened at Blendworth on 20 January 1901. A year later at the mature age of 73 George finally had a son who was to survive. David Alexander was christened in the same church as his sister on 21 January

1902.[63] At last George had a male heir, but ironically not until well after he had sold his other major creation, the Horndean Brewery.

Despite his now being a septuagenarian with a household containing two small children George involved himself increasingly in local community work. For those less fortunate than himself, various bodies received his assistance, albeit in a somewhat attenuated form. While he maintained his life subscription to the Portsmouth and Gosport Hospital, later to become the Royal, the company supported a separate 1-guinea subscription. From 1907 onwards he also provided a separate 2-guinea subscription towards the Mayor's Hospital Building Fund for Operating Theatre and Corridors.[64] The Hampshire and Isle of Wight School and Blind Home also benefited from his kindness, with a 3-guinea subscription received in June 1888.[65] His good works embraced other forms of charitable donation as well.

Living and working in and near a naval town, supplying the navy with various alcoholic requirements, from at least 1888,[66] it was only natural that he would wish to contribute to the relief funds raised in the aftermath of naval tragedies. In October 1870, as has been shown above, he contributed towards the relief fund for HMS *Captain*, as he also did for HMS *Cobra*, lost in 1901, to which he contributed 1 guinea.[67] On 18 September that year the *Cobra*, a turbine torpedo-boat destroyer on her way from a Newcastle shipyard to Portsmouth, was totally wrecked off the Lincolnshire coast with considerable loss of life.[68] George Gale and Co. was also to contribute 3 guineas to the Mayor's Naval Disaster Fund in 1908.[69]

On a totally different front he had made a further contribution to local affairs from at least the 1870s, if not before, through the volunteer movement. To the Annual Prize Meeting of the 5th Hants (Portsmouth) Rifle Volunteers, held at Browndown in late October 1879, he had subscribed 10s. 0d.[70] In the 1880s it was to the 3rd Hampshire Volunteer Battalion of the Hampshire Regiment that the subscription went. The company subscribed 1 guinea in both November 1888 and November 1889.[71]

For someone so wealthy these charitable contributions could no doubt be easily made, but perhaps were carried out for Christian reasons since he was an active church-goer, serving as a churchwarden. At a Blendworth vestry meeting on 25 March 1886 Gale consented to act as Clergyman's Churchwarden, taking over the office from his father Richard.[72] For the next 28 years he was to hold this office, discharging it as a good and faithful servant.[73]

For many years George Gale was also to be involved in local Poor Law administration. In March 1889 he was nominated as Guardian for Blendworth within the Catherington Union. His nephew, Richard Rogers

Gale, was nominated as one of the four for Catherington itself.[74] When
the Horndean Board of Guardians met in January 1910 they considered, amongst other items, a letter from Baldwyn Fleming, Local
Government Board Inspector, pointing out that his appointment terminated on the eighteenth of that month. The clerk, Mr Longcroft, noted
that this marked 40 years' service: 'Mr George Gale, the Chairman, said
that he could boast of even longer service on that Board; he had
belonged to it for 55 years.'[75] Just a few months later, Gale was himself
to be the recipient of fulsome praise and recognition of his services. At
the mid-April meeting of the Horndean Board of Guardians Mr Whalley-
Tooker submitted Gale's name as Chairman of the Guardians and District
Council, paying tribute to his handsome record of public service. Returned to the chair, Gale thanked members for the compliment, praised
their achievement, welcomed the new members on the Board, and more
especially the old members, the great desire of whom in the past had
been to do the business of the council to the satisfaction of all.[76]

George Gale was to continue in his chairman's role until the end of
his days.[77] Membership and Chairmanship of the Board of Guardians
was to result in a 59–year contribution from him, by any standard no
mean achievement. Furthermore, Chairmanship of the Guardians had
been combined, from 1896 onwards, with that of Catherington Rural
District Council and service as a magistrate[78] and he was also Chairman
of Catherington Parish Council from its inception to his death in 1914.

By the second decade of the twentieth century George Gale was in his
eighties and as he and his then 47-year-old wife Miriam, shared Christmas in 1913 their thoughts must have been concerned both with the
omens for change coming to the world, as well as George's mortality.
The old Queen Empress, a reference point in so many people's lives, had
long since gone. Born before her accession, George had seen two Jubi-
lees and outlasted her reign to witness the dawning of a new age. And
from the summer of 1914 onwards, that age would look particularly
bleak, as the world plunged into war. Doubtless he thought, too, of his
family, of the children who had predeceased him, and his first wife with
whom he had spent so many years. It is by no means impossible that he
grew both tired and disillusioned.

In its issue for 31 October 1914, the *Portsmouth Evening News*
carried the simple entry: 'GALE – On the 30th October at 'Crookley',
Horndean, George Alexander Gale, J.P. , passed peacefully away in his
86th year. No flowers, by special request.'[79] Having undergone an
operation, he had died the day afterwards. He was buried on 3 November 1914 along with Hester in their grave in Catherington churchyard.[80]

'The village of Horndean was absolutely deserted on Tuesday afternoon, on the occasion of the funeral, which attracted a very large

1 The brewery and oast-house *c.* 1900, prior to traction engines, when deliveries were only by horse-drawn vehicles, but after the arrival of telephones in Horndean, although only four lines exist on the telegraph pole

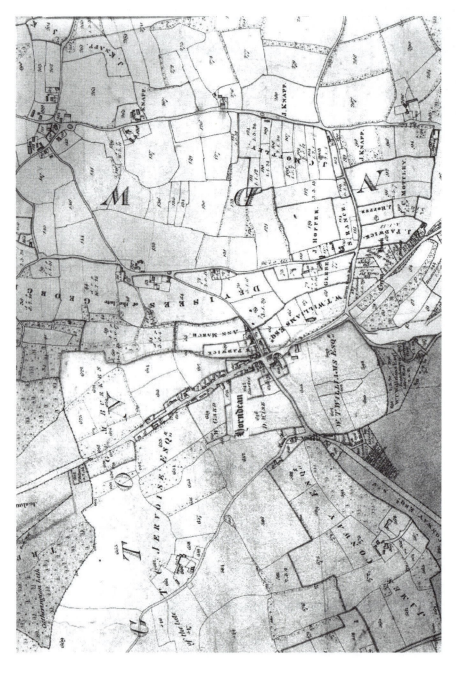

2 Catherington and Blendworth Enclosure Maps, 1816. The Portsmouth–London road comes into Horndean from the south-west.

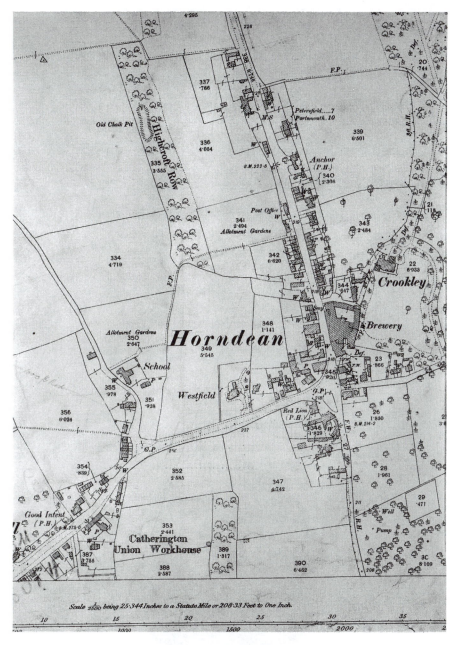

3 Horndean in 1897, showing the brewery, 'Crookley', 'Westfield' and related buildings

4 Richard Gale, who bought the *Ship and Bell* in 1847, during his retirement at 'Crookley'

5 George Alexander Gale, developer of the Horndean brewery which still bears his name, probably at about the time he sold the company

6 George Alexander Gale looking great-grandfatherly but actually with his second wife Miriam, daughter Marjorie and son David

7 Herbert Frederick Bowyer as a successful business man in the inter-war period. He acquired the Horndean Brewery in 1896 and was its Chairman from then until 1938.

8   Frederick Hugh Bowyer, Chairman of Gales between 1938 and 1981

9 Owen Leonard Noel Chambers, Chairman of Gales between 1981 and 1987

10 Reginald George Bowyer, Chairman of Gales since 1987

11 A gathering of brewery notables in May 1937. Left to right are William Barton Mears, Head Brewer and Director, Richard Newman Gale, Director and Company Secretary, Frederick Hugh Bowyer, Chairman, Richard Walter Gale, Director, and W. B. V. Knight.

12 A generation later in 1980. Left to right, current Chairman Reginald George Bowyer, Richard Evans Gale, Managing Director, Owen Leonard Noel Chambers, Chairman 1981–87, Clive Maurice Jones, Company Secretary, Frederick Hugh Bowyer, Chairman 1938–81, and Edward Thomas 'Ted' Argyle, Head Brewer and Director.

13   Gales' workforce in the mid-1990s

14 'Crookley', built by Richard Gale for his retirement and after his death the residence of George Alexander Gale

15 'Westfield', the Bowyer family residence

16   Horndean, *c.* 1900, with the brewery clearly visible to the right of the road

Ship & Bell Tea Gardens, Horndean
Proprietor: E. Grinstead.

17   The *Ship and Bell* tea gardens at Horndean, n.d.

18 The cooperage at Gales Brewery

19 The cooperage with a cooper at work

20 A rare photograph of a Foden steam motor wagon, probably in 1904, delivering to the *Little Brown Jug* in Havant (later the *Brown Jug* and afterwards a furniture store), acquired by Gales in 1903. Note the considerable quantity of bottled beer.

21 A brewery outing in 1925 at the *New Inn*, Chichester

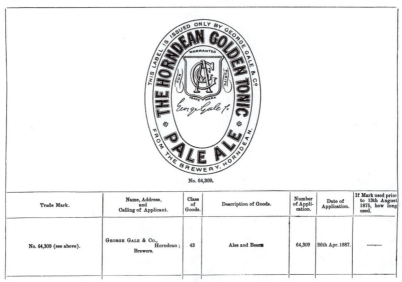

No. 64,309.

Trade Mark.	Name, Address, and Calling of Applicant.	Class of Goods.	Description of Goods.	Number of Appli- cation.	Date of Application.	If Mark used prior to 13th August 1875, how long used.
No. 64,309 (see above).	GEORGE GALE & CO., Horndean ; Brewers.	43	Ales and Beers	64,309	26th Apr. 1887.	————

22 and 23   Trade mark material for George Gale and Co.

BREWERS' EXHIBITION, 1930.

SECOND PRIZE FOR STOUT.   SECOND PRIZE FOR BOTTLED BEER.   THIRD PRIZE FOR BOTTLED STOUT.

Brewers' Exhibition, London, 1926.

Previous Awards:-
BREWERS' EXHIBITION, LONDON.
1902, 1904, 1906, 1908, 1921,
1923, 1924, 1925, 1926, 1928.

Branch Offices & Stores:
18, OSBORNE R? SOUTHSEA.
SQUARE BREWERY,
PETERSFIELD.
Off Licence,
NORTH ST, MIDHURST.

CHAMPION GOLD MEDAL & DIPLOMA 1926.   FIRST PRIZE SILVER MEDAL & DIPLOMA 1926.

CHAMPION CHALLENGE CUP   & DIPLOMA 1926.

Registered
George Gale & Co Ltd
TRADE MARK

George Gale & Co., Ltd.,

Brewers, Wine & Spirit Merchants,

HORNDEAN, PORTSMOUTH, HANTS.   *August, 1933.*

Telephone : N? 10.
Telegrams : GALES, HORNDEAN.

REVISED TIED PRICES.

CASK BEER :—		Per Barrel Nett.
" XX " Beer	(4d.) ...	... 72/-
" BBB " Ale	(7d.) ...	... 132/-
" XXXXX " Ale	(8d.) ...	... 152/-
Stout	(6d.) ...	... 111/-
P.A.	...	... 112/-

BOTTLED BEER :—		Per Doz.
Quarts, Golden Tonic Ale ...	...	10/3
" Nourishing Stout ...	...	11/6
" A1 Ale and Digestive Stout		9/-
Pints, Golden Tonic Ale ...	...	5/6
" Nourishing Stout ...	...	6/-
" A1 Ale and Digestive Stout ...		4/8
" Nut Brown Ale ...	...	5/3
½ " Golden Tonic Ale and Nut Brown Ale	...	3/4
" " Nourishing Stout ...	...	3/10
" " King Cole Ale ...	...	4/-
" " Special Champion Cup Ale, naturally conditioned	...	4/6
" " Prize Old Ale ...	...	8/-
" " Bass, Worthington & Guinness		5/-
Pints, Guinness	...	9/6
Nips " ...	...	3/6

CYDER :—		Per Doz.
Reputed Pints, Henley's Cyder	...	4/-
Half Pints, " "	...	3/3
Nips, Cyder	...	2/6

BULK WINES AND SPIRITS :—		Per Gall.
Irish, Scotch and Rum ...	...	66/-
Gin and British Brandy ...	...	65/-
French Brandy ...	...	72/6
Glenlivet Whisky ...	...	68/-
Port	...	20/-
Best Port	...	25/-
Sherry	...	25/-

AUSTRALIAN WINES :—		Per Doz.
Austavin Red and White ...	...	33/-

BOTTLED WINES AND SPIRITS :—		Per Doz.
Fine Old Blended		
Glenlivet Whisky (over 10 yrs. old)		**136/6**
" " ½ Botts.	...	71/3
" " ¼ "	...	37/2
" " Miniatures	...	12/5
Proprietary Whiskies	...	143/6
" " ½ Botts.	...	75/-
" " ¼ "	...	39/3
" " Miniatures	...	14/-
Rum, Gin and British Brandy	...	137/6
Cognac Brandy	...	150/-
Orange Bitters and Cloves ...	...	66/-
Peppermint	...	57/-
Ginger Brandy	...	81/-
Otards Brandy	...	165/-
Port, Black Cap	...	42/-
½ Bots. Port, Black Cap ...	...	23/-
Sherry	...	42/-
Booth's and Gordon's Gin ...	...	140/-
Coates' Gin, and Nicholson's	...	137/6
Hollands Gin (De Kuyper)...	...	150/-
" " (Gale & Co.'s)	...	140/-
Martells or Hennesseys * ...	...	185/-
" " ***	...	195/-
" " *** ½ Botts.		102/-
" " *** ¼ "		54/9
White Port, No. 1	...	48/-
Litres, French Vermouth ...	...	62/-
" Italian " ...	...	45/-
" British (Italian Style)	...	25/-

Other Wine and Spirit prices on application.

25   The *Ship and Bell* and brewery at Horndean: a recent view

number of villagers, who came to take part in the farewell to one of their most respected neighbours.' The service was well attended, with relatives, business associates, friends and representatives of the bodies upon whose behalf he had worked so long, and with such vigour. The coffin was borne into church by some of his employees, the service being conducted by Blendworth's incumbent, the Reverend E. J. Nelson. Although George's widow, Miriam, had expressed a wish for no flowers, handsome wreaths of arum lilies, chrysanthemums, roses and carnations were sent by mourners. He was buried, at his request, with his first wife. This fact, plus overwhelming grief, could perhaps explain the absence of his second wife, Miriam, from the service, although it must be borne in mind that it was then quite usual for widows not to attend. As the mourners filed respectfully from the church to the graveside in the crispness of that November day in 1914 they must have realised, in more ways than one, that they had witnessed the end of an era. Some six or seven weeks later, the final chapter in George Gale's story was made public in *The Times*: 'Mr. George Alexander Gale, J.P. , aged 85, of Crookley, Horndean, Hants, formerly of Messrs. George Gale & Co, brewers and wine and spirit merchants, of Horndean and Southsea. £93,177.'[81]

Notes

1. See for example some of the cannons found on the sixteenth century warship, *Mary Rose*, which sank in 1545. They are on show in the Mary Rose Exhibition Hall, Portsmouth R.N. Dockyard.
2. For much of the early history of the Bowyer family, as well as for his hospitality and that of his wife Sylvia, we are greatly indebted to Paget Bowyer of Corfe Castle, Dorset.
3. PRO Prob 11/1667, Will of Michael Bowyer dated 30 March 1822, proved at London 1 March 1823, for all information on legacies.
4. Guildford Muniment Room (GMR) Bowyer MS. RB 670
5. See Appendix 1: Bowyer family tree.
6. *Kelly's Directory of Surrey* (1853).
7. GMR PSH/STK/5/3, Stoke Parish Register of Burials 1867–78.
8. *Sussex Advertiser* 30 June 1863; 6 October 1863.
9. We are greatly indebted to H. F. and Elsie Bowyer's niece, Doreen Carlos Perkins, for providing information about her aunt and uncle's life in Horndean as well as H.F. Bowyer's early employment with Lord Beresford.
10. PCRO CHU. 4/18/4, Catherington Parish Baptism Register 1894–1927.
11. Gale and Co. Minute Book 1888–1927, p. 1. A mortgage of £11,250 at 4 per cent was also involved.
12. M. Dunn, *Local Brew: Traditional Breweries and their Ales* (London, 1986), p. 63, states that there were nine.
13. What follows is derived from the deeds for the eight specified sets of premises.

14. Deeds in the care of Barclays Bank, Commercial Road, Portsmouth.
15. K. H. Hawkins and C. L. Pass, *The Brewing Industry: A Study in Industrial Organisation and Public Policy*, (London, 1979), p. 31.
16. J. Vaizey, *The Brewing Industry 1886–1951: An Economic Study* (London, 1960), p. 16.
17. Ibid., p. 17.
18. Ibid.
19. H. F. Bowyer's Pocket Book, 1896–1935.
20. T. R. Gourvish and R. G. Wilson, *The British Brewing 1830–1980* (Cambridge, 1994), p. 340.
21. Private Ledger No. 3, 1903–11.
22. Journal 1888–96; Private Ledger No. 2, 1895–1902; Private Ledger No. 4 1912–19.
23. B. Stapleton, *Waterlooville: A Pictorial History* (Chichester, 1996), n.p.
24. Whitbread Archive 365/2 Brickwood and Co. Ltd, Directors' Minute Books 1900–29, p. 175, 8 May 1907. We are most grateful to Philip Eley for this and the following reference.
25. Ibid., p. 270, 9 November 1910.
26. Gale and Co. Minute Book 1888–1927, p. 14.
27. Ibid., p. 18.
28. Ibid., p. 10.
29. Ibid., pp. 111, 113.
30. *Post Office Directory of Wiltshire* (1875), p. 617. We are obliged to Lorna Haycock for drawing this item to our attention.
31. *Kelly's Directory of Wiltshire and Dorsetshire* (1895) makes no mention of it.
32. *Kelly's Directory of Hampshire, Isle of Wight, Wiltshire and Dorsetshire* (1895), p. 617; *Kelly's Directory of Hampshire and the Isle of Wight* (1898), pp. 621, 1012; *Kelly's Directory of Hampshire and the Isle of Wight* (1903).
33. Agreement to rent, 24 March 1893 and notice of sale for 8 August 1910. By December 1910 the premises had been converted into two cottages: Gale and Co. Minute Book 1888–1927, p. 155.
34. *HT*, 6510, 4 August 1906.
35. Private Ledger No. 6, 1929–35. The Southsea branch kept a horse and dray for deliveries until 1934 (see Chapter 5).
36. Gale and Co. Minute Book 1888–1927, *passim*; Private Ledger No. 3 1903–11; Private Ledger No. 4 1912–19; *HT*, 5964, 28 December 1895.
37. Private Ledgers No. 2 1895–1902, No. 3 1903–11, No. 4 1912–19.
38. *HT*, 5964, 28 December 1895.
39. *HT*, 6549, 4 May 1907.
40. Private Ledger No. 3, 1903–11.
41. H. F. Bowyer's Pocket Book 1896–1935.
42. N. Barber, *Where Have All the Breweries Gone?* (Swinton, Lancs., 1981) p. 18.
43. *British Parliamentary Papers (BPP): Reports from Select Committee on the Telephone Service, 1895–8* (Dublin, 1971), p. 972.
44. Private Ledger No. 3 1903–11. Even so, Gales board meeting minutes were not typed until the 1930s.
45. For details about the life of H. F. Bowyer in Horndean we are most grateful to his niece Doreen Carlos Perkins.

46. Whitbread Archives, 365/1, Brickwood and Co. Ltd, Directors' Minute Books 1891–1900 p. 110, 21 December 1896. We are grateful to Philip Eley for drawing our attention to this and the next two references.
47. Ibid., p. 113, 10 February 1897.
48. Ibid., p. 159, 8 February 1898.
49. Ordinary Share Certificates 1888–1927, *passim*.
50 Gale and Co. Minute Book 1888–1927 p. 105.
51. Ibid., *passim*.
52. Dring and Fage's, *Almanac and Brewer's Directory* (1876), p. 59. McMullens still brew in Hertford.
53. Gale and Co. Minute Book 1888–1927 gives 124 shares from G. A. Gale and 376 from R. R. Gale. The Share Transfer Ledger gives the figures as 125 and 375 respectively.
54. Gale and Co. Minute Book 1888–1927, p. 72.
55. Ibid., p. 85.
56. Share Certificates and Minute Book 1888–1927.
57. George A. Gale, Private Ledger 1888–1914, p. 120. We are greatly indebted to Major W. R. N. Ladds for allowing access to this ledger.
58. Gale and Co. Minute Book 1888–1927, p. 83.
59. George A. Gale, Private Ledger 1888–1914, p. 130.
60. Ibid., *passim*.
61. *HT*, 6073, 12 February 1898; *Hampshire Post*, 1232, 11 February 1898.
62. PRO RG 12/944 Census of Great Britain 1891.
63. David Alexander Gale lived until 1984, residing in Ireland.
64. PCRO PR/H7/2/1/3–8, Hospital Annual Reports 1879–88; 1889–95; 1896–1902; 1907–1910; 1911–14. The company would continue its subscription beyond 1914.
65. *HT*, 5581, 9 June 1888.
66. Ibid.
67. Ibid., 6263, 19 October 1901.
68. Some 60 or more lives were lost: *AR for 1901* (1902), pp. 24–5; *HT*, 6273, 28 December 1901.
69. *HT*, 6603, 16 May 1908. The total raised was close to £6,000.
70. *HT*, 4924, 25 October 1879.
71. Ibid., 5602, 3 November 1888; 5655, 2 November 1889.
72. PCRO CHU 40/2/3, Blendworth Churchwardens Account and Vestry Minute Book 1865–1896, n.p.
73. Ibid., CHU 40/3/7, 'Blendworth Transcripts and Monumental Inscriptions', typescript study, 1973, p. 28.
74. *HT*, 5624, 30 March 1889.
75. Ibid., 6688, 15 January 1910. The Chairman of the Portsmouth Board, E. S. Main, had also written, suggesting a testimonial from all the Boards of Guardians.
76. *HT*, 6702, 23 April 1910.
77. Ibid., 6854, 11 April 1913; 6869, 25 July 1913; 6883, 31 October 1913.
78. *The Hants and Dorset Court Guide* (1897), p. 219.
79. *Portsmouth Evening News*, 11595, 31 October 1914. The issues for 2 and 3 November 1914 carried the same entry. See also *PT*, 4111, 6 November 1914.
80. What follows is derived from the account of the funeral contained in *PT*, 4111, 6 November 1914.

81. *The Times*, 40, 738, 30 December 1914. At his death, his wife, Miriam, was to receive all his personal leasehold property, cars etc., and an annuity of £800 with residence at Crookley for life. Daughter Marjorie was to receive £20,000 at age 24 or on marriage. His daughters by his first marriage had received the Chichester and Southsea estates between them. The rest was to go to David when he reached the age of 24. There was no specific mention of the Manchester estate. At the age of 25 David sold off the Crookley estate and his mother moved to Compton near Winchester where she lived until her death aged 85 in 1952. She remained a widow for 38 years and perhaps it says something of her character, as well as the love she had for her husband, that it was in the grave, with both George Alexander and his first wife Hester, in Catherington churchyard that she found her final resting place. She left her estate to her daughter Marjorie, stating that her son David was amply provided for by his father.

CHAPTER FIVE

The company in war and peace: 1914–39

The First World War 'came to be regarded as an unqualified misfortune by Britain's brewers'.[1] It was to have profound effects on the brewing industry with the establishment in 1915 of a Central Control Board under the Defence of the Realm Act. The board imposed shorter licensing hours, a reduced gravity of beer and restricted output in order to reduce the amount of land used for barley and hop growing and to save shipping space for food. Higher costs resulted and the trend of declining output and consumption was strongly reinforced, particularly since there was a reduction in the quality of materials used, much higher wartime duties on beer were imposed (the tax burden rose 430 per cent in real terms) and raw material prices increased, all leading to more expensive beer that was weaker in strength and lower in quality. In early 1917, further restrictions on output were ordered with a reduction to 10 million standard barrels per annum being specified – less than half the pre-war output. In the event this trough was not reached, almost 14 million barrels being produced in 1917, but still much below the pre-war average of nearly 23 million (see Table 5.1). Restrictions also applied to opening hours for public houses, thus opportunities for

Table 5.1 UK beer output and consumption, 1910–39 (five-year averages)

Years	Output: standard barrels (millions)	Consumption per head (gallons)
1910–14	34.70	26.90
1915–19	21.74	15.80
1920–24	20.93	17.68
1925–29	19.91	16.65
1930–34	15.50	12.88
1935–39	17.71	14.09

Source: Gourvish and Wilson (1984), pp. 24, 30, 320, 618–19. The figures of consumption per head for 1915–19 are an estimate calculated from the output in barrels and estimated mid-census population figures.

drinking were reduced and convictions for drunkenness fell by 84 per cent in England and Wales between 1914 and 1918,[2] there being a marked improvement in Portsmouth. Manpower shortages, first through volunteers and secondly through conscription, added to the problems faced by brewers.

Gales did not escape the effects of war, but they appear to have had contradictory consequences. In the two years immediately preceding the war, their output reached entirely new levels as a result of increases in the production of both casked and bottled beers, the latter of which reached almost a quarter of total production. It is tempting to suggest that the preparations for war which led to feverish activity in the naval dockyard at Portsmouth, with 15,000 men constructing the Super Dreadnoughts, had meant a rising demand for beer in Gales' marketing area. By 1917 dockyard employment had risen to 23,000[3] and resulted in growth for Portsmouth's two largest brewers, Brickwoods and Portsmouth United Breweries, the latter's sales almost doubling between 1913 and 1918.[4] Gales could not match such performance, for in 1917 their output fell to levels which had been common before 1912. This suggests, first, that Gales were not too closely tied in with dockyard and naval activity and, secondly, that the 1917 government order that output be reduced was having some effect. In addition, it was a cold, wet year[5] and the summer's production was appreciably below that of both previous and succeeding years.[6] Some recovery was effected in 1918, but the consequences of war for Gales were not as severe as had been felt in the industry generally where reduction in output had been considerable (see Table 5.1). However, for most brewers the decline in supply had been more than offset by higher prices per bulk barrel which rose from 58s. 0d. to 144s. 0d. in 1917 and led to higher profits. Gales was no exception. Even though output in 1917 fell by the equivalent of almost 4,600 barrels, some 26 per cent less than in 1916, income rose by more than £1,000.[7] In fact, income rose every year throughout the war and continued to do so until 1922 when, keeping pace with the growing tax burden, it was over four times greater than it had been in the last peacetime year, whereas output had risen by only 19 per cent in the intervening decade.[8] Behind this growth in income from sales lay the rising cost of raw materials – sugar, malt and hops – since the shortages did not disappear after the war. Control over hop growing and marketing was continued to assist in the restoration of hop production, thus barley prices were seen to rise much higher.[9] More importantly, however, was the escalating beer duty. In 1914 duty payments probably represented less than 15 per cent of total costs, but by 1920 they were nearly 40 per cent, the duty having been raised in both of the first two post-war budgets.[10] In fact the excise duty was quadrupled after 1918, making beer 7 pence a pint in 1922 — double the pre-war level. Almost 4 pence of this price was duty, and since this happened at a time when some workers' wages were actually cut in money terms, it made beer overpriced.

Not surprisingly, then, the consumption of beer nationally in the inter-war period continued the decline that had been seen since the 1890s, reaching levels which brewers would have regarded, before 1914, as economically unsustainable. From 1920 to 1929 consumption per head was 39 per cent below the pre-war level of 1910–14, and in the early 1930s (1930–34) it was almost 52 per cent lower. The fall in national output over the same period also approached 52 cent (see Table 5.1).

Such remarkable reductions in output and consumption cannot be explained simply in terms of price, particularly since breweries like Gales did not experience any such collapse in either output or sales. In fact, until the early 1930s, apart from the war period, the brewery's output increased steadily, and by 1930–34 it was averaging 28 per cent above its First World War level and by the Second World War output had risen by 41 per cent (see Table 5.2). Even in the midst of the world's greatest economic recession, only 1932 saw any real fall in production and that was no more than 12 per cent below the average for the years immediately preceding. Had the depression year of 1932 been excluded from the figures, then Gales would have continued their steady increase in output (see Table 5.2). Remarkably, once again, in the inter-war period, the Horndean company defied the national trends. These trends were the result of a number of factors, the most important being social change, for the old pre-war order exemplified by Victorian and Edwardian society was gone for ever.

Improvements in urban living conditions meant that the Victorian connection between heavy drinking and poor housing was reduced. Consequently, the proportion of working-class expenditure on alcohol fell from around 15 per cent in the 1870s to 8.5 per cent by the outbreak of the First World War,[11] and continued its downward path in the inter-war period reaching 6.5 per cent in 1938.[12] The growing aspirations of workers were broadening their consumer horizons and brewers had to compete with the growth in popularity of the radio, cinema, teashops, ice-cream parlours, coffee bars and spectator sports, as well as participatory ones. These activities could be undertaken on a family basis so the new breed of working-class fathers could just as easily be found taking their offspring to the cinema or the local football ground as visiting the pub. Such working-class changes were more noticeable in the Midlands and the north of England than in the south, so Gales were geographically more favourably placed to avoid the

Table 5.2 Beer output: Gales Brewery, 1910–39

Year	Barrels		Bottles (doz.)		Equivalent no. of barrels		Total (barrels)	
1910	9,943		52,960		2,407		12,350	
1911	10,474		73,119		3,323		13,797	
1912	11,316	11,773	81,966	79,360	3,725	3,607	15,041	15,383
1913	13,446		91,888		4,176		17,638	
1914	13,688		96,867		4,403		18,091	
1915	11,875		89,769		4,080		15,955	
1916	13,816		84,960		3,862		17,678	
1917	11,036	13,699	45,255	58,715	2,057	2,669	13,093	16,368
1918	13,670		37,167		1,689		15,359	
1919	18,098		36,423		1,656		19,754	
1920	17,738		35,856		1,630		19,368	
1921	18,334		36,277		1,649		19,983	
1922	19,534	19,034	31,762	36,025	1,444	1,638	20,978	20,672
1923	19,560		32,683		1,486		21,046	
1924	20,006		43,547		1,979		21,985	
1925	19,675		47,371		2,153		21,828	
1926	19,245		54,913		2,496		21,741	
1927	18,214	18,557	57,100	58,723	2,595	2,669	20,809	21,226
1928	18,258		64,001		2,909		21,167	
1929	17,393		70,231		3,192		20,585	
1930	17,942		79,926		3,633		21,575	
1931	18,281		72,396		3,291		21,571	
1932	16,188	17,958	55,011	65,100	2,501	2,959	18,689	20,917
1933	18,257		55,265		2,512		20,769	
1934	19,120		62,901		2,859		21,980	
1935	19,833		64,649		2,939		22,772	
1936	19,566		78,643		3,575		23,131	
1937	18,573	19,057	92,115	88,800	4,187	4,037	22,760	23,091
1938	18,342		97,558		4,435		22,777	
1939	18,969		111,037		5,047		24,016	

Source: 1910–34, H. F. Bowyer's Pocket Book 1896–1935; Cash Summary Book 1932–66.

worst effects of this declining expenditure on alcohol. Even so, Portsmouth was very much a working-class town, but one in which, with the end of hostilities, the need for dockyard employment diminished so that by 1921 only 9,000 workers were required, 14,000 less than the wartime peak.[13] By 1924 contracts to supply the forces fell by 80 per cent, leaving Portsmouth United Brewery with such financial problems that it was only rescued, four years later, by a merger with the Rock Brewery of Brighton.[14] Gales clearly had avoided the mistake of placing too many of its eggs into a single basket, and thus was not seriously affected by the high levels of unemployment that many brewers regarded as a reason for their reduced performances.

Nevertheless, the company would have been concerned about the obvious weaknesses in the local, as well as the national, economy and this is reflected in the fact that on 12 May 1926 it was reported to Portsmouth brewery Brickwoods' board of directors that their Mr Bonham Carter had been discussing with Mr Bowyer the possibility of amalgamating with Gale and Co. Brickwoods wished to 'take advantage of every opportunity' to follow up the conversation'.[15] Although the amalgamation did not take place, the proposals may well have led to further developments, for in less than two years Brickwoods were discussing an offer from Gales for the sale of their business. In a year when Gales were valued at £256,000 the Brickwoods board proposed a price of £280,000 with the possibility that the Horndean Brewery be withdrawn from sale.[16] Clearly, Brickwoods were more interested in Gales tied houses than the production plant. On 17 May 1928 it was reported by Harry Brickwood that Gales had refused the offer, but he considered that negotiations would shortly be reopened.[17] His optimism was not misplaced, for a year later, on 4 June 1929, Brickwoods were considering a renewed offer for the purchase of the Horndean business and decided to set a purchase price of £290,000 made up of £200,000 in debentures and £90,000 in cash. Masons, Gales' auditors, were to conduct the negotiations.[18] On 26 June, Masons wrote to Brickwoods to say that their offer was not acceptable to Gales, whereupon a resolution was passed that the board would not entertain a cash purchase of Gales. No more was to be heard of this matter, and once again not a word of these negotiations appeared in the board minutes of Gales brewery! There is no doubt that Herbert Bowyer wished to keep the matter secret since, on 8 June he wrote to his son Hugh that Brickwoods were interested in making a substantial offer and to 'peruse at your leisure and *tell not a soul*'.[19]

With the welcome return of peace in 1918, life in Horndean began to resume its normal tenor. Located at the northern end of the light railway's route from Cosham, Horndean, in contrast with the war years, began receiving influxes of visitors again. The initial year of peace brought some unusual and unexpected visitors to this small Hampshire community. In late February a Japanese squadron arrived in Portsmouth for a short goodwill visit. A fairly intensive programme was arranged for the oriental visitors for their five-day stay. Imagine the scene, therefore, when on the afternoon of Monday, 3 March, five flag-bedecked tramcars arrived in Horndean and discharged their cargo of 190 Japanese and 80 British seamen. The country ride was thoroughly enjoyed, and fortunately the weather was fine, observed the local press. The officers, accompanied by Portsmouth's Mayor, arrived by car. They were all marched to the gardens of the *Red Lion* (unfortunately not a Gales house) where light refreshments were served and photographs taken. The visitors then returned to Portsmouth for afternoon tea.[20] Fine weather at Easter 'brought the usual large crowds to Horndean, and the cars were crowded with visitors from Portsmouth'. Similar conditions in early June and the psychological impact of the first Whitsun break since the war's end, attracted further crowds to the rural community. The light railway, 'was taxed to the full, and the queues were very long, but all were safely away' by about 10.30 p.m. In mid-July visitors included members of the Hampshire and Isle of Wight branch of the Institute of Journalists. Having first been received by Portsmouth's Mayor, they were subsequently hosted for tea at the *Good Intent*, Horndean, by Portsmouth branch members. Tea and business were followed by a short ramble round the village.[21] Such considerable numbers of visitors could only have helped to increase the local consumption of Gales ales.

Visitors apart, the community needed to do two other things to lay the wraith of war – erect some sort of memorial and arrange a celebratory event. Catherington's contribution was a lych-gate, to be erected at All Saints' Church. By late April collections, proceeding apace, had topped £200, to which George Gale's widow contributed 2 guineas.[22] In Horndean's case, the decision for a memorial was marked by indecision. At an August meeting in the Parish Hall four suggestions were put forward – a shrine, cross, clock, or a figure on a plinth. When the last suggestion was voted for the Chairman, Sir Dudley Clarke-Jervoise, stated that it was possible that this might be beyond the community's financial power and the knowledge of a second choice would be wise. It was accordingly decided that 'failing the Figure, a Clock should be erected'.[23]

By the time this meeting took place, Catherington and Blendworth parishes, united for the event, had officially celebrated peace. The local press announced that on 19 July, nationally designated as Peace Day, all children between the ages of 5 and 15 would be entertained. There would be a bonfire on nearby Windmill Hill and fireworks in the evening. Demobilised troops, it was stated, would be entertained later in the year.[24] For the sports events, H. F. Bowyer lent a meadow 'at the top of Horndean Hill'. Weather changes, however, led to an impromptu concert in the Parish Hall until teatime, when the children were marched off in three parties to the *Ship and Bell*, the *Good Intent* and *Red Lion*. Between 8.00 and 11.30 in the evening it was the adults' turn to celebrate with dancing and singing in the hall. A break at 10 p.m. enabled everyone to enjoy a grand firework display. Afterwards many moved to the top of Windmill Hill to watch a large bonfire, more fireworks and to partake of refreshments provided by Sir Dudley Clarke-Jervoise. The heady atmosphere of Peace Day was also extended to Catherington Union's Workhouse inmates, for whom all regulations were relaxed and two sumptuous meals provided. Even those on out-relief were remembered, 6 shillings being distributed to each adult and 3 shillings to each child.[25] Celebrations are always good for brewers and it was noticeable that Gales output of both casked and bottled beer was at its highest in 1919 in the month of July.[26]

In the brewing industry there were changes almost as soon as peace had been concluded. In February 1919 the government announced they would permit the brewing of greater quantities of stronger beer. G. H. Roberts, Controller of Food, declared cheaper prices for beer brewed later than 1 January 1918, except for 'the sale of beer on passenger vessels, and for the sale of beer in Ireland for delivery in Ireland'.[27] At the same time, public house and club evening opening hours in England and Wales were extended by half an hour, to run from 6.00 to 10.00 in the evening.[28] Some wartime restraints were beginning to disappear, thereby increasing the demand for beer. Coincidentally, doubtless encouraged by manpower losses sustained during the struggle of 1914–18, the national brewery workers' branch of the Workers' Union began to flex its muscles to acquire better conditions for those engaged in the industry. The government convened national industrial conferences and propitious agreements were reached by the union in Burton upon Trent, London, Sheffield, Llanelli, Manchester and other notable brewing centres. Brewery workers in the Portsmouth area attended a meeting convened by district organiser S. N. Warsnop, where it was agreed that the disparity between these agreements and the local position should be the subject of negotiations between the union and local brewing firms. He also remarked upon increased branch membership, doubtless a sign of changing times.[29]

Gales' performance during these years was marked by steady, sustained growth. Indeed, the company embarked on the post-war period from a position of strength, as H. F. Bowyer's solicitor, T. Blanco White, observed in April 1919: 'I think it is clear that the Company is in a very strong position and you certainly are in a position to pay a bigger dividend if you wish to.' To emphasise the point, he concluded: 'Altogether ... I think you are to be much congratulated on the result.'[30] Certainly, from the point of view of profits Gales had confounded the

industry's gloom and had a good war. In 1914 profits had topped
£6,000 and then rose fluctuatingly until, in 1919, they reached £9,345.
The following year was to bring an astonishing change. The dramatic
fall in profits for 1920 could have been ascribed in part to wage and
salary increases and expenditure on repairs at Horndean, as well as by
increased expenditure at their Southsea branch. That branch was involved in handling a substantial consignment of American whisky, 75
barrels from Peters and Company at 8s. 9d. per American gallon,[31] a
transaction in which something went radically wrong. From his home
in Leyburn near Richmond in Yorkshire, Frederick Riddell wrote to
Herbert Bowyer in September 1920:[32]

> Dear Bowyer,
>
> Thanks for your letter and balance sheet. Mason seems to consider
> it in reality better than last year which is satisfactory. I conclude
> from his letter that he considers in a normal year that the freight
> should be spread over a certain number of years and the same with
> regard to bottles, jars, etc. I gather also that the stock has been
> written down some £1120 which is pretty drastic, but as you say,
> that will come back to us and if we can dodge excess profits it is all
> to the good. What is the loss of 1,421 galls American Whiskey, did
> it disappear in transit. How about the Meeting. We are having
> some fine weather at present but cold.
>
> Kind regards to M[rs] Bowyer.
>
> Y[ou]rs sincerely
>
> Frederick Riddell

But these were minor matters and the major reason for the decline in
profits was the quite phenomenal expenditure on raw materials, especially malt. Some £39,000 was spent on sugar, hops and malt. Whereas
in the previous five years expenditure on sugar had averaged around
£2,650, in 1920 over £7,000 was spent. Expenditure on hops was over
£5,300, whereas in the previous five years it had been not much over
£2,000 per annum. But it was in the purchasing of malt where the
largest amounts were spent, over £26,500 by comparison with less than
£7,000 per annum over the previous five years.[33] A major cause of this
increase was the very high price which barley reached in 1920. Whereas
before the war it had averaged around 27 shillings per quarter, its price
rose consistently during the war and immediately afterwards, peaking
in 1920 at over 89 shillings.[34] Even so, it seems an error of judgement
was made at the brewery, probably by the brewer Sydney Steel, since
over £10,000 worth of malt was left in stock and carried over to 1921
when purchases were therefore only a little over £2,000. But in that
year the price of barley had fallen substantially to just over 52 shillings,

so considerable savings could have been made. The result of this error was that for the only time since records began in 1886 the Horndean account actually showed a net loss of £466 8s. 9d. and only the Southsea branch's profit of over £2,000 brought the final account into the black. The error was never repeated (see Table 5.3).

The dip in profits for 1923 was also explained, in part, by problems with materials supply. A contract for Pacific Coast hops had produced difficulties in both 1922 and 1923, with money having to be set aside to cover losses. Despite the fact that costs of materials and duty per barrel of beer were much lower in 1923 than in 1922 (62s. 5½d. as against 79s. 3½d.), profits had seen a shortfall of nearly £3,000 in the year ending 31 December 1923 (see Table 5.3). This, however, was probably the result of the very inclement weather, the wettest year since 1916 with excessive rainfall almost everywhere.[35] Profits rose steadily in 1925 and 1926, to stand at over £22,000 in the year of the General Strike. In 1927, however, they fell back to £20,520. Movements in material costs and duty per barrel of beer had been such as to arrive at a steady state by comparison with 1926. Trade expenses had gone up through expenditure on trade cards, advertising to celebrate the company's recent Exhibition success (see below) and increased outlay on cars. Expenditure on the Southsea branch had also increased, due chiefly to repair works 'which were exceptionally light in 1926'. Yet again, however, the weather would have depressed beer consumption.

Table 5.3   George Gale and Co.: net profits, 1917–34

	£		£
1917	7,755	1926	22,081
1918	6,972	1927	20,520
1919	9,535	1928	23,321
1920	1,614	1929	24,065
1921	11,768	1930	22,488
1922	18,212	1931	23,057
1923	15,347	1932	22,644
1924	16,148	1933	23,488
1925	18,533	1934	25,942

Source: Balance Sheets and Annual Accounts.

It was a year of considerable rainfall with a summer which was 'not only wet but very deficient in sunshine. The period June to September was the wettest since 1879'.[36] Despite the Wall Street crash of 1929 and the subsequent world economic depression, profits during this period were hardly affected, suffering only minor variations. Apart from the fact that in 1933 the wages and salaries bill for Horndean went down 'on account of less number of Men employed and decreased in salaries £38' the company seems to have come out of the world's greatest economic recession virtually unscathed. In fact profits continued to rise until the Second World War, except for 1938 when the installation of new bottling and electrical plant costing £16,384 caused a temporary decline, assisted by some lesser factors. Malt prices, wages and salaries had all risen, two houses had been bought, the *King's Arms*, Fernhurst, and the *Woodman*, Purbrook, and income in the form of interest had been lost through adjustments in the company's investment portfolio.

A new aspect of the company's activities was investment in the stock market. Company balance sheets indicate that in 1907 Gales purchased £600 worth of Cape of Good Hope 4 per cent stock and in 1915 New South Wales 4 per cent stock was acquired.[37] The company's investment portfolio during the two decades after 1919 (see Table 5.4) revealed an intriguing pattern of stability and change. At a national level, there was a holding of £50 of War Stock throughout the period, of £7,300 of 5 per cent National War Bonds, split after 1921 into £300 in Bonds and £7,000 in 3½ per cent Conversion Loan, disposed of in 1927. The National War Bonds were switched, in 1928, for 4 per cent Consolidated Stock, held for the ensuing ten years. Some investments were made in other branches of the drinks industry. Hence, there were two investments in distilleries for most of the 20 years. By the same token, there was investment in the Portsmouth Bonding Company from 1922 onwards and in two bottle-manufacturing companies. For five years, between 1923 and 1927, the company also invested in Southern Railway 4 per cent Debenture Stock, an investment which incurred a loss of over £1,000. The other investments reflected the company's community 'face' and interest in sport, as well as a modest attempt to involve themselves in the growing club trade, although this was always stronger in the north of England. Hence, sums of money went into Portsmouth Swimming Club, Cowplain Social Club, quadrupling between 1924 and 1939, and the Alexandra Bowling Club, a modest, steady, investment between 1930 and 1936.

For 4 per cent Debenture stockholders (see Table 5.5) the Company maintained a second investment portfolio, the characteristics of which were rather different. Invested funds were again divided, but this time between internal and external sources. Sums involved remained almost constant, except for a doubling in the 3 per cent Conversion Loan Stock from 1936 onwards and an increase with regard to 4 per cent Consolidated Stock from 1930 onwards. The substantial difference, however,

Table 5.4   George Gale and Co.: investment portfolio, 1919–39 (£)

	1919	1920	1921	1922	1923	1924	1925	1926	1927	1928	1929	1930	1931	1932	1933	1934	1935	1936	1937	1938	1939
Debenture Stock. G. A. Gale	2,910	2,910	2,910	2,910	4,300	4,700	5,000	5,000	4,758	5,102	5,644	6,169	10,017	10,578	10,578	10,578	10,879	11,583	11,783	11,783	11,783
Powell & Rickets War Stock	250	250	250	250	—	—	—	—	—	—	—	—	—	—	—	—	—	—	—	—	—
5% National War Bonds	7,300	7,300	50	50	50	50	50	50	50	50	50	50	50	50	50	50	50	50	50	50	—
Portsmouth Bottle Co.	250	250	250	—	—	—	—	—	—	—	—	—	—	—	—	—	—	—	—	—	—
4% Consolidated Stock	—	—	—	—	—	—	—	—	—	300	300	300	300	300	300	300	300	300	300	300	—
Langley Distillery Co.	—	—	250	250	250	250	250	250	250	250	250	250	250	250	250	250	250	250	250	250	250
D. P. Macdonald & Son Distillery	—	300	300	300	300	300	300	300	300	300	300	300	300	300	300	300	300	300	300	—	—
3½% Conversion Loan	—	—	7,000	7,000	7,000	7,000	7,000	7,000	7,000	—	—	—	—	—	—	—	—	—	—	—	—
Portsmouth Swimming Club	—	—	25	25	25	25	25	25	25	25	25	25	16	16	16	16	16	16	16	16	16
Hampshire Bottle Company	—	—	—	167	136	136	136	136	136	136	—	—	—	—	—	—	—	—	—	—	—
Portsmouth Bonding Company	—	—	—	500	500	600	600	600	600	600	600	600	615	615	615	615	615	615	615	615	615
Southern Railway 4% Debenture Stock	—	—	—	—	5,000	5,000	5,000	5,000	4,295	—	—	—	—	—	—	—	—	—	—	—	—
Cowplain Social Club Debentures	—	—	—	—	—	50	100	100	100	100	100	100	100	100	100	150	200	200	200	200	200
Alexandra Bowling Club Debentures	—	—	—	—	—	—	—	—	—	—	—	75	75	75	75	75	75	75	—	—	—
3½% Conversion Stock	—	—	—	—	—	—	—	—	—	—	—	—	—	—	—	900	900	—	—	—	—

Source: Balance Sheets and Annual Accounts 1919–39.

Table 5.5 George Gale and Co.: investment portfolio – trustees for 4% debenture stockholders (£)

	1919	1920	1921	1922	1923	1924	1925	1926	1927	1928	1929	1930	1931	1932	1933	1934	1935	1936	1937	1938	1939
Cape of Good Hope & New South Wales 4% Stock	1,676	1,676	1,676	1,676	—	—	—	—	—	—	—	—	—	—	—	—	—	—	—	—	—
5% National War Bonds	650	650	650	650	650	650	650	650	650	—	—	—	—	—	—	—	—	—	—	—	—
Union of South Africa 5% Inscribed Stock #	—	—	—	—	350	350	350	350	350	350	350	350	350	350	350	350	350	350	350	350	—
New South Wales 4% Stock	—	—	—	—	730	730	730	730	730	730	730	730	730	730	730	730	730	730	730	730	—
3½% Conversion Loan	—	—	—	—	—	720	750	720	720	720	720	720	720	720	720	720	720	720	720	720	—
4% Consols	—	—	—	—	—	—	—	—	—	807	807	900	900	900	900	900	900	900	900	900	—

Note: # Altered in 1935 to 3½ per cent.

Source: Balance Sheets and Annual Accounts 1919–39.

between what might be termed the company's 'ordinary' investment portfolio and that for 4 per cent debenture stockholders was the placing of money overseas. Not only were funds invested in Cape of Good Hope and New South Wales stock but also, from 1923, in Union of South Africa 5 per cent stock.

More importantly, on the production side in the inter-war years, the brewery continued to generate high quality and well regarded beers. The company collected a series of Exhibition awards and diplomas, very clear evidence of the maintenance of high standards and a dynamic approach to fresh challenges undertaken, particularly by the brewer. Having done handsomely at the Brewers' Exhibition, London, in 1902, 1904, 1906 and 1908, the company went on to excel itself at the Exhibitions of 1921, 1923, 1924, 1925, 1926, 1928 and 1930. The tally of awards from the 1926 Exhibition was impressive – Champion Gold Medal and Diploma, First Prize Silver Medal and Diploma and Champion Challenge Cup and Diploma. As a memento of securing the Championship Gold Medal and B. J. Challenge Cup, H. F. Bowyer was presented with a double-handled silver tankard. Though the company may not have done as well at the 1930 Exhibition, there were still some awards in which to take pride – Second Prizes for Stout, for Bottled Beer and for Bottled Stout.[38] In a period when there was a reduced demand for beer, breweries generally, notably Guinness, attempted to build brand loyalty.[39] There is little doubt that Gales successes indicated their response to the need for product differentiation as well as to be known for the excellence of their beers.

In no small measure were these successes thanks to the two formidable Head Brewers of this period – Sydney Steel and Barton Mears. Steel had joined the company at the turn of the twentieth century and guided the brewing operations successfully through both the Edwardian period and the strains of 1914–18. During the war he had developed 'process brewing', a method of producing alcohol from making best possible use of such brewing materials as were available. Widely adopted by other breweries, the method was also recognised by HM Customs and Excise. To him went the credit, in the first decade of the century and in the early 1920s, of winning almost every top award for his beers. The glitter of the prizes and awards was somewhat dimmed, however, when shortly before Christmas 1922 Steel was found 'drowned in a vat of beer at the brewery'. Seen at his desk at 8.15 on the morning of 21 December by employee John Murrant, Steel took his own life shortly afterwards. County Coroner Leornard Warner returned a verdict of 'suicide whilst temporarily insane', pointing out that Steel had been under great stress.[40] It proved to be not only a tragic but difficult time for the brewery management.

His successor, William Barton Mears, came from a notable Yorkshire brewing family. One of three brothers, all of whom entered the brewing industry, Mears was to be successful in his own right. Matching Steel's record of award-winning beers, successes were achieved at the Brewers' Exhibition every year from 1923 to 1926 and also in 1928 and 1930. In the early 1930s Gales were brewing five cask beers, 'XXXXX' Ale, the most expensive, 'BBB' Ale, Pale Ale, Stout and 'XX' Beer and eight bottled beers – Golden Tonic Ale, Nut Brown Ale, Nourishing Stout, AI Ale, Digestive Stout, King Cole Ale, Special Champion Cup Ale and Prize Old Ale, the most expensive. Mears's successes, along with his steadfast character, led to his appointment as an Exhibition judge in 1939. At Gales he was conscientious and level-headed, and these qualities were recognised when in January 1936, along with Richard Walter Gale, he was made a director of the company.[41] That November he was appointed one of three trustees for the newly introduced Staff Pension Scheme. He oversaw the extension and improvements to the Bottling Store in 1936–37 which, along with the rise in the company's value, may have encouraged him in January 1937 to apply for a salary increase, a request that was acceded to the following month. An increase of £70 per annum took his salary to £1,050 with a house at £50. At the board meeting in January 1938 he intimated that he was contemplating the purchase of a house at Havant. Would the directors sanction his living away from Horndean? Fellow director Hugh Bowyer stated that 'providing Mr Mears felt that he could carry out his duties and the Business would not suffer in any way there would be no objection'.[42]

Although unemployment was regarded by the brewers, in the inter-war period as a major cause of falling consumption, its effect should have been at least partially offset by the rising real incomes and standards of living of those in work. But beer consumption still declined. Generally, it was a period of smaller and healthier families, and one in which over 4 million new houses were built. With the cheap money policy of the 1930s it was possible to obtain mortgages at 4 per cent. Thus, expenditure not only went on houses but also their contents. Sales of vacuum cleaners, radios, cookers and refrigerators, not to mention furniture and furnishings, were becoming the norm for many who now moved to become suburban dwellers since this was where many of the new houses were erected. Clearly, fundamental changes in the patterns of expenditure were taking place, but not ones that had anything but a marginal effect on Gales' output. This was not a matter entirely of geographical good fortune, as the problems of Portsmouth United Breweries demonstrate, but resulted from some positive responses made by the brewery in Horndean. Most progressive breweries in the inter-war period invested in bottling plant, motorised distribution and improved the standards of their public houses.[43] Gales were no exception.

Whereas other breweries in the 1920s found themselves surprised by the growing demand for bottled beers,[44] Gales had already introduced their new bottling facilities before the First World War and reaped the rewards of the rise in the drinking of bottled beer. Curiously, however, the wartime decline in bottled-beer drinking by Gales customers which led to a fall in output of nearly 62 per cent at Horndean, was not halted after the war, but continued until 1922, when output was less than one-third that of 1914. The rest of the 1920s, nevertheless, saw a recovery that peaked in 1930, but still at more than 17 per cent below the 1914 figure, and in the early 1930s output began to decline again, despite the general trend towards the drinking of more bottled beer. Since at this time brewery output was being maintained at a fairly steady state, it could mean that the existing facilities had reached their maximum productive capacity, particularly since in 1930 replacement bottling plant machinery costing not far short of £2,000 was installed. Even so, a new bottling plant, budgeted for in 1936, was introduced in 1938 at a cost of over £15,600.[45] Clearly much more extensive bottling facilities were needed, especially since, nationally, the popularity of bottled beers saw them accounting for only 20 per cent of the industry's sales by 1939.[46] Gales had surpassed this figure as early as 1914, but thereafter sales declined in importance so that by 1934, they represented only 13 per cent of total output.[47]

With rising living standards it was necessary to modernise older public houses or even replace them and Gales must have had their share of ageing properties since, under the compensation scheme introduced in 1904, three were closed – the *Foresters Arms* in Havant in 1910, the *Bricklayers Arms*, Hambledon in 1914, both being sold in 1920, and the *Queens Hotel*, Ryde in 1932, being sold six years later. But Gales recognised that their houses should be decent, comfortable and pleasant places, long before the Royal Commission on Licensing (1931) indicated they should be so, as well as places of general refreshment.

Consequently, between the wars, a policy of modernisation of public houses was pursued. At least £24,500 was spent on improvements to 19 of the company's houses. Moreover, presumably in order to ensure that output was maintained, at least another 20 houses were added to Gales growing list, plus at least two off-licences and a brewery (see Table 5.6). The total investment in these premises was approaching £90,000. Most of the improvements and purchases took place in the 1920s and early-1930s. In fact, after 1930, only five houses were improved and only three new additions purchased.[48] Even so, in his annual report for 1933 the Chairman, H. F. Bowyer, stated that for the 'extension of the

Table 5.6   George Gale and Co.: property acquisitions, 1919–39

Years	Licensed premises	Other
1919–24	11	2
1925–29	6	—
1930–34	4	2
1935–39	4	—
Total	25	4

Source: Company Records Listing, pp. 29–39.

business it is desirable that the policy of past years of acquiring additional licensed houses and rebuilding of present properties as opportunity offers be continued'. Profit was to be retained for this purpose.[49] That Gales were most active in house purchases in the years immediately following the First World War represents not only the inability to buy in wartime, but also their rising output and profits, the former requiring outlets and the latter providing the means to acquire them. The geographical extent of expansion is an indication of Gales confidence in a period of increasing economic uncertainty.[50] The years 1919–24 were marked by expansion into Sussex, seven of the nine houses purchased being located there. The other two were placed strategically close to the brewery at Horndean. On 27 January 1919 the company purchased the *Farmer* at Catherington from Sir Dudley Clarke-Jervoise. Lessees since mid-September 1905, the company paid £2,376 for the inn and other properties. At the end of that year, in a second transaction with Clarke-Jervoise they purchased, for £1,275, the *Red Lion* at Chalton. In February 1920 Gales purchased the *Wickham Arms* in Chichester. Since late December 1912 the company had leased the premises, with the *Cattle Market Inn*, Chichester, and the *Royal Oak* at nearby Lagness from London china and glass merchant George Collins. The properties had originally been acquired by a namesake ancestor, a Lagness brewer, in 1853. Although the lease still had half its span to run, the company pressed ahead and purchased all three houses for £5,100. In September 1921 Gales and Co. made a further purchase in Chichester by acquiring, for £1,550, the *New Inn*. Erected by 1851, the building stood on land known in the late 1770s as 'The One Acre'.

In December 1923 the company made its major property purchasing move of the entire decade with the acquisition of the Angel Brewery, Midhurst, and six associated premises. For £13,600 they obtained at auction the brewing premises, the *Angel Inn*, an adjoining off-licence, three other Midhurst inns, the *Ritz* at Chichester and the *Railway Inn* at nearby Elsted. The history of the *Angel Inn* itself can be traced back to October 1699 and rents regarding the land on which it stood for a century or more before that. By 1875 the inn was owned by Henry Capel, wine merchant of Seething Lane in London. He leased it to Midhurst resident John Parker whose role was to be an important one as he acquired nearly all the premises that, subsequently, would pass to Gales. In 1872, for example, he had acquired both the *Oxford Arms* in Midhurst, built *c.* 1830, and the *Ritz* in Chichester, the third name by which that public house had been known. Originally the *Same Place Inn*, it had then become the *Park Tavern* before being known as the *Ritz*. In 1888 Parker had also obtained the *Three Horseshoes* in Midhurst, which had been in local doctor John Robinson's possession since 1875. The *Railway Inn* at Elsted, 5 miles east of Petersfield, was in widow Mary Parker's tenancy when purchased by Gales.

During the second half of the 1920s the company turned its gaze southward. Having purchased a private residence, 'Clydesdale' in Ryde in 1922, the company made a further acquisition there in June 1925. Built about 1860 on land that was once part of the Lind estate, the *Castle* had been leased by the company since October 1898. Rather than continue with the 990–year lease, the company paid £702 for the freehold. In the following month, back on the mainland, they added to their inns in the Meon Valley by purchasing the *Roebuck*, located north of Wickham on the road to the market town of Alton. Built by September 1841 and insured against fire for £500 five years later, the *Roebuck* was, by 1909, in the hands of Emily and John Didymus. In July 1925, Emily Didymus, by now a widow, sold to Gales and Co for £5,000. That October the company made a further purchase – the *Horse and Jockey* at Curbridge, midway between Wickham and Southampton. The premises had been leased by the Hyde Street-based Winchester Brewery Company since May 1901 from the owners of Upham House. Early in October 1925 the company paid out £2,150 to the owners and thus acquired yet another outlet in their growing empire. The following month purchase of the freehold of the *Queen's Hotel*, was noted. Two years later came two further purchases, this time to create 'northern outposts'. The *Three Horseshoes* at Thursley near Frensham Common, had been leased by its owner, Captain W. H. Rushbrooke, to Lascelles, Tickner and Co. of the Castle Brewery, Guildford on 29 September 1922 for 14 years at £55 per annum. Five years later, the Guildford brewers having surrendered the property, Gales purchased it for £2,750. Four days later they procured the *Fox Inn* at Cane End, Oxfordshire. The company's first venture so far afield, it stands as proof of their growing success and enterprise. The property was owned by Henry

Vanderstegen of Cane End House who had let it, in 1924, for £35 per annum, all the liquors to be obtained from the Wallingford Brewery Company. On 13 December 1927 Gales purchased it for £1,700. In 1939 a new *Fox Inn* was constructed on the site and in December the old premises were demolished by Oxfordshire County Council to make way for a road improvement scheme.

Between March and September 1930 Gales acquired a further four houses, two in Surrey and two in Hampshire. That May, for £850 in the Isle of Wight, the Company bought 'Albert Villa' in Sandown, located next to their *Commercial Hotel*. On 14 March they acquired the *Newport Inn* at Braishfield, near Romsey, two cottages and 49.5 acres of land, for £2,000 from the authorities of New College, Oxford. That June Gales purchased the *Sea Horse* at Shalford in Surrey, a short distance to the south of Guildford. The property had been let out by the owner, retired Major Robert Godwin-Austen, to Hodgsons (Kingston) Brewery Co. Ltd. In mid-June, however, he and his associates conveyed it to Gales. Two more purchases were made that year – the *Three Horseshoes* at East Worldham and the *Red Lion* at Milford in Surrey. The history of the former property can be traced back to 1771. In 1860, it was in the possession of Crowleys, the Alton brewers, but by mid-August the property was acquired by Gales. The *Red Lion* was bought in mid-September 1930 for £7,750 along with a house and shop, both of which were subsequently sold off. Thus, by the early 1930s Gales had some 67 tied houses and half a dozen off-licences to supply,[51] as well as their free trade and private customers who took approximately half their output.

Between 1935 and the outbreak of the Second World War the Company purchased another four licensed houses. While the acquisitions were scattered in terms of time, they were, with one exception, concentrated in Hampshire. In January 1935 the *Chairmakers Arms* at Hipley near the village of Hambledon, not far from Horndean, was acquired. The premises, originally a beerhouse called the *Pig and Whistle*, had been held by the Ecclesiastical Commissioners as lords of Hambledon manor who, in mid-October 1923, had sold the beerhouse to F. Hartridge. His two sons, Edward and Austin, sold it to Gales early in January 1935 for £3,000. Twelve months later the company were again in the market for property, this time purchasing the *Portland Hotel* in Fareham. Located in Portland Street, the premises had been in use since the mid-1870s. They were acquired by Gales for £10,500. Then, in January 1939, they obtained the *Dolphin* at Havant, subsequently to be the subject of rebuilding after the Second World War. In addition to these purchases of licensed premises, the company bought Flint Farm, Purbrook, as a new site for the *Woodman* and removal of its licence to the new site was sanctioned. The old premises were demolished and a new inn built. To finance this rebuilding, and that of the *Spotted Cow* at nearby Cowplain, all the invested stock held by the Debenture Trustees had to be sold off in 1938.

The acquisition of some 25 new licensed houses plus other properties inevitably had a considerable effect on the value of the company's assets. Between 1918 and 1939 it rose by an impressive 77 per cent. (see Table 5.7) with property accounting for some 70 per cent of the total.

Table 5.7   George Gale and Co.: asset value, 1918–39 (£)

1918	191,709	1929	262,375
1919	197,235	1930	288,498
1920	215,281	1931	292,982
1921	202,095	1932	298,629
1922	209,467	1933	297,165
1923	213,674	1934	293,963
1924	225,598	1935	281,328
1925	242,427	1936	302,127
1926	246,571	1937	331,358
1927	255,235	1938	331,507
1928	256,497	1939	339,137

Source: Balance Sheets and Annual Accounts.

With increasing output to supply the growing number of tied houses came an expanding workforce, thus the company also began to buy into non-licensed local property to house some of its workers. In September 1919 four properties, numbers 32 to 38 Five Heads Road, Horndean, were acquired and in the early 1930s a further purchase of three adjoining houses in London Road, Horndean, was made.

One other way in which the company demonstrated a progressive approach was in its attitude towards transport changes. The policy of continuing to maintain a modern transport fleet with constant upgrading of vehicles was maintained. At least four new lorries and the same number of cars were bought in the 1920s, and five lorries, a van and three cars in the 1930s. There was no sentimental attachment to brand names. From the 1920s Fodens were replaced by Dennis lorries and a Morris van was acquired in the 1930s. A Talbot car from the 1920s was replaced by an Alvis, but it was a Rover that was the final purchase before the Second World War. During the decade after 1919 the use of horses at Horndean declined quite sharply, depreciation in 1929 being a mere 10 per cent of what it had been ten years earlier, and accompanied by a commensurate increase in the use of motorised transport, indicating that the policy of constant upgrading of vehicles was continued. In contrast, the use of horses at the Southsea branch remained steady, if meagre, and only came to a halt in 1934 when the one remaining beast died and deliveries were taken over by a lorry from Horndean.[52]

Over the years horsekeep at Horndean, on balance, went down. Standing at £69 in 1923, it decreased to £45 in the following year, but increased in 1925 to £61. In 1925 another new lorry was purchased. The 1931 accounts revealed decreased expenditure on coal and petrol of £388 'partly due to use of Petrol Lorry in place of two Fodens'. Carriage costs were also down by £64, explained by 'Increased use of our own Lorries'. Carriage expenses for the Southsea branch were £524 in 1934, compared with £377 for 1933, the £147 rise being explained by 'Increases in Shipments of Whisky, Port and Guinness and Hire cost £69 on account of the death of the horse in July'. In 1937, as evidence of changing circumstances £29 13s. 0d. was spent on purchasing time recorders for lorries. Carriage expenses rose by £92 in 1939, explained by 'Additional Hiring contracts due to the War Department taking over one of the Companies lorries for some weeks'.[53]

Progress in relationships with the workforce also continued. Apart from the introduction of an annual bonus scheme, mindful of its social responsibilities, the Gales' Board of Directors turned their attention in the mid-1930s to a staff pension fund. Discussed at a meeting on 20 November 1936, an explanatory letter to employees, demonstrating the care and consideration of the company, was approved on 16 December:

> The Directors for some time have been carefully considering the adoption of a scheme to assist members of the staff to make provision for their old age and to benefit their dependents in the event of earlier death. We are now glad to be able to inform you that arrangements have been made with the Eagle, Star and British Dominion Insurance Company Ltd., to put into operation such a scheme providing pension and assurance benefits as described on a subsequent page.
>
> The scheme will apply to all male employees on the staff over age 20 and under age 64 and will be put into operations as from the 1st January next. Medical examination will only be required in exceptional cases but those who fail to join now may be required to provide evidence of good health at their own expense if they wish to join at a later date.
>
> The scheme has been drafted on the basis of joint contributions by the employees and the Company, but I am pleased to say that the Directors are prepared to increase employees' wages as from the 1st January next by the amount of the contributions they will then make so that actually the scheme will not cost anything to employees who join now, The Directors paying the whole cost,

including additional pensions in respect of past service and death and disablement benefits.

Whilst the present intention of the Directors is to continue their contributions from year to year, it is impossible to guarantee what may happen in the future and they therefore reserve the right to discontinue or modify the Scheme at any time on giving six month's notice to the employees. Should the scheme be discontinued, each employee would receive from the normal pension age such pension as had been secured by both the employee's and the Firm's contributions up to the date of discontinuance.[54]

At the same meeting the board decided that as from 1 January 1937 employees' wages would rise by the amount of their contribution to the new scheme.[55]

In June 1937 agreement was reached on further wage rises for some staff – F. A. Childs by £10 per annum, five men by 1 shilling per week each, two by 2 shillings and one, C. Eames, by 5 shillings. One request was denied, while attention was also paid to Richard W. Gale's salary. He had asked that his salary and commission be consolidated into a single payment. It was agreed that his salary be set at £600 from 1 July 1937, to be reviewed again in January 1938 'with a view to ascertaining what his Commission for 1937 would have been'.[56]

Staff were certainly looked after by the company. When, in late January 1938, it was reported that Mrs Minkey had to retire, through ill health after 27 years' service, it was decided to grant her a weekly allowance of 5 shillings. When negotiations were in hand to secure new premises to be known as the *Woodman*, provision was made with regard to Miss K. Smith's 'long service of 48 years'. She would receive a weekly pension of 8 shillings 'or allowed to live in the old "Woodman" as long as it remained'. When she decided not to remain in the old premises, the pension was raised to 10 shillings.[57] There was other evidence of caring too. Late in March 1939 it was decided 'to place a Notice in the Brewery Yard regarding Employees' Wages during sickness as suggested by The Brewers' Society'. One employee – Harry Sheppard – broke his leg while delivering beers. 'It was decided to make his Wages up to the full amount whilst he was away.'[58] Caring could also be shown by the company's patronage of, and contribution towards, worthy causes. While it could be argued that such a policy presented a slightly less than hard business face, it nevertheless represented a very genuine concern, which was to be one of the company's twentieth-century hallmarks (see Table 5.8). Clearly a range of interests and concerns attracted the company's attention.

During the inter-war years change was also to be observed within the context of the Bowyer and Gale families. With the change of control at the brewery in the 1890s it was the Bowyers who became more

Table 5.8 Gales' contribution to causes, 1936–39

Date	Cause	Amount
May 1936	Airspeed Sports and Social Club	Loan of further £300
June 1936	George V. Memorial Fund	£21
February 1937	Coronation Donations	10s. 0d. per house where company owned licensed premises
May 1937	Portsmouth Cathedral Fund	£50
August 1937	Trade Union Club, Cosham	Loan? Interest charges to be remitted until 31 Dec. 1939
January 1938	Portsmouth Coronation Homes	£21
February 1938	Nash Memorial Hall	£21
September 1938	Royal West Sussex Hospital	£5
September 1938	Rothampstead Institute	£3 3s. 0d.
October 1938	Barclay Gretton Fund	£10 10s. 0d.
January 1939	Prize Fund, Royal Counties Show	£5 5s. 0d.

Source: Gale and Co. Minute Book March 1936–November 1965, *passim*.

important. H. F. Bowyer certainly made an active contribution in terms of community work. In 1919, for example, he served on both the Horndean Board of Guardians and the Rural District Council. When nominated for Catherington Rural District Council six years later he was described as of 'Westfield', Horndean, brewery managing director.[59] Mrs Elsie Bowyer, H. F. Bowyer's wife, made a similar community contribution through the activities of the local Women's Institute. In 1925, as President, she agreed to act as delegate at the May Annual Meeting in London. She provided the garden at 'Westfield' for the September meeting, marred by inclement weather and the need to hold it in the Parish Hall instead. The same thing happened in June 1926 'when the stormy weather made the looked for rally in the garden impossible'. For the Armistice Day meeting that year she provided both prizes and refreshments.[60] Whilst involved with the Women's Institute, Elsie would almost certainly have been familiar with George Gale's widow, Miriam, who also assisted in the local community.[61]

Miriam's son, David, appears to have been somewhat elusive. In July 1925 he received a vote of thanks for placing the family home, 'Crookley' in Horndean, at the Women's Institute's disposal. In the same month he was a guest at the Amalgamated Friendly Societies' Fete at Horndean, designed to raise money for the Portsmouth Hospital, the Eye and Ear Infirmary, the Surgical Aid Society, and the local Nursing Fund. The event drew over 3,000 people.[62] Having sold off the Crookley estate in

1929, he was absent from many local and family funerals,[63] and certainly avoided H. F. Bowyer's in 1938. He appears to have left the Horndean area completely.

Much more of a contribution, by virtue of both action and presence, was made by Richard Newman Gale. Born in 1879 and educated at Portsmouth, he went to live with his great uncle, George Alexander Gale, at 'Crookley', perhaps as a surrogate son. Soon after, in 1897, he started to work in the brewery, being a brewery traveller initially, but rising to become a director and then Secretary. He began acquiring shares in 1905 and slowly increased his holdings in the 1920s, doubtless as a result of becoming a director in 1925 and of assuming the mantle of Company Secretary from Ernest H. Taylor in 1927.[64] He took a great interest in church, sport, local and national affairs. A deputy warden and member of Havant Parochial Church Council, he was also Rector's warden at Blendworth. His other interests included politics, serving as Chairman of the Horndean Conservative Association. Additionally, he was Treasurer of the Hampshire Brewers' Union. He also demonstrated a very great interest in sport, as well as participating himself, being a keen cricketer. He was an ardent supporter of Portsmouth Football Club, took a very active role as a referee in many local games, frequently putting up the prize for the participants[65] and was President of Horndean Football Club. He also found time in his busy schedule to act as Chairman of the Horndean and District Horticultural and Allotment Society in 1925. During the 1920s he regularly made the arrangements for local Sunday School outings to nearby Hayling Island.[66] The euphoria of such occasions may be adduced from the following account of the 1920 visit:

> We had a long and happy day, cricket, (a feature of this was a magnificent catch by Mr Nelson in the middle of the sea!) An interminable game of Rounders, Football in which Catherington had to own to defeat by Blendworth, bathing, paddling, sticky sweets, ginger beer, 'Souvenirs for Mother', and not least a jolly good tea.[67]

The marriage of Richard Newman Gale and Alice Mary Brown resulted in one child – a son Richard Walter, baptised at Blendworth on 22 January 1907. By the time the First World War ended he was attending his third school. Having initially been at Miss Maunder's School for girls and boys in Waterlooville, he then went to Mr Hill's school for boys in the same community. On 1 May 1917 he began at Forest School in North London where his uncle, Bill Dawe, had taught science. A noted footballer, Dawe had played for England, captained Southampton and also played for the Corinthians and the Casuals. Between 1919 and 1924 Richard Walter Gale served in the school Officers' Training

Corps before joining P. Marsland and Sons, Watergate Brewery, in Huddersfield as a pupil brewer.[68] While there, he also joined the Huddersfield Old Boys Rugby Club and the Territorial Army (5th Battalion, the Duke of Wellington's Regiment) as a lieutenant from 9 July 1925. Pupilage complete, he moved to Peters and Co. in Southsea in order to learn about wines and spirits. His move also occasioned a transfer into the 6th (Duke of Connaught's Own) Hants Battalion, the local Territorial Army regiment, serving as lieutenant from 9 July 1927.[69] On 18 May 1933 he married Thelma May Evans, daughter of Mr and Mrs Harry Evans of Waterlooville, at St Judes Church, Southsea, subsequently joining George Gale and Co., where he became a director in January 1936.[70]

The inter-war period in the brewing industry was one of adjustment to lower production levels of what were weaker strength beers. Higher excise duties and higher prices did not help to alleviate the problems. The declining national demand for beer created a problem of over-capacity resulting, inevitably, in increasing concentration through mergers and acquisitions. At the end of the first decade of the twentieth century there were 4,482 breweries in Britain. Ten years later, in 1920, these had been reduced to 2,889 and another decade saw them depleted to 1,418. By the beginning of the Second World War only 840 remained, representing a massive reduction of 80 per cent of all breweries in thirty years.[71] The number of brewing companies, as distinct from breweries, fell by more than half from 941 to 428 in the same period.[72] In the process, some important regional breweries emerged such as Greene King in East Anglia, Simonds at Reading and, in Gales own area, Strongs of Romsey and Brickwoods in Portsmouth, which had absorbed six other breweries.[73]

To have survived this period of intense concentration was some achievement, to have done so and had a larger and stronger company at the end, testifies to some considerable quality of management at Gales. In this respect the whole of the twentieth century almost to the outbreak of the Second World War was dominated by one man, Herbert Bowyer. He had commenced his four decades at the helm with some cautious financial management exemplified by the reduction in directors' fees, dividend payments and in his new Company Secretary's salary. Ernest Taylor was appointed at £115 per annum, £85 less than his predecessor.[74] By comparison, the workforce were provided with incentives. This rationalisation in wages and salaries was accompanied by a similar approach to the company's organisation. By 1901 Bowyer had taken the decision to sell off the loss-making Newport branch and, when eventually a buyer was found in 1904, its sale price covered almost all the losses made during his period of management. On the production side he had appointed in 1900 an exceptional brewer, Sydney Steel so that in 1912, despite the problems caused by the increased cost of raw materials, the 'excellent qualities of the Beer'[75] meant that output had increased. These 'excellent qualities' meant Steel won many awards for his beers at the Brewers' Exhibition. Even so, Bowyer's innate cautiousness meant that in 1915 he reduced dividend payments 'to provide against the anticipated restrictions threatened by the Chancellor of the Exchequer affecting the hours of trading'.[76] The result was, that despite 'immense difficulties of labour, transport, office-work and of meeting the requirements of government authorities',[77] Gales came out of the First World War a more successful company.

In the early 1920s Steel's tragic death was to prove a 'very trying time' for the brewery but one in which the experienced Managing Director 'showed a calm determination to carry on' and the brewery 'pulled through without a single complaint from any of our customers as to the quality of our Beers'.[78] Perhaps that last comment was a reflection on the appointment of the replacement brewer, William Barton Mears, who proved outstanding, maintaining the quality of Gales' beers and, following in Steel's footsteps, winning national championships at the 1926 Brewers' Exhibition in London as well as carrying on the tradition of process brewing instigated by Sydney Steel in the First World War.

Herbert Bowyer was by now in his sixties, and having piloted the brewery through the 'very troublesome times' of the General Strike, and with some long-serving friends departing – 1927 saw the last mention of F. W. Riddell and also of Ernest Taylor, the Secretary for 30 years[79] – he needed to consider the future management of the company. His only son, Hugh, had been brought up in Horndean attending Sullivan's Preparatory School before going on to Haileybury. Aged 16 when the First World War began, he enlisted in the Royal West Surrey Regiment, and then transferred to the Royal Flying Corps. He was reported missing in September 1915, whilst still only 17, when he was shot down over Germany and became a prisoner of war. Because of his injury – he had suffered a bullet wound in the left ankle – he was repatriated on 7 January 1918 coming home on crutches, and entering Netley Hospital for an operation. However, the bone was so badly damaged that the ankle could not be properly repaired and Hugh was left with a limp and had to wear a built-up boot for the rest of his life. With the foundation of the RAF on 1 April 1918 he became a lieutenant in the Aeroplane and Seaplane branch.[80]

However, by June 1922 he had left the service and joined the brewing industry, not in his father's firm, but at Barclay Perkins,[81] no doubt through the influence of his mother's family and Charles Carlos Perkins. He became a director responsible for their managed houses and lived in a flat over the gatehouse at Barclay Perkins' Anchor Brewery in South-wark. It was thus as a 30-year old, with several years' experience in the brewing industry, that he was elected a director of Gales on 2 March 1929. Shortly afterwards, on 17 September 1931, he married Katherine Henrietta Clare Mason, a young lady some 11 years his junior. In parental footsteps, the couple were married in Southwark cathedral, the service being conducted by Reverend A. A. Evans, assisted by three other clergymen. The bride's parents, Mr and Mrs Reginald Maxwell Mason of 'Westland', Chailey, 6 miles north of Lewes in Sussex and of Birling Gap, East Dean, lived in some style. And by coincidence Reginald Maxwell Mason just happened to be one-half of the accountancy firm in King William Street, London, that looked after the Gale company accounts. The newspaper accounts of the wedding were fulsome:

> The bride, who was given away by her father, wore a gown of parchment satin. A train of old Brussels lace was draped from the shoulders over a satin train and held in place by a cluster trail of orange-blossom. Her veil of parchment silk net was held in place by a coronet of seed pearl leaves, and she carried a sheaf of Madonna lilies and white heather. There was one grown-up bridesmaid, Miss Betty Mason, the bride's sister, who carried the train and wore a frock of lily-green silk tulle trimmed with petals of ring velvet. She was followed by six little girls – Miss Dawn Drake, Miss Rosemary Bovill, Miss Alison Perkins, Miss Eva Symonds, Miss Mary Symonds, and Miss Betty Nelson. They wore picture frocks of the same green, and had wreaths of lily-green painted crystal flowers. All the bridesmaids carried posies of white roses and lilies of the valley.

The guest list was both extensive and impressive and included brewing associates of both families, service personnel, some of whom had probably served with the groom, along with a 'sprinkling' of clergy, titled guests and medical men.[82]

Reginald Mason was to remain a family friend for the rest of his life and a major influence, as auditor, on Herbert Bowyer's business affairs. In fact, the Masons were to remain a pervasive factor in the decisions and direction that the company took throughout the twentieth century. As specialist auditors to many brewing companies, such as Brickwoods in Portsmouth, they were able to recommend to Gales quality personnel for recruitment, new share structure proposals to minimise the impact of death duties and the establishment of a family trust related to the introduction of a dual share voting system among other aspects of business, all of which were instrumental in contributing to the company's survival and development.

The wedding demonstrated that links between the Gale and Bowyer families had developed on a personal as well as business level after

Herbert Bowyer had acquired the Brewery and settled in Horndean. There his son had grown up alongside David, the young son of the ageing George Alexander. That a close friendship developed between the two boys is demonstrated by the fact that Hugh Bowyer's best man, surprisingly omitted from the comprehensive newspaper account, was David Alexander Gale, a young man of considerable means after his father's death in 1914, who had a passion for cars, motorcycles and horses. That Hugh Bowyer had been working away from Horndean for some time, but his best man came from the community, is an indication of his regular visits to his childhood home and his parents, indicating a considerable attachment to the place of his birth.[83] From 1929 as a director he was to be a regular visitor at the board meetings of the brewery where his father remained in control. In the early 1930s the elder Bowyer, then over 70 years old, was to succinctly express the philosophy behind his company's success when he stated: 'that for the extension of the business it is desirable that the policy of past years of acquiring additional licensed houses and rebuilding of the present properties as opportunity appears be continued'. It was also advisable, he said, that a reasonable amount of profit be retained to carry on the policy.[84] It was the only time his policy and the need for it to continue was ever referred to in a board meeting and it may be that he was beginning to consider his own mortality. If so, it was timely, for late that year, 1934, he was to be ill, the December board meeting having to be held at his home, 'Westfield'. In May 1935 pleasure was expressed at his recovery – he was back in the chair – but it was a short-lived one for 'a long and trying illness' followed later in the year and extended into 1936. In his absence his son Hugh took over the chairmanship of the board. By mid-1936 Herbert Bowyer was back in harness and coinciding with his return two new directors were created, W. Barton Mears, the brewer, and Richard Walter Gale, aged 29.[85] It seems that Bowyer was preparing the way for the next generation of the company's management and his new directors were to see just two years of his management technique, for in August 1938 he was laid to rest in Blendworth churchyard after 40 years of considerable achievement.

The feeling of loss for many at the Horndean Brewery was perhaps best encapsulated by Company Secretary Richard Newman Gale. Great-nephew of George Alexander, he paid tribute to 'H.F.B.' at the board meeting held on 8 August 1938:

> Before we proceed to Business I would like to express on behalf of my Colleagues, the Staff and Myself our deepest regret at the death of our late Chairman and Managing Director and to convey to Mrs Bowyer and her Son our sincere sympathy in their Bereavement. Having had the pleasure of being very closely associated with him,

both as a Servant and Colleague for over 42 years I do know what
he did to make Gale and Company the prosperous business it is
and personally I feel his death very deeply, in fact he has been quite
a Father to me and it is through his kindness that I hold the
position I now do.[86]

The funeral took place on 5 August 1938 and was conducted by
Blendworth incumbent Reverend H. Lake. Six brewery employees bore
the coffin into church that summer's day as a final act of respect for
their employer. Blendworth church was filled with mourners – family,
friends, colleagues from the brewery, representatives of the clerical staff
at both the Horndean and Southsea branches of the firm, the four
domestic staff and three outside staff who had cared for him and his
wife at 'Westfield', and associates from the brewing industry locally.
Also present were mourners reflecting Bowyer's community interests –
W. Hammond, assistant secretary of Horndean Football Club, C. W.
Seward, JP, Chairman of the Petersfield Rural District Council and
Lieutenant W. H. Sheppard, RN, representing the Horndean branch of
the British Legion. The floral tributes were equally as profuse.[87] Three
months to the day after H. F. Bowyer's death, the following brief notice
appeared in *The Times*: 'BOWYER, Mr. Herbert Frederick (77), of
Horndean, Hants, chairman and managing director of George Gale and
Co. Limited, brewers and wine and spirit merchants, of Portsmouth
(net personalty £131,820) £141,007.'[88]

It is difficult to know precisely why, in these turbulent years in the
brewing industry when 80 per cent of breweries disappeared, Gales not
only survived but gathered in strength and size until they had over 70
tied houses at Bowyer's death. Perhaps the real answer lies in the
personality of the individual entrepreneur. He had failed to reach agreement with Brickwoods over both amalgamation and sale, probably
because he valued the brewery much more highly than his rivals. Certainly it would have been impossible for them to succeed unilaterally,
since the Bowyer family retained the equity and hence shares could not
be acquired from what was a private limited company without his
support. He was an astute and perceptive manager both of materials
and men, and, although few personal comments appear in the pages of
the records of business companies, two significant statements perhaps
summed up his approach to both the company and particularly its
workforce. In 1912 it was said that the 'happy relations that existed
between the Managing Director and the Staff was [*sic*] in no small way
responsible for the success of the business'.[89] He had then been in
charge for 15 years, but at the first annual general meeting after his
death in May 1939 thanks were given "to all those who work for our
Company and show such excellent "Team Spirit"'.[90] Such team spirit

could only have been developed by someone with a considerable regard not only for the company, but especially for the workforce, and it is particularly significant that it was six of his employees who carried his coffin into church. It was under his stewardship that Gales became known as a company for which generations of the same families were pleased to work. His death was undoubtedly a major loss but he had as carefully managed his succession as he had the business. His son Hugh had not only his Barclay Perkins experience but also ten years as a director of Gales to call on when he eventually took over the Horndean company at a very uncertain time as the storm clouds of war once again gathered over Europe.

Notes

1. T. R. Gourvish and R. G. Wilson, *The British Brewing Industry 1830–1980* (Cambridge, 1994), p. 317.
2. Ibid., p. 326.
3. B. Stapleton and J. H. Thomas (eds), *The Portsmouth Region* (Gloucester, 1989), p. 168.
4. Ibid., p. 170.
5. J. M. Stratton, *Agricultural Records 220–1977*, (2nd edn, London, 1978), p. 137.
6. H. F. Bowyer's Pocket Book 1896–1935.
7. Private Ledger No. 4, 1912–19.
8. Ibid., and No. 5, 1920–27.
9. J. Vaizey, *The Brewing Industry 1886–1951: An Economic Study* (London, 1960), p. 25
10. Ibid., pp. 24–5.
11. A. R. Dingle, 'Drink and Working-Class Living Standards in Britain 1870–1914', *Economic History Review*, 2nd series, 25 (4) (1972), pp. 608–22.
12. K. H. Hawkins and C. L. Pass, *The Brewing Industry: A Study in Industrial Organisation and Public Policy* (London, 1979) , p. 153.
13. Stapleton and Thomas, *Portsmouth Region*, p. 168.
14. Ibid., p. 170.
15. Whitbread Archives 365/2, Brickwood and Co. Ltd., Directors' Minute Books 1900–29, p. 503, 12 May 1926. We are indebted to Philip Eley for drawing our attention to this and the next four references.
16. Ibid., p. 529, 3 April 1928.
17. Ibid., p. 531, 17 May 1928.
18. Ibid., p. 558, 4 June 1929.
19. Whitbread Archives 365/2, Brickwood and Co. Ltd., Directors' Minute Books 1900–29, p. 560, 28 June 1929; H. F. Bowyer to F. H. Bowyer, 8 June 1929. We are indebted to Group Captain R. G. Bowyer for a copy of this letter, found amongst his father's papers.
20 *HT*, 7196–7, 28 February, 7 March 1919. The squadron, consisting of the cruiser *Irzumo*, three destroyers including the *Kashiwa* and *Kashi*, and three submarines, was commanded by Rear Admiral K. Sato. For his

letter of gratitude to Portsmouth's Mayor, see *Minutes of the Meetings of the Town Council 1919*, p. 108.

21. *HT*, 7204, 25 April 1919; 7211, 13 June 1919; 7216, 18 July 1919; 7204, 25 April 1919; PCRO CHU 41/13/14 Catherington Parish Magazine for April 1919, n.p.
22. *HT*, 7219, 8 August 1919.
23. *HT*, 7216, 18 July 1919.
24. Ibid., 7235, 28 November 1919. For one thing, not all troops were yet back. Lieutenant A. J. Austin did not return home to Horndean from Germany until late November 1919.
25. *HT*, 7217, 25 July 1919.
26. H. F. Bowyer's Pocket Book, 1896–1935.
27. *HT*, 7193–4, 7 and 14 February 1919.
28. Ibid., 7206, 9 May 1919.
29. Ibid.
30. T. Blanco White to Herbert Bowyer, 8 April 1919: Enclosure in Balance Sheet and Annual Accounts for 1919.
31. Gale and Co. Minute Book, 1888–1927, p. 199, minute of 11 April 1919.
32. Frederick Riddell to Herbert Bowyer, 7 September 1920: Enclosure in Balance Sheet and Annual Accounts for 1920.
33. Private Ledger No. 4, 1912–19; No. 5, 1920–27.
34. B. R. Mitchell and P. Deane, *Abstract of British Historical Statistics* (Cambridge, 1962), p. 489.
35. Stratton, *Agricultural Records*, p. 141.
36. Ibid., p. 143.
37. Balance Sheets and Annual Accounts for 1907 and 1915.
38. Information derived from printed price list, August 1933.
39. Gourvish and Wilson, *British Brewing*, p. 346.
40. Typescript notes on Head Brewers of Gales by E. T. Argyle, n.d.; *HT*, 3859, 29 December 1922.
41. Board meeting Minutes (looseleaf), 15 May 1936.
42. Typescript notes by E. T. Argyle, n.d.; Gale and Co. Minute Books, March 1936–November 1965, pp. 23, 26, 29, 32, 33, 59.
43. Gourvish and Wilson, *British Brewing*, p. 346.
44. For example see R. G. Wilson, *Greene King: A Business and Family History* (London, 1983), pp. 195–6, one of the best histories of a British brewery.
45. Private Ledger No. 7, 1936–44, p. 69.
46. Gourvish and Wilson, *British Brewing*, p. 340.
47. H. F. Bowyer's Pocket Book, 1896–1935.
48. All information on compensation improvements and purchases extracted from Private Ledger No. 4, 1912–19; No. 5, 1920–27; No. 6, 1928–35 and No. 7, 1936–44.
49. Gale and Co. Minute Book: Minutes of Forty-Sixth Annual General Meeting, 12 May 1934.
50. The ensuing comments regarding acquisitions between 1919 and 1939 are based on a detailed analysis of 435 deeds and related documents in the Deeds Collection of George A. Gale and Co. and of Gale and Co. Minute Book, March 1936–November 1965.
51. List of Properties and Consumption, 1930–34.
52. Balance Sheets and Annual Accounts, 1919–39, *passim*.

53. Material in this paragraph is derived from an analysis of the Reports on Company Accounts for the appropriate years.

54. Gale and Co. Minute Book, March 1936–November 1965, pp. 27–8.

55. Ibid., p. 29.

56. Ibid., pp. 43–44.

57. Ibid., pp. 57–9, 61.

58. Ibid., p. 99.

59. HT, 7208, 23 May 1919; 7210, 6 June 1919; 7226, 26 September 1919; 7230, 24 October 1919; 3975, 20 March 1925.

60. PCRO CHU 41/13/14, Catherington Parish Magazines for May, June, October 1925; July, December 1926, n.p.

61. Ibid., *passim*. In her early fifties, when peace was concluded and with both children off her hands, Miriam naturally had more time to devote herself to such work. She belonged to the Horndean Women's Institute, was treasurer in 1925 and, earlier that year, came second in a show of bulbs. She offered the facilities at Crookley on occasion for institute meetings. She took an active role in prize-giving at Horndean School in June 1926 and contributed 5 shillings to the local churchyard fund that December. Daughter Marjorie, a teenager in 1919, ran the 1st Horndean Girl Guides in 1923, staging a play called *A Defensive Alliance* early that April. She was also involved directly in local amateur dramatics. At the Women's Institute meeting at Crookley in July 1925 a play regarding 'one of the many legends of Queen Elizabeth' was staged, Miss Gale participating, though in what precise role was unknown.

62. PCRO CHU 41/13/14, Catherington Parish Magazine for August 1925; HT, 3992, 17 July 1925.

63. When the funeral took place at Catherington of J. S. Stares, Relieving Officer to the Guardians, rate collector and registrar, David Gale was away and was represented by Richard W. Gale; HT, 4046, 6 August 1926.

64. Typescript notes by E. T. Argyle, Head Brewer of Gales. R. N. Gale obtained 50 Preference Shares between 1926 and 1929, 10 in 1931 and another 10 in 1940 (Preference Share Certificates 1888–1955). He acquired 100 Ordinary Shares in 1905, 40 in 1922 and another 10 in 1925 (Ordinary Share Certificates 1888–1927).

65. Information derived from obituary (HT, 8287, 28 November 1941). Prizes proffered included the Gale Charity Cup, played for at Havant (ibid., 7852, 5 May 1933).

66. HT, 3986, 5 June 1925; PCRO CHU 41/3/14, Catherington Parish Magazines for September 1920 and August 1926.

67. PCRO CHU 41/3/14, Catherington Parish Magazine for September 1920.

68. Registered in 1899, Marsland's was taken over by Wilson's Brewery Ltd of Manchester in September 1930, with 30 public houses and the brewery was shut (N. Barber, *Where Have all the Breweries Gone?* (Swinton, Lancs.), 1981, p. 43).

69. *Army List* for January 1927, p. 530; Army List for January 1930, p. 545.

70. Information derived from typescript notes by E. T. Argyle and biographical note issued by the company following R. W. Gale's death in 1983. HT, 7854, 19 May 1933, which included a wedding photograph. Shortly before their marriage the couple had attended a Territorials' dance at Horndean and presented prizes for spot dances. Company employees

presented the groom with a silver entree dish: *HT*, 7852, 5 May 1933; 7854, 19 May 1933.

71. Hawkins and Pass, *Brewing Industry*, p. 48.
72. Gourvish and Wilson, *British Brewing*, p. 346.
73. Ibid., p. 349.
74. Gale and Co. Minute Book, 1888–1927, p. 63.
75. Ibid., p. 161.
76. Ibid., p. 178.
77. Ibid., p. 183.
78. Ibid., p. 220.
79. Gale and Co. Minute Book, 1927–78. At the board meeting of 27 June 1927 Ernest Taylor was said to be ill and Richard Newman Gale, also a director, took on the Secretary's job. Taylor never returned. R. N. Gale appears to have continued as Company Secretary until his death in November 1941, when F. A. Childs was appointed.
80. *Royal Air Force List* for April 1918 (1990 reprint), cols. 237, 1106; *Royal Flying Corps: Casualties and Honours during the War of 1914–17* (comp. G. L. Campbell) (1987 reprint), p. 237. RAF Archives, official service record supplied by Group Captain R. G. Bowyer.
81. Gale's Preference Share Certificates 1888–1955, certificate for 15 June 1922. Founded in 1781 and registered in June 1896, Barclay Perkins and Co. merged with Courage and Co. Limited in 1955 to form Courage, Barclay and Co. (Barber, *Breweries Gone?* p. 23). In 1972 they were in turn taken over by Imperial Tobacco Group.
82. *The Times*, 45931, 18 September 1931. The same account appeared in *HT*, 7,768, 25 September 1931. The three assisting clergy at the ceremony were Canon Haldane, Reverend W. Marshall Selwyn and Reverend T. H. L. Jellicoe.
83. Minute Book 1927–78, 46th Annual Meeting, 12 May 1934.
84. Gale and Co. Minute Book, March 1936–November 1965, Minutes of General Meeting, 18 October 1935 and Extraordinary General Meeting, 17 January 1936.
85. Ibid., forty-eighth annual meeting, 15 May 1936.
86. Gale and Co. Minute Book, March 1936–November 1965 (loose leaf), pp. 77–8.
87. *HT*, 8123, 12 August 1938.
88. *The Times*, 48142, 3 November 1938.
89. Gale and Co. Minute Book 1888–1927, p. 161.
90. Gale and Co. Minute Book 1927–78, fifty-first Annual Meeting, 20 May 1939.

CHAPTER SIX

Problems and progress: 1939–84

At the age of 40, Hugh Bowyer took over the chairmanship of Gales. He was then a family man, Hugh and Katherine's marriage having been blessed with two children – a son, Reginald George, was born in late August, 1932 and destined to follow his father into the Royal Air Force, and a daughter, Patricia, arrived in late July 1935 to complete their family.

In the 1930s Hugh's main occupation was in London as a director of the large Barclay Perkins brewery, where he was responsible for their managed houses. Being not only a director of a major London brewing company, but also holding other directorships through the Barclay Perkins connection, meant that he spent much of his time in the metropolis. When he joined the Gales board, his patterns of work and residence were already established in the capital and necessarily had to continue. His visits to Horndean in the 1930s were mainly in connection with his duties as a director of Gales.

However, when Hugh Bowyer took over as Chairman of Gales, it was at a most inauspicious and critical time generally. Within months the world was plunged into global warfare which presented the brewing industry with new and unwanted problems. As in the First World War, there were material and personnel shortages, increased government controls and higher duties. At the outbreak of war, beer duty per barrel was doubled. It was increased again in 1940, 1942, 1943 and 1944, when it was 486 per cent higher than before the war. Even though war ended in 1945, a period of ensuing austerity saw beer duty continue its upward climb, rising in both 1947 and 1948, until it was 645 per cent above its pre-war level. Even taking into account inflation, the duty was 339 per cent higher in real terms.[1]

Inevitably, there were sharp increases in beer prices, but the climate of controls over the industry was very different in the Second World War from that in the First World War. Beer consumption per head had declined in the inter-war period and so had drunkenness, thus in 1939, national beer output was only just over half what it had been in 1914 (see Table 5.1). As a consequence, it was possible for the drinking of beer to be considered as beneficial to the war effort. Nevertheless, there were increasing problems for brewers. Not only did duties rise alarmingly, but so did the price of barley until, in early 1942, it reached a peak. In March, that year, the government fixed a maximum price of

27s. 6d. per hundredweight at which it remained until after the war. Quotas were fixed on malt, sugar and hops, and petrol was controlled. Labour supplies were affected by enlistment and more women had to be employed. Overtime was frequent, and emergencies commonplace, with brewers having to make the best of the shortage of supplies of such items as casks and bottles, as well as raw materials. In addition, publicans had to take beer from the nearest brewing source to conserve fuel and brewers resorted to exchanging beers.

But the war also brought an end to unemployment for the first time in 20 years, leading to both rising demand and rising wages. However, strict rationing and controls meant there were limited opportunities for spending, hence the pub re-established its place as a centre of leisure. Consequently, beer output rose by some 32 per cent between 1938 and 1945,[2] although the beer was weaker in strength (see Table 6.1).

Table 6.1   UK beer production and consumption, 1938–45

Year	Bulk barrels (million)	Standard barrels (million)	Consumption per head (galls)
1938	24.7	18.4	14.2
1939	25.4	18.7	14.6
1940	26.2	18.4	14.2
1941	26.9	19.3	15.0
1942	29.3 〉29.4	18.3 〉19.0	14.1 〉14.6
1943	30.5	19.2	14.6
1944	31.3	19.7	15.2
1945	32.7	20.6	16.3

Source: Gourvish and Wilson (1984), p. 619.

In 1939, apart from the increase in beer duty, Gales faced two immediate problems – the likely loss of personnel to the forces and the possibility of becoming a target for the Luftwaffe, given the growing number of its licensed houses in southern Hampshire as well as the relative proximity of Horndean to Portsmouth with its defence establishments and substantial dockyard complex. In the event, however, fewer than ten company personnel were to enlist in the armed forces. Some, such as R. D. Berry and F. Kill of Horndean and B. Prentice of the Southsea branch, received a company allowance of £1 per week during their military service.[3] S. W. H. Eager joined the services in late October 1942, receiving a company weekly allowance of 10s. 0d. starting from the first of the month. When the board met on 29 December 1944, his

safe return was reported and it was decided to provide him with a
second-hand Hillman car as it would be necessary 'for him to spend a
certain amount of his time visiting the Company's properties and customers'.[4] In November 1940, Mr Smeaton, tenant of the High Street
off-licence at Selsey, began service in the Royal Air Force.[5] Three
former employees, Messrs Wood, Tayler and Tanner, decided not to
come back to the company once demobilised and the board accordingly
repaid their contributions to the staff pension scheme.[6] On 1 November
1945 Richard W. Gale returned to the Company, his 18 months' service
having taken him to North Africa, Italy and Austria.[7]

With the struggle of 1939–45 being fought in the air, as well as on
land and at sea, the war was brought home, literally, to English men,
women and children. Thus, complying with black-out regulations, the
board decided, in late August 1940 to accept the Portsmouth-based
Landport Drapery Bazaar's (now Allders) estimate of £66 19s. 6d. for
black-out curtains and, three months later, an estimate of £42 13s. 9d.
for an air-raid shelter for Fratton Road, Portsmouth.[8] As further evidence of the fact that this was a different kind of war, the company was
appointed by the Ministry of Food as a storage location for unsweet-
ened condensed milk, and by mid-February 1942, some 10,000 cases
had been received for storage at owner's risk. Charges imposed were 6s.
0d. per ton for the first week and 6d. per week thereafter. That June a
further 5,000 cases arrived for storage at comparative rates.[9] In late
June 1940 R. N. Gale had attended a meeting of brewers at Henty and
Constable, Chichester, to discuss a scheme in the event of breweries
being put out of action as a result of enemy bombing. When he reported
upon his visit to fellow directors at Horndean, they decided to support
the scheme fully.[10]

It was without doubt, however, the extensive effect of Luftwaffe raids
that caused most problems for the company. With long-range bombers
capable of delivering a lethal load, few locations could be considered
safe, as the devastating damage of the London, Coventry, Southampton
and Portsmouth blitzkrieg raids made abundantly clear. Raw material
stores, bonded wines and spirits warehouses, licensed premises – all
were hit. As direct spin-offs, air-raid insurance had to be introduced[11]
and fire insurance policy coverage was increased in February 1941,[12]
while trade generally contracted in Portsmouth owing to the implemen-
tation of an evacuation policy. Thus, in November 1940 traders such as
wholesale and retail butchers Parkers (Portsmouth) Ltd, successfully
sought a rent reduction on this count.[13] In August 1940 the International Cold Storage and Ice Company, located at the docks in
Southampton, where Gales kept some of their hops, was hit. While,
fortunately, the hops were undamaged, alternative storage had to be

Table 6.2   War-damaged properties and effects, 1939–45

Date	Premises	Damage
August 1940	*Shakespeare's Head*	Unknown
	Harlequin	Minor
	Cox's Hotel	Windows, ceiling and roof
	Ship and Castle	Windows, ceiling and roof
	Horndean House	Windows
	Others	Windows
February 1941	*York and Pier*	Extensive
May 1941	Brewery – loose plant and effects	£17,850
	Furniture and fittings in licensed houses	£2,650
	Five motor lorries	£4,000
December 1941	*Bay Tree*, Southampton	Extensive
July 1943	*Bevois Castle*	£69

Source: Gale and Co. Minute Book March 1936–November 1965, *passim*.

found.[14] By late March 1941 store losses, through enemy action, amounted to over £11,500 and replacement space had to be rented in the premises of Portsmouth brewers Brickwoods and Co.[15] Some of the company's licensed premises were also seriously damaged or destroyed by enemy action (see Table 6.2).

Damage apart, such raids caused copious extra work. R. N. Gale had to view the premises and inspect the damage. Discussions were needed with Portsmouth's Chief Constable with a view to formally closing premises, as happened with the *York and Pier*, declared unfit to live in. Builders had to be called in, premises examined and damage made good. Some thought had to be given to the sufferings experienced by the staff. Mr Reddington, who ran the *Bay Tree* at Southampton, applied for assistance 'as the living part of this house was no longer tenable owing to war damage'. Reimbursement of half his rent to the date of the blitz ensued, while the company agreed to pay two-thirds of the Excise Licence.[16]

The company sustained one further major loss during the Second World War – the death of its capable and experienced Secretary, Richard Newman Gale. Before formal business commenced at the board meeting on 16 December 1941, Chairman Hugh Bowyer addressed the meeting: 'It is with the deepest regret that the Directors have to report the death of the Company's Secretary and Director Mr R.N. Gale, which occurred suddenly in November after 44 years of loyal and energetic service to the Company.'[17] It is very likely that, with Hugh Bowyer being frequently away, the day-to-day administration of the company had recently been in R. N. Gale's capable hands. He had died from heart trouble, aged 62, at his home, 'Ardingly', in Horndean. The funeral took place at Blendworth on Monday 24 November and was attended by a substantial congregation of mourners. His community allegiance had never been in doubt. A former manager of Cowplain Senior School and Chairman of Horndean Conservative Association, he had also been Treasurer of the Hampshire Brewers' Union and a county delegate to the National Brewers' Society. Family mourners included his son Richard W. Gale, his brother 'Rex', who worked for Lloyds Bank, and his sister 'Kathleen', otherwise known as 'Queenie', with her husband George Aylward, a Cosham lime merchant. Fellow directors and staff from Horndean attended, as did representatives of organisations with which the deceased had either been involved or with which he had done business. A. J. Hall represented United Brothers (1069) Lodge of Freemasons, while S. G. Marsh represented Horndean Home Guard, Richard Newman Gale having been a member of both organisations. Two directors of Portsmouth Football Club attended, as did representatives from Portsmouth Trade Union Clubs, Cowplain Social Club, the local Wine and Beer Retailers' Association and the Portsmouth and Gosport Licensed Victuallers Association. Private mourners were just as numerous and the wreaths 'numbered nearly 150'.[18]

At the December board meeting the question of a replacement as Secretary was resolved. Chairman Hugh Bowyer proposed, and his wife seconded, that Frederick Ammon Childs be appointed Acting Secretary at a salary of £500 with effect from 1 December 1941. He would reside at 'Southfield', rent-free, and the company would pay the rates. His pension fund contribution would also be paid by the company and the position be reviewed after six months. Accordingly, in June 1942 it was decided to appoint Childs as Secretary. The Chairman expressed the directors' appreciation of his work and, in recognition of this fact, they wished to make him a present and 'it was left to him to decide what form this should take'.[19]

Two other wartime changes were noticeable – in terms of transport and bonus payments. Wartime transport austerity became apparent from September 1941 when two lorries were noted as being out of commission through difficulties in obtaining the necessary spare parts. An application was made to the Divisional Transport Officer for a licence to purchase, for about £400, a Morris Commercial lorry, only to have the request denied. In spring 1942 enquiries were made as to whether transport manufacturing concerns were accepting orders for post-war deliveries and two AEC Monarch (Petrol) Chassis were ordered via Horndean supplier S. G. Marsh. In the mean time, petrol shortages meant that other appropriate measures were needed and the company decided to purchase a horse and trolley to handle local deliveries. Richard W. Gale was instructed to make contacts in Chichester and Hawkley, to the north-east of Petersfield, 'with a view to purchasing a horse and to obtain prices for a trolley from any source available'. A month later he reported no purchase of a suitable horse, but partial success otherwise. A set of harness had been purchased for £15 and a four-wheeled pneumatic tyred trolley had been ordered from the Fleet-based firm of Stevens and Sons at a cost of £92 10s 0d. Delivery would take place in six weeks. All that was needed now, was the power to pull it! By mid-June this, too, had been obtained. A horse had been bought from J. Church of Alresford for £110, a spare set of harness purchased for £12 and a spring cart from G. Carpenter of Durrants, at nearby Rowlands Castle, for £10. To save on both petrol and tyres, and to conform with government requests, Gales negotiated with Brickwoods 'for the exchange of Bulk Beers only and with Henty and Constable for the exchange of Bulk and Bottled Beers'. Agreement had been reached by mid-May, the exchange commencing from 1 June.[20] The agreement with Brickwoods was in respect of 3,500 barrels of beer and bitter.[21] Thus, in the face of wartime stringency the company had shown a necessary degree of flexibility.

That same characteristic was to be demonstrated with regard to bonus payments. At the board meeting on 20 March 1940, one of Hugh Bowyer's first acts as Chairman was to recommend the discontinuation of the yearly bonus payments that his father had introduced, and which had reached £600 per annum. Instead, weekly wages would be increased 'by the proportionate amount of the Bonus each man receives'. Clearly, the new Chairman considered the old incentive scheme was no longer appropriate and that wages should be raised in lieu. Even so, an alternative to the bonus was introduced as well. In December 1941 it was agree that staff Christmas presents 'should take the same form as last year, namely Cash, and that they should receive double the amount of that year'.[22] Benign paternalism was just as apparent in 1942, when at the October board meeting it was decided to give all weekly wage employees 'one full week's wages as a Christmas present. Off-Licence and Managed House Managers to receive 30s. each'. Similar moves were made in December 1943, when salaried staff and wage earners with a year's service each received a full week's salary or wage, as also happened in 1944.[23] At the November meeting in 1945, with the war over, a slightly different, but nevertheless appreciative, tack was tried:

'It was decided to give all salaried staff and wage earners with twelve months service one full week's salary or wage as a Xmas Bonus together with another week's pay for V.J. Day. Employees with six months service half week's bonus and V.J. Day.'[24]

Unlike the First World War, and confounding all expectations, the Second World War had been beneficial to the British brewing industry as a whole. Although beer was weaker, much more of it was brewed so that by 1945 output had reached 32.65 million barrels, the highest output since 1914 and an increase of 32 per cent above that of 1938[25] (see Table 6.3). Those breweries situated where demand from armed forces personnel had grown, such as Greene King in the midst of the East Anglian airfields,[26] did particularly well. Gales' proximity to the naval dockyard and port, in addition to other shore establishments in and around Portsmouth, gave them a similar advantage.

However, whereas the output of the brewing industry as a whole had declined considerably in the inter-war years, that of Gales had

Table 6.3   UK beer production and consumption, 1945–59

Year	Bulk barrels (million)	Standard barrels (million) 1055'	Consumption gals. per head	
1945	32.7	20.6	16.3	
1946	29.3	17.3	13.4	
1947	30.4	18.1	13.5	
1948	27.0	16.4	12.1	
1949	26.5	16.3	11.7	
1950	24.9	16.7	12.3	
1951	25.2	17.0	12.5	
1952	24.9	16.7	12.2	
1953	24.6	16.5	12.1	
1954	23.9	16.2	11.8	
1955	24.6	16.6	12.0	17.85
1956	24.5			17.75
1957	24.7			17.76
1958	23.8			17.13
1959	26.1			18.46

Source: Gourvish and Wilson (1984), p. 619, 1945–55; p. 630, 1955–59 when standard barrels are not given; consumption is in pints per head (converted to gallons above). Eire appears to be included in the UK since consumption figures are higher than they should be for the UK alone. See Table 6.1 for wartime data.

consistently risen, so that there were few underutilised resources at Horndean. Hence, the rise in the company's output during the war years was only 6 per cent. Even so, this meant the brewery produced over 25,000 barrels a year in 1944 and 1945 (see Table 6.4). Of this output casks represented approximately three-quarters of production and bottles one-quarter throughout the war. However, the tied trade became increasingly important, rising from about 50 per cent of output in 1939 to nearly 70 per cent by the end of the war. It was supplies to stores and shops which suffered – some 14 per cent of output provided to them in 1939 disappeared from the Summary Book in 1943, although private sales rose from one-tenth of 1 per cent to 2.5 per cent.

In the days of victory celebrations in 1945 optimism in the brewing industry was high and the Second World War was to be followed by half a century of momentous history. Unfortunately, optimism was soon

Table 6.4   Beer output: Gales Brewery, 1939–59

Year	Barrels		Barrels (dozen)		Barrels equivalent of bottles		Total	
1939	18,969		111,037		5,047		24,016	
1940	18,812		116,289		5,286		24,098	
1941	21,140		118,636		5,393		26,533	
1942	19,162	19,606	109,421	118,853	4,974	5,402	24,136	25,008
1943	19,054		127,039		5,774		24,828	
1944	19,863		122,880		5,585		25,448	
1945	20,051		109,819		4,992		25,043	
1946	17,412		103,369		4,699		22,111	
1947	16,308	15,844	96,278	95,068	4,376	4,321	20,684	20,165
1948	14,427		83,853		3,811		18,238	
1949	11,020		82,021		3,728		14,728	
1950	9,959		80,633		3,665		13,624	
1951	10,171		95,338		4,333		14,504	
1952	9,508	9,130	96,881	90,735	4,404	4,124	13,912	13,254
1953	8,664		94,498		4,295		12,959	
1954	7,349		86,324		3,924		11,273	
1955	7,685		92,370		4,199		11,884	
1956	7,633		84,763		3,853		11,486	
1957	8,048	7,710	83,281	84,343	3,785	3,839	11,833	11,544
1958	7,157		78,658		3,576		10,733	
1959	8,026		82,639		3,756		11,782	

Source: Cash Summary Book 1932–66.

dissipated as a period of stagnation, followed by decline, lasted until the late 1950s. From 1948 demand for beer fell continuously until 1959 when output in England was 17 per cent below the level it had been at the end of the war.[27] Excess profits tax, introduced in the war, was extended in 1948 so that some brewing businesses considered that up to 60 per cent of their profits were absorbed by taxation. In addition, the continuation of wartime restrictions and high duties in peacetime did not help. Although beer duty did fall from its peak in 1949, the new low reached in 1960 was still almost three and a half times higher than the pre-war duty level. Moreover, personal attitudes and tastes were changing. In the post-war years came a major growth of television, being especially boosted in the Queen's coronation year of 1953, and a consequent decline in the popularity of public houses. One of the major priorities of brewing companies after 1945 was to attempt to improve their houses, which had suffered from unavoidable wartime neglect.

Old houses in particular needed to be modernised, but building licences were in short supply until 1951, so little real progress could be made. Then, in the early 1950s, district councils began to insist on basic standards of cleanliness and sanitation. But, as profits were squeezed after 1948, finances for many breweries were tight. Even so, with declining output, competition was becoming fiercer and public houses had to be upgraded in order, not only to retain existing customers, but also to attract new ones. This time, Gales were not to escape from the industry's problems. Output at Horndean fell rapidly from over 25,000 barrels in the last of the war years to under 15,000 in 1949. Over the five post-war years (1945–49) a 20 per cent decline was experienced.[28]

The year-on-year decline, however, was much more disturbing, for by 1949 output had fallen 42 per cent from its 1944 level (see Table 6.4). Profits fell even more dramatically. Although affected by excess taxation during and immediately after the war, they were still at a modest £17,695 in 1947. The next two years were to see them collapse to less than £4,000. Hugh Bowyer explained the poor performance in his Chairman's Report to Shareholders for the Accounts to 31 December 1949:

> You will see from the Profit and Loss Account and Balance Sheet enclosed herewith that the Company has experienced a disappointing year; the Net Profits after providing for Taxation but before charging Preference Dividend amount to £3,840 as compared with £11,127 for 1948, a reduction of £7,287 following a reduction last year on the same basis of £6,568. The Taxation charge is considerably reduced this year, following the decline in Income, so the Profits before Taxation disclose an even greater reduction.[29]

This situation, he went on to explain, was caused by two factors – a further considerable reduction in the cask beer trade, and a fall of over

50 per cent in gross profits on wines and spirits 'by reason of the new price arrangement now in force with our tenants which was arranged by the Brewers' Society'. As some small consolation, he pointed out that the cask beer decline was experienced 'by nearly all Brewery Companies in Southern England'.[30] In fact, sales of beer at Wadworths of Devizes fared even worse, falling by over 70 per cent.[31] It was, however, the first time in the twentieth century that Gales had not bucked the trend.

While the 1949 budget reduced beer prices by 1d. per pint or 24s. 0d. per barrel, brewers still found themselves in difficulties. Having withstood wartime problems of sugar shortages, even with beet sugar, declining barley supplies, particularly after 1942 when acreage had been reduced, devastation of extensive hop acreage during the Battle of Britain and the quadrupling of beer duty between 1938 and 1944, they found themselves faced by just as many new ones after 1945. Duty levels in the 1949 budget were reduced by only 21s. 0d. a barrel so that brewers bore the difference of 3s. 0d. a barrel at an estimated cost of £4 million. To add to their worries, new transport and plant were 'rationed' in terms of supply, while the rebuilding and restoration of licensed premises was hampered by difficulties in obtaining the necessary building licences.[32]

Doubtless directorial minds turned to Joseph's gloomy prognostications of seven lean years and hoped that the second part of the story would come true. Unfortunately, the next decade was to prove even worse for Gales in terms of lost output. Whereas the British brewing industry as a whole managed to stabilise output at or near 25 million barrels in the next decade (see Table 6.3), Gales' production fell until it reached a trough of only 10,733 barrels – a decline of 60 per cent from the wartime peak (see Table 6.4). The last time the Horndean Brewery had produced so little had been as long ago as 60 years earlier at the very beginning of the twentieth century! The five-year average shows that output had fallen by 54 per cent (see Table 6.4) in 15 years. Unsurprisingly, profits remained depressed only reaching their 1947 level in 1958 (see Table 6.5) and, in view of the large decline in production, it is remarkable that they made any profit at all in the early and mid-1950s. All that Herbert Bowyer had achieved in the first 40 years of the century appeared to have been lost.

Clearly, one major cause was the difficult times through which the industry as a whole was passing, but it would seem not to be the sole explanation, since Gales' performance was twice as poor as the industry's average. There is no doubt that smaller breweries generally had a relaxed management style and brewers could survive without demonstrating exceptional entrepreneurial talents. There was limited technological change in the industry. Long-serving managers and

Table 6.5   George Gale and Co.: net profits, 1947–58 (£)

1947	17,695
1948	11,127
1949	3,840
1950	7,280
1951	12,573
1952	13,304
1953	12,404
1954	13,626
1955	8,288
1956	12,924
1957	14,569
1958	19,624

Source: Balance Sheets and Annual Accounts.

directors were common, particularly from founding families. However, outsiders were beginning to be brought in to assist with management. For example, Barclay Perkins, with whom Hugh Bowyer had his director's employment, had long-serving family members such as Lieutenant-Colonel H. F. Barclay and Major Charles Augustus Carlos Perkins, Hugh Bowyer's uncle, but they also brought in Colonel T. B. Bunting, a chartered accountant, to be Company Secretary in 1931. He joined the board as director in charge of sales to the free trade in 1945 – a more executive style was emerging.[33]

By comparison, Gales had a largely absentee Chairman who had to leave the day-to-day management in the hands of others, not a situation conducive to establishing recognised chains of command. It would seem that the auditors, Masons, had identified this problem in a stringent report attached to the Directors' Report and Accounts for 1955. Among other things, they suggested that 'an Order Book should be instituted in which *all* orders are to be recorded, large or small, without fail ... '. They continued by stating that it was most essential that the number of every invoice received must be included as 'this year in a number of cases, especially for large contracts, invoices and statements were *not* available for production to us'. The report went on to state that some of the general expenses of the company 'seem to have got out of hand' and recommended 'closer supervision of expenditure'.

Furthermore, Masons added, for wines and spirits 'the system of stock control appears to have broken down'. Recommendations included Mr Chambers visiting Horndean to explain in detail if required. Among other suggestions was that more detailed minutes should be

kept of matters approved by F. H. Bowyer at his visits to Horndean and
that a competent assistant to the Secretary should be appointed as soon
as possible. The whole tenor of this report implied a need for a considerable tightening up of operations at Horndean, as well as offering
some explanation for the substantial decline in profits that year (see
Table 6.5).

For much of the period of decline, the production side of the brewery
was in the control of the Head Brewer, Barton Mears, with Company
Secretary F. A. Childs being responsible for administration. Both were
in the last years of their working lives in a traditional brewery with no
individual in overall control. It seems likely that these circumstances
were partly responsible for the decline. There was little or no technological progress and, possibly, some problems with the beer. At the end
of the Second World War about 68 per cent of Gales' income came from
their tied houses, 28.5 per cent from the free trade and 3.5 per cent
from private customers. By 1958, at the bottom of the trough, the
private customers represented only 1 per cent, the free trade 12 per cent
and the tied houses were responsible for 87 per cent of Gales' income.
Thus the private customers and the free trade were mainly the ones who
had chosen not to continue purchasing Gales' beers. Even so, sales in
Gales' own houses had fallen substantially from 11,600 barrels in 1946
to 6,730 in 1957.[34] It seems an inescapable conclusion that some problems existed with beer quality especially since, in 1951, for example,
almost £3,000 worth of Gales' own output had been returned to the
brewery, almost 3 per cent of total sales. Mears had been at Gales for
23 years when the Second World War ended and would have been
unlikely to be looking for new methods of production or new beers in
the nine years between the war's end and his retirement in 1954. Childs
had fewer years' service but within three years followed Mears into
retirement.

Another link with the past had been broken in early 1949 when the
Chairman informed his fellow directors at the board meeting on 19
January: 'It is with the deepest regret we have to report the death of our
Director and good friend Mrs E. A. C. Bowyer, who passed away on the
14th January 1949'.[35] As a mark of respect, the Directors stood in
silence. Elsie Bowyer had been a director for almost a decade, attending
her first board meeting on 14 June 1939. Her presence ensured some
continuity of family interest during her son's absences between February 1940 and October 1941.[36]

Two months after Mrs Bowyer's death occurred came the first mention of the much younger, but nevertheless, experienced, man who was
to replace Barton Mears, and have a profound influence on the company's reputation and success – Edward Thomas Argyle.[37] Born on 9

October 1918 and raised in Staffordshire, he had attended Shardlow Hall Preparatory School and Westminster School before becoming a pupil at Offilers Brewery at Derby in 1934.[38] Two years later he entered the School of Malting and Brewing at Birmingham University from where he moved, in 1938, to train with maltsters Yeomans, Cherry and Curtis. With the outbreak of war he joined the Army, rising to the rank of major. When demobilised in 1946 he began work as Assistant Brewer with Border Breweries at their Mount Street site in Wrexham.[39] On 6 April 1949 a service agreement was signed between him and Gales and on 24 August that year he was in attendance at a board meeting in his capacity as Assistant Brewer.[40] The agreement was to run for three years and on 26 August 1952 was extended for a further three years on the same terms. On 30 March 1954 he succeeded Mears as Head Brewer, the latter having reached retirement age. On 15 May 1956 it was agreed that Argyle be appointed to the board of directors subject to confirmation at the annual general meeting.[41] Argyle worked hard to develop the quality and character of cask-conditioned beers, launching in 1959 Horndean Special Bitter or 'HSB' which was an instant success.

Another key staff change, and a reflection of the planning for replacement, was the appointment of an Assistant Secretary. On 1 May 1956, Cecil George Martin, late of Adnam and Co. Ltd, the well-established brewers of Southwold, took up his duties with a salary of £650 and a house free of rent and rates.[42] Frederick Ammon Childs, Company Secretary, was due to retire early in autumn 1957 and steps were taken to provide him with a £350 pension and a similar arrangement for his wife.[43] Once again the company showed it was prepared to look after loyal staff. In July 1957 the board agreed that C. G. Martin would take over as Secretary from 1 October. On 27 September Childs attended his last board meeting as Secretary, at the end of which he was presented with a television set and the company's thanks 'for his many years of loyal and conscientious service'.[44]

Meanwhile, this period of post-war decline in the brewing industry generally, saw the beginnings of substantial structural change taking place, with mergers and take-overs occurring in the late 1950s and early 1960s. In 1955 there were ten mergers, of which that of Courage with Barclay Perkins, forming Courage and Barclay, was the most notable. The following year came 18 mergers with probably the most important being Friary, Holroyd and Healy's Breweries merging to form Friary-Meux. The next two years each saw ten mergers, the most spectacular being Watney Combe Reid's with Mann, Crossman and Paulin to become one of Britain's biggest brewers with over 3,600 tied houses. The following year, 1959, the new Watney Mann found itself the unwelcome recipient of a surprise hostile take-over bid of £20.7 million from Charles Clore, whose main interest was in their undervalued property assets. The bid was resisted but Watney Mann's shares rose from 51s. 3d. to 77s. 0d. The offer had been 60s. 0d. per share and Clore, unwilling to pay an unrealistic price, withdrew and took his profit. Watney Mann, however, reacted rapidly and began to acquire other breweries outside the metropolitan area in which Clore had caused much alarm to brewers.

In the same year, 1959, E. P. (Eddie) Taylor, the Canadian who had built up the Canadian breweries combine, took a major stake in Hope and Anchor Breweries of Sheffield and shortly after, in February 1960, created Northern Breweries. By October of that year he had taken over five Scottish breweries and formed United Breweries. Scottish and Newcastle were created simultaneously as a defence against Taylor's activities and other smaller and regional breweries also felt the need to combine to counter Taylor. Thus, the years 1959–61 were to see the peak of merger activity, with over 70 mergers occurring, including Ind Coope's take-over of Taylor Walker (1959), Courage and Barclay's of H. and G. Simonds (1960), Joshua Tetley's absorption of Walker Cain forming Tetley Walker (1960), Ind Coope, Tetley Walker and Ansell's merger (1961), renamed Allied Breweries in 1962 and Bass with Mitchells and Butler (1961). Although the peak of merger activity was over, other important mergers occurred in the 1960s. Charrington merged with United Breweries in 1962 to create Charrington United and, in 1964, Allied Breweries took over Friary-Meux.

This decade of merger activity saw the number of brewing companies fall from 305 in 1954 to 117 in 1967,[45] as well as the emergence of the 'Big Six' – Allied, Bass, Courage, Scottish and Newcastle, Watneys and Whitbread. The late 1960s and the 1970s were quieter years, but even so the latter decade saw the emergence of the big conglomerates. Imperial Tobacco took over Courage in 1970, Grand Metropolitan absorbed Truman and Watneys in 1971 and Allied did the same with J. Lyons and Co. in 1978.[46] The cosy world of family-run breweries had gone but, throughout, Gales remained independent. It could be considered that a company which had just experienced 15 years of declining output and profits was particularly vulnerable to take-over. But for such to have happened it would have needed a prospective purchaser to have been invited to place a bid by Gales' board of directors. For Gales, like Brakspear of Henley and Hall and Woodhouse of Blandford Forum, retained all their ordinary share capital in the hands of the Bowyer family and directors. Thus, any potential predator could not buy voting shares unless invited to do so by the board.

Although, it seems, no competitor was invited to buy, discussions were held well before the merger mania beginning in 1955, considering a possible amalgamation with Portsmouth and Brighton United Breweries Ltd. Negotiations commenced in 1951 and were reported to the Board of the Portsmouth brewery on 27 August 1952. The Chairman of George Gale and Co. Ltd (Mr F. H. Bowyer) and his co-director (Mr R. W. Gale) had put proposals for:

the acquisition of the whole of the Ordinary Share Capital of George Gale & Co. Ltd. by this Company and stated that Mr Bowyer was prepared in principle to submit to his shareholders an offer in the following terms:

1. *That the Portsmouth* and Brighton United Breweries Ltd. should acquire the whole of the issued Ordinary share capital of George Gale & Co. Ltd consisting of *5,000* shares of £10 each fully paid up, in consideration of the issue of *250,000* Ordinary shares of 5/- (25p) each fully paid up, and *75,000* 6% Preference shares of £1 each fully paid up in the capital of The Portsmouth and Brighton United Breweries Ltd.

2. *That on completion* Mr F. H. Bowyer was to become Chairman of the Joint Companies at a fee of £1,000 per annum and Mr R. W. Gale to become a full-time working Director for a minimum period of five years at a salary of £1,800 per annum exclusive of Directors' fees.

3. *That the employees* of George Gale and Co. Ltd. who may become redundant as a result of the merger shall be compensated as follows:

    (a) *As to those* with service of five years or less, no compensation

    (b) *As to those* with five to ten years service, such compensation as may be awarded out of the sum mentioned in paragraph (d) below

    (c) *As to those* with service of ten years or more a sum equal to one month's salary for each year's service with George Gale and Co. Ltd or such other amounts as may be agreed, out of which where applicable (and subject to the consent of the Insurance Company and the approval of the Inland Revenue authorities) there will be withheld and paid the pension contributions payable by the employer and employee until such time as the employee becomes pensionable under the existing pension scheme of George Gale and Co. Ltd. with the Insurance Company.

    (d) *Special cases* referred to in correspondence (and in particular those referred to in Mr Frost's letter to Mr Bowyer and the schedule thereto of 21st August 1952) to be dealt with at the discretion of the Board by payment of pensions or otherwise but that so the total amount of the commitment in this regard will not exceed £3,000 and that the commitment shall end at the expiration of ten years from completion of the merger.[47]

This offer was approved subject to a general meeting of the Portsmouth brewery's shareholders agreeing both to an increase in capital and to the number of directors. A request to acquire the whole of Gales' preference shares to avoid stamp duty and obviate any requirement to guarantee the shares was also to be made to Bowyer.

The preference shares became an issue between the two companies and at their meeting on 24 September the Portsmouth board stated that 'the maximum concession we are prepared to make in order to acquire Gales Preference Shares is a 2% Conversion Cash Bonus (involving £500) on a straight exchange of 5% Shares'[48] and waited for a response. Hugh Bowyer was clearly not enchanted by the offer. Thus when he and R. W. Gale met representatives of the Portmouth brewery on 6 November an additional inducement was 'to be offered to the holders of Gales 2,500 5% Preference Shares of £10 each of a 3¾% *cash bonus (or 7s./6d.) per £10 Share* to exchange into a Portsmouth issue of 25,000 5% Preference Shares of £1 each'.[49]

This further inducement proved to be insufficient for, although the Portsmouth board approved the main agreement at their meeting on 10 December they were 'quite unable to make the further substantial concessions asked for',[50] indicating that Bowyer had raised his requirements with relation to the preference shares to an unacceptable level. Nine days later the Portsmouth board were facing 'the possibiity that the deal with Gales would fall through',[51] and, since their Chairman, Sir William Dupree, was going abroad he wrote, noticeably to Bowyer's home address, the following letter:

19 December, 52

F. H. Bowyer Esq.,
Yew Tree Farm,
Scaynes Hill
HAYWARDS HEATH
Sussex   *Personal*

Dear Mr Bowyer,

As you know I am going abroad for a couple of months on the 5th prox. – and you also very soon afterwards – and my Board have been giving close consideration to the trend of events following the hoped-for merger of our Companies.

After the recent correspondence which has taken place between our respective Solicitors the position seems to emerge that an impasse has been reached after your second thoughts following the provisional agreement arrived at when you came to see us.

Mr Blanco White had no further comments to make to our Solicitors yesterday in the absence of your instructions on their last letter to him, in which it was stated we could not in the main, agree to the amendments which were now proposed.

My Board feels, in the absence of agreement in principle which we thought had been achieved, that no good purpose can be served by a continuance of the negotiations. If however, on our return from holiday the matter can fruitfully be reopened, we can get together again.

I am sorry we have reached this stage after so much time and money has been expended, and if you have any other views I shall be pleased to hear from you before I go away.

Yours sincerely

WD

Bowyer replied, on 24 December, stating that the cancellation of the meeting arranged for 15 December had been rather abrupt, since numerous discussions were needed in mergers of this kind and 'give-and-take' on both sides. On the last day of 1952 Sir William once more wrote to Bowyer's home address and not to the Horndean Brewery, saying it was a pity that negotiations 'over the last eighteen months should, after provisional agreement be so considerably revised to our detriment', and this was why the 15 December meeting had been deferred in the hope that Bowyer would reconsider demands made in his solicitor's letters. He ended 'our points of view unfortunately appear, at the moment, to be irreconcilable'.

Fortunately, for the Horndean staff, who were the only ones for whom redundancy was discussed, no more was heard of the proposed merger. Yet again, not a single word about the matter appeared in the Minute Books of the Horndean company, despite the fact that, during the period of negotiations, other correspondence with the Portsmouth brewery dealing with Gales sale of its shares in Portsmouth Bonding Stores was included in full.

With the catastrophic fall in output experienced by Gales between 1945 and 1951 when it was almost halved in six years (46.5 per cent) (see Table 6.4) it seems more than likely that Hugh Bowyer would have become increasingly concerned with the company's survival. Thus it may well have been his desire to save something of the business which induced him to open merger discussions with the Portsmouth brewery.

In the next two decades, when the British brewing industry underwent profound change, through mergers and amalgamations, Gales were unaffected, even though their Chairman was largely an absentee and personally involved with merger activity as a director of Barclay Perkins. Perhaps too, the very smallness of Gales helped their survival – many larger companies may have thought a 10,000-barrel annual output as too insignificant to be worth the price – although small size did not save other companies! Perhaps also, the number of Gales' tied houses was thought to be too small. Thus, small size and especially financal strength through control of the equity would seem to be the reasons for Gales' continuing independence.

The company could not, of course, ignore the massive transformation that the industry was undergoing, and signs of changing times and approaches to business began to be seen at Horndean. Representatives of Mason and Son, the company's auditors began, in May 1959, to attend board meetings. Their presence was explained by the need to take directors through the accounts, after which they withdrew and business carried on as usual. Representing the firm in March 1960 were R. Wallis Mason and O. L. N. Chambers, who drew attention to the fact that the 1959 accounts showed a pre-tax profit for the year of £50,042 (net £25,122), an increase of £8,850 on the position in 1958. In April 1961 Mason and Chambers repeated the performance. The accounts for 1960, they explained, showed a pre-tax profit of £58,440 (net £27,774), an increase of £8,398 over 1959.[52] With good reason the board would come to appreciate the advice proffered by the auditors, especially that of Noel Chambers.

In the 1960s evidence of diversification at Gales can be seen in the range of their products. In the period of decline up to the late 1950s, the company continued to produce its traditional drinks, including pale and mild ales, for which malt was purchased from the Ipswich Malting Company and E. T. Argyle's former employers Yeomans, Cherry and Curtis Ltd. From 1958 onwards, however, changes in trend, direction and tastes became apparent. In January of that year Argyle was given permission to let Metal Box Co. Ltd can a small quantity of Champion Ale as an experiment on their pilot plant, though similar trials with Prize Old Ale were considered inadvisable. Seemingly Gales anticipated something of the growth of canned beer which was to be a feature of the British industry in the 1960s and 1970s. In September 1958 it was resolved to increase the price of XXX Light Mild Beer which 'would have the effect of bringing our Mild Beer price into line with nearly every other Brewer'. The following July the board agreed to stock Carlsberg Lager, in addition to Harp Lager which had been supplied, at least since 1955, by Barclay Perkins, part of a consortium headed by Guinness, provided there was sufficient demand. Problems with the bottling of Bass led to the discontinuation of sales, leaving Guinness, by far the most popular, Mackeson, Worthington E, Carlsberg and Harp as the 'foreign' beers sold in 1961. In July 1960 the Chairman raised the issue of producing keg beers in future, arguing that this may be forced on the company 'owing to the general trend of demand'. By Christmas of that year a new product would be on the market – Tudor Ale.[53] Difficulties experienced in early 1961 with the production of bottled beer had been resolved by June following a stringent cleansing of the entire bottling plant. In June 1964 the decision was taken that Horndean Special Bitter and the company's Champion and Tudor Bottled Beers would be entered in the autumn Brewers' Exhibition. Progress was not without its hitches. The bottled beer, particularly Champion and Tudor, began throwing a heavy deposit after a relatively short shelf-life, a careful analysis revealing an excess of air in each bottle.

From 1965 came further signs of future trends. It was agreed, admittedly with some reservations, to try a small quantity of hop pellets submitted by Wigan, Richardson and Co. as an experiment, while the final minute for the board meeting of 20 May that year read 'The matter of Gaming Machines in Houses was raised and discussed but no decision was reached'.[54] At the very least, these aspects show that there was at Gales an awareness of changes taking place in the British brewing industry and the emergence of the need for entertainment provision in public houses.

To cope with change and product range, the Horndean plant had to be monitored constantly and updated where necessary. Outlay in the late 1940s on bottle-washing machinery and a Super Head filler for pints, the latter originally at a cost of £4,330 and subsequently scaled down, was followed by disposal of the replaced machinery. Thus the 24–head Pontifex filler was sold to Plowman, Barrett and Co. in Wandsworth Road, Vauxhall for £350 early in March 1950. The two boilers at Horndean needed attention four years later, while in 1955 it was decided to proceed with the purchase of Yeast Collecting Plant for £1,322 and Yeast Filtrate Sterilizing Plant to be used in conjunction with it for another £1,141. Outlay on plant and its updating grew between 1958 and 1963 (see Table 6.6).

It was resolved to purchase the bottle-washing machine in 1958 'as in spite of the difficult cash position at the present it would be the most economical in the long run'. There was a limit to the amount of repair work that could be carried out on it. Purchase of another would be simpler, quicker and, in the long run, more cost-effective. The larger total for that year was explained by the eventual cost of the bottle-washer amounting to £5,181. The volume meter ordered in March 1961 would test the carbon dioxide content in bottled beers and assist elmination of uneven saturation. With the proposed plant installation of 1962 'considerable economies could be made in steam usage owing largely to the shorter time the plant would be at work'. The following year saw even more substantial improvements, most notably boiler plant repair work, designed to give increased capacity taking into account likely increases in kegging and bottling.[55] It was no surprise to discover, therefore, that Messrs Mason and Chambers observed of the company's 1962 accounts that the adverse cash position as compared

Table 6.6   Expenditure on plant, 1958–63

Year	Plant	Expenditure	Total
1958	Bottle-washing machine	£4,546	
	Essex Brine Injection Softener	£562	£5,743
1960	Pasteurising plant incorporating	£4,005	
	chilling unit	+c. £1,200	£5,205
		for alterations	
1961	Volume meter	£38	
	3 × 50 barrel storage tanks	£210	
		£60 removal	£523
	Air compressor, air filter and	£215	
	after cooler		
1962	Cask-washing machine	£3,975	
	Heating Coils	£250c.	
	Insulation and pipework	£227+	£5,000
	Hot liquor tank	£100	
	Structural repairs to barrelway	£1,200	£1,200
1963	New hop store	£700	
	Bottled beer cooling equip.	£500	£1,450
	Keg cooling equipment	£250	
	Boiler plant repair work inc.	£9,710	£9,710
	replacement oil-fired boiler		
	Second-hand filter and sheets	£800	£800

Source: Gale and Co. Minute Book March 1936–November 1965, passim.

with 1961 reflected amounts spent on capital improvements and property purchases.[56]

Gales were certainly active in acquiring extra licensed premises between 1950 and 1965, whether through new building programmes, purchase, leasing arrangements or through acquisitions from other brewing concerns (see Table 6.7). Nineteen premises were obtained in all; five were newly built and necessitated a total outlay of £94,845. A further seven involved deals with other brewing companies. Thus acquisition of the *Gun* at Stedham may have been explained by Watney shedding some Tamplins houses following their take-over of that brewing concern six years before. In addition, Gales were further consolidating in Hampshire, with only four purchases outside the county – three in Sussex and one in Surrey. Furthermore, two of the three Sussex acquisitions were by lease. The one Surrey purchase – the *Woodcock* – had been an inn since at least 1906.[57] Of all the acquistions, however, it was

Table 6.7 Acquisition of licensed premises, 1950–65

Year	House	Location	Type	Cost	Opened
1951–57	Dolphin	Havant	New Build	£23,700	28 March 1958
1954	Curlew	Havant	New Build	£15,320	8 December 1954
1958	Fairfield	Havant	Licence transfer from *Little Green*, Emsworth	£11,020	—
1955	Three Horseshoes	Bighton	Purchase from Crowley & Co. Alton	£2,750	—
1957	Woolpack	Totford ⎱ Longstock ⎰	Purchase from The Brewery, Blandford	£10,250	—
	Peat Spade				—
1958	Lifeboat	Hayling Island	Taken over from Whitbreads	?	—
1958	Jubilee Tavern	Dundridge	Licence obtained by surrendering that on *Plough* Soberton obtained from Watneys	£250	—
1959	Fox and Pelican	Grayshott	Purchase from Peoples Refreshment Houses Ass.	£13,250	8 May 1959
1953–59	Kittiwake	Hayling Island	New Build	Stores bought for £7,500	—
1959	Gun Inn	Stedham	Bought from Tamplins	?	—
1961	Sociable Plover	Paulsgrove	New Build	£24,091	1 December 1961
1962	Shamrock	Bepton	14 year lease from Cowdray Estate	£1,000 p. a. for 7 years and £250 for 7 years	—
1962	Harrison's Bars	Brighton	14 year lease from Brighton Council	£100 p. a. rising by £50 p. a. to £1,200	—
1962	Red Lion	Southwick	21 year lease from Borthwick-Norton Estate	£1,000 p. a.	—
1963	Grey Friar	Chawton	Leased from Whitbreads	£1 p. a. to 1979	—
1964	Black Horse Inn	Binstead	Portsmouth United Breweries	£2,000	—
1964	Ark	Park Estate, Southampton	New Build	£24,234	21 July 1964
1964	Woodcock Inn	Beacon Hill, Hindhead	Bought from Trust Houses Ltd	£35,150	—

Source: Collection of Property Deeds; Archival Listing; Gale and Co. Minute Book March 1936–November 1965, *passim.*

the *Fox and Pelican* at Grayshott that had the most unusual history. Erected for about £2,000, it was opened on 23 August 1899 by Mrs Randall Davidson, wife of the Bishop of Winchester, and was run mainly on temperance lines. Lemonade, ginger beer and beer were all available, but the manager, Mr Wallace, would only supply the last item when pressed. The salaried manager received a commission, not upon the sale of intoxicants, but upon profits arising from the sale of other kinds of refreshment! The other unusual feature about the house was George Bernard Shaw's involvement. Having purchased shares in the Grayshott and District Refreshment Association, Shaw, with his Fabian and temperance sympathies, presented a small library to the new establishment. Thus, while downing a thirst-slaking lemonade, customers could peruse Kipling's *Day's Work*, Du Maurier's, *Peter Ibbotson* or Tolstoy's *The Gospel in Brief*. In 1913 the house was transferred to the People's Refreshment House Association,[58] from whom Gales purchased it in 1959. With these acquisitions Gales' asset value steadily increased reaching £500,000 by 1955 and over £600,000 by the early 1960s.

Additionally, the period between the end of the Second World War and 1960 saw the persistence of the traditional brewery's benign paternalism in its attitude towards the workforce, as noted in earlier decades. This was reflected in a number of ways. That some of the workforce were at Horndean for half a century or more and that the company employed second- and third-generation staff, was ample testimony in itself of a generally congenial working environment. Pensions were paid to brewery staff and long-serving tenants, such as A. P. Buckett who retired owing to ill health after over 20 years as Manager and three as tenant of *Cox's Hotel* in Charlotte Street, Portsmouth in September 1952 and Mrs D. A. Catchlove, retiring after 35 years as tenant of the *Brewer's Arms*, Horndean, who received a pension of £52 per annum for life. The company pension scheme was revised upwards and in 1960 it was decided to contract into the State Pension Scheme that would operate from the following April. Wages and salaries were reviewed and increased regularly and the brewery foremen, cooper, bottling foreman and engineer were placed on the salaried staff in May 1963. There was the regular Christmas gift to staff, usually in the form of an additional week's wages or salary, and the provision for retired staff, in 1961, of two bungalows.[59] Time and time again, however, it was the degree of loyalty and long service that was evident and rewarded by the company (see Table 6.8).

That 11 men should complete a total of 366 years loyal work for a company engaged in an industry that had witnessed many changes was impressive. Of particular note was brewery foreman Arthur Purnell who went on to complete nearly 52 years' service before retiring at the

Table 6.8   Long-service employees, 1950–61

Year	Name	Length of service	Gift
1950	E. Thompson	25 years	Clock
	F. Hayter	25 years	Clock
	E. Longhurst	25 years	Clock
1952	H. Holland	50 years	Case of pipes and £10
	F. A. Childs	25 years	Wrist-watch
	C. Belcher	25 years	Clock
	C. Dunford	25 years	Clock
1957	R. D. Berry	25 years	Clock
1959	A. Purnell	50 years	?
1961	F. Stubbington	41 years	Radio
	F. Tilbury	50 years	Two armchairs

Source: Gale and Co. Minute Book March 1936–November 1965, *passim*.

end of July 1961. It was with much regret that the board noted, at its meeting on 10 June 1964, his passing away two days before 'after fifty two years exemplary service'. A further example of loyal service could be seen in W. G. E. Elliot's case. In October 1957 the Board resolved that being well over 70 and having worked for the company since 1941 he should retire at the end of the year with a gift of £200.[60] In March 1963 it was decided that Gale's employees in the Services Reserves could attend their fortnight's camp or exercises on full pay and receive a further week's holiday in addition, while there were also staff outings to provide light relaxation.[61] 'Life and soul' of many an annual outing, organised by Ted Argyle, was Frank Tilbury who completed his 50 years' service in 1961 (see Table 6.8). Argyle was subsequently to recall:

> The back of the 'chara' was loaded with crates of beer, and the first stop was always at Butser Hill on the A3, where the beer was sampled. We always seemed to be lucky with the weather in those days, and the outing was a real family affair, starting many romances between the bottling girls and the brewery men, ending in happy marriages and children who work at the brewery to this day. Frank would entertain us by removing his glass eye and false teeth, lighting his little clay pipe and impersonating Popeye the Sailor man to perfection.[62]

In the early 1970s, however, with the increasing ownership by staff of motor vehicles, the long tradition of brewery outings was discontinued.

As with Gales Brewery, so 1958 proved the low point in output for the British brewing industry as a whole. In that year only 23.8 million barrels of beer were produced nationally, but 20 years later, in 1979, output had risen by 75 per cent to 41.7 million barrels (see Table 6.9). It is tempting to suggest that such a recovery was the result of all the merger activity creating economies of scale, but this would be too simplistic an explanation in view of the smaller independent breweries

Table 6.9   UK beer production and consumption, 1960–84

Year	Production Bulk Barrels (million)	Consumption (pints per head)
1960	27.1	151.6
1961	27.5	157.0
1962	27.8	156.0
1963	29.0	156.6
1964	29.5	163.0
1965	30.0	161.7
1966	30.4	164.9
1967	30.5	166.8
1968	31.6	170.0
1969	32.9	176.7
1970	34.4	181.3
1971	35.0	186.9
1972	35.3	189.4
1973	37.9	199.3
1974	38.2	204.4
1975	39.2	208.6
1976	40.4	212.4
1977	40.3	209.6
1978	40.6	213.6
1979	41.7	217.1
1980	39.0	208.3
1981	37.1	198.8
1982	36.6	193.2
1983	37.0	195.6
1984	36.6	194.3

Sources: Gourvish and Wilson (1994), p. 630, for production; BLRA (1995), p. 7, for consumption.

that survived, although it has to be said that by 1980 only 81 brewing companies were left in existence.[63] However, the recovery coincided with a period of increasing incomes and population, the latter rising by 10 per cent from 50.9 millions in 1955 to 56.2 millions in 1979. With more consumers, and the numbers in the 15–24 age group enlarged by a third as a result of the post-war bulge in births at a time when American youth culture of pop music, clothes and drink, such as Coca Cola and lager, was exported to Britain, the demand for certain alocholic beverages was bound to rise. However, not only the young in larger numbers became customers of the brewing industry, so did the middle class and women. These latter two groups were more likely to be found drinking in hotels and restaurants, since the 1961 and 1964 Licensing Acts included new restricted on-licences for these establishments. Such licences increased about tenfold between 1962 and 1989 from around 3,000 to over 31,000. Similarly the Acts also helped the expansion of off-licences from around 26,000 in 1951 to, probably, 51,000 in 1989, including large food supermarkets that appealed more to women and stimulated the growth of alcohol-drinking at home. By 1979 there were 170,000 outlets for the sale of alcohol and probably 200,000 by 1989.[64]

This increased consumption, however, was accompanied by substantial change in the patterns of alcohol consumption, particularly in relation to the growth of brewery conditioned draught beers in the 1960s and 1970s and the decline in bottled beers. Simultaneously, came an increase in the sales of canned beer stimulated by increasing take-home sales, especially from supermarkets. On the whole, this meant a substantial growth in the free trade, not only in supermarkets but also in clubs and at off-licences as well as in pubs. The number of brands of beer also fell from some 3,000 in 1966 to less than half that number in 1976. Even so, the tied house remained the principal source of beer sales, although in relative decline.

The 1970s ended with economic recession in Britain from 1979 to 1981. The demand for beer fell from its 1979 peak of 41.7 million barrels to a trough of 36.6 millions in 1982, a fall of some 12 per cent, before stability about the 1982 level was maintained (see Table 6.9). However, the demand for cider and wines was much more buoyant, cider sales increasing by 43 per cent between 1980 and 1983 and wine by 40 per cent between 1980 and 1986.[65] The reason for beer consumption falling was strongly related to the decline in Britain's manufacturing industries which caused a fall in the number of unskilled and semi-skilled manufacturing workers, especially in areas of traditionally heavy consumption in Yorkshire and the West Midlands. Unemployment nationally rose from 1 million in October 1979 to 3 million by October 1985, and the manufacturing districts fared worst. In addition, in a period when consumers had less to spend, duty on beer was raised by 90 per cent between 1978 and 1982 and value added tax raised from 8 to 15 per cent in 1979.[66] Meanwhile, the duty on wine had to be lowered in 1984 to conform with European Community requirements, whilst the beer duty was raised again. Hence, beer was becoming relatively overpriced. Social influences, such as the campaign against drinking and driving and greater health and figure consciousness also worked against beer sales.

In this period of rapid change and diversification came the beginning of the recovery of Gales' fortunes. It coincided not only with the recovery in the brewing industry nationally, but also with the decision to install new bottle-washing machinery which cost over £5,000 in 1958. More importantly, came an APV bulk pasteuriser in 1960 – an expensive piece of equipment for a small brewery – but it was important for ensuring that the beer was right. Problems had certainly existed with bottled beer through inadequate pasteurisation,[67] and as Ted Argyle had introduced Horndean Special Bitter (HSB) in 1959, it was even more important to ensure its success. In fact HSB spearheaded Gales' resurgence assisted by increasing sales of other producers' beers, especially Guinness and Mackeson and lagers – Harp plus Carlsberg from 1959. With the introduction of HSB Gales were producing six draught beers in 1960 – XXX Light Mild, XXXD Dark Mild, BBB Bitter, XXXXX Winter Ale and PA Pale Ale were the others, although PA was quickly phased out in 1961. A similar situation existed with bottled beers. Five were produced in the 1950s – Light Ale, Brown Ale, Nourishing Stout, Champion Ale and Prize Old Ale. To these Argyle added Tudor Ale in 1960. Thus, a new draught beer and a new bottled beer were introduced in successive years along with new plant.

In 1962 Gales introduced their own keg bitter – cask conditioned beer. Like HSB it was a success with over 1,100 casks being produced in 1966. Coincidentally, a cask-washing machine and its ancillary equipment, costing about £5,000, were purchased (see Table 6.6). It is clear that the brewery was recognising the consumer trends towards lager and lighter beers, and reacting positively to them.

In 1964 Ted Argyle decided that more had to be done to improve and stabilise the quality of the beer. HSB had been giving problems in summer. There was no recognised quality control at Horndean, the brewery being operated in a traditional manner and on limited scientific principles. Thus Argyle advertised to start a laboratory, to which Chris Winchell was appointed. He was responsible for advising on appropriate equipment and dealing with microbiological infection. Thus quality control began to be established in 1964. Winchell left in 1966 to be replaced by Derek Lowe, who ran the laboratory until 1968 when he became Assistant Brewer.[68]

The early 1960s thus laid a solid foundation for recovery so that by 1974 Gales had again reached an output of 20,000 barrels (see Table 6.10). This revival was assisted by changing the yeast supplier in 1969 to Whitbreads who provided better quality yeast. Furthermore, in 1972, Gales developed their own facility for the culture of yeast, giving them better control over the yeast quality. Thus, by the early 1970s, Gales' beer was recognised as of good quality, endorsed by CAMRA (Campaign for Real Ale) and consequently sought out by traditional beer drinkers.

Meanwhile, Derek Lowe, who had become second brewer in 1971, moved on to Theakstons in 1976, being replaced by Mike Lunney. Five years later, however, Lowe returned to replace Ted Argyle who was

Table 6.10　Beer output: Gales Brewery, 1960–84

Year	Barrels	(group)	Keg	(group)	Bottles (barrel equivalent)	(group)	Total (barrels)	(group)
1960	8,158				4,114		11,782	
1961	8,677				4,047		12,724	
1962	9,130	8,966	390		4,427	4,303	13,947	13,567
1963	9,130		687	660	4,395		14,212	
1964	9,735		902		4,531		15,168	
1965	9,645		1,137		4,554		15,336	
1966	9,389		1,466		4,408		15,263	
1967	9,292	9,273	1,865	1,920	4,334	4,502	15,491	15,695
1968	8,945		2,397		4,412		15,736	
1969	9,096		2,752		4,082		16,650	
1970	9,263		2,834		4,893		16,990	
1971	9,542		3,087		5,022		17,651	
1972	9,733	9,829	3,465	3,619	5,630	5,207	18,828	18,675
1973	9,772		4,263		5,396		19,531	
1974	10,836		4,446		5,091		20,373	
1975	14,586		4,736		5,043		24,365	
1976	17,792		4,321		4,321		26,434	
1977	20,294	19,432	3,996	4,011	3,804	3,927	28,084	27,368
1978	22,198		3,632		3,318		29,148	
1979	22,292		3,372		3,147		28,811	
1980	23,922		3,036		2,847		29,805	
1981	24,036		2,553		2,766		29,355	
1982	26,550	28,038	2,341	2,414	2,265	2,265	31,156	32,717
1983	30,451		2,154		1,850		34,455	
1984	35,232		1,985		1,597		38,814	

Sources:　Monthly Returns (sales) 1959–64 and 1965–84.

retiring as Head Brewer. By then Argyle had presided over a revolution in Gales brewing and seen their output rise to new heights, having not ony introduced HSB draught beer and Tudor bottled beer, but also keg bitter in 1962 and keg mild (777) in 1972. Of these by far the most successful in terms of output, once initial problems had been overcome, was HSB which, introduced in 1959, had reached an output of over 2,000 barrels in 1971, before exponential growth took place to over 10,000 barrels by 1978 and over 20,000 in 1984. More than half Gales' total output was then HSB. By 1977 Gales had surpassed their previous best year, 1941, with an output not much less than 27,000 barrels. By 1984 this was made to look a much more modest achievement when nearly 39,000 barrels were produced (see Table 6.10). In 25 years, not only was depression lifted, but quite unprecedented levels of production had been achieved, with an overall increase in output of 229 per cent between 1960 and 1984.

Within these total production figures, however, are hidden some substantial changes indicating shifts in consumer tastes. While Gales' bottled beers continued to be sold in increasing quantities up to 1972, a 56 per cent increase occurring between 1960 and that year, a dramatic fall then ensued so that by 1984 some 72 per cent of output had been lost. A similar pattern can be discerned with Gales' keg beers. Output of keg began in 1960 with keg bitter (named Southdown in 1984), and keg mild (777) introduced in 1972. Thus it is tempting to think that the decline in bottled beer was the result of the introduction of keg mild. However, only three years after it was marketed keg output reached its peak, when some 4,736 barrels were produced. A decade later only 1,985 barrels, representing a fall of 58 per cent, were sold.

While keg and bottled beers were expanding in the 1960s and early 1970s, sales of Gales' traditional ales were sluggish. In the five years 1960–64 their output averaged under 9,000 barrels. Clearly, from 1960 until the mid-1970s, Gales expansion of output, which in total approached 40 per cent, had been very much the result of growing production of keg beers and, to a lesser extent, bottled beers. After that, however, as has been shown, output of both keg and bottled beers fell catastrophically in the late 1970s and early 1980s.

Consequently, it was the traditional draught beers that, from the mid-1970s, contributed everything to Gales' outstanding growth. The output of these beers in the decade 1974–84 rose by a phenomenal 225 per cent. Clearly, while national output of beer was being seriously affected by the economic recession, Gales had no such problems, exiting from the recession with higher production levels. Not being located in a manufacturing region would have helped but this was not the only reason.

The emergence of CAMRA in 1971, a mainly middle-class movement in favour of traditional mild and bitter beers, at a time when working-class drinkers were turning to keg and lager, helped to retain a market share for traditional beers. In the industry nationally, it was a time of increasing concentration when the Big Six brewers were supplying a greater proportion of the market and the conglomerates emerged. These created more competition in the leisure market, linking food and drink, tobacco and hotels and restaurants. It was a period dominated by the sale and advertising of the keg and lager beers of the big breweries – Bass's Worthington E, Allied's Double Diamond, Courage's Tavern, Watney's Red Barrel, Whitbread's Tankard, Scottish and Newcastle's Tartan, plus draught Guinness, which Gales sold, were the keg beers. Carling and Tennent lagers were supplied by Bass, Skol by Allied, Carlsberg by Watneys, Heineken and Stella Artois by Whitbread, and Harp by a consortium led by Guinness and also sold by Gales. By 1972 the Big Six plus Guinness accounted for 80 per cent of beer production in the UK.[69] In such an environmet, CAMRA's advertising of traditional ales helped to boost the smaller breweries, Gales even getting a recommendation from CAMRA at a time when maintaining a toehold in the market was becoming increasingly difficult. But CAMRA's support was only one factor in allowing breweries like Gales to survive in the face of the massive investment programmes of the giant combines.

There were, of course, internal factors as well. Gales diversified, not only by introducing new beers, but also by extending the sale of other breweries' beers. Harp keg was sold from 1970 and to this was added Worthington White Shield and Pils Gold Label by 1975, Ritter in 1976 and Tuborg Gold in 1979. In the early 1980s Tennents E and Carlsberg, replacing Harp, were introduced. By 1984 over 8,000 barrels of 'foreign' beers were sold.[70] In a separate development, a sister company, Horndean Hotels Limited, was established in 1973, to run managed houses, and it widened the opportunities for customers to eat in Gales tied houses. Another innovation was the introduction of electronic gaming machines, a development that was widespread, there being 121,000 in Britain by 1980.[71] Further diversification came with the development of Country Stores through the acquisition of retailing outlets which could then become a range of off-licences. In all this change one trend remained constant – the increasing importance of the tied trade and corresponding decline of the free and private ones. By 1966, some 98 per cent of Gales income from their own beers came from the tied trade and, from 1972, earnings in the free trade were so insignificant that they were omitted from the draught beer sales' accounts. As bottled beer sales became trifling the same policy was followed, in their case from 1976.[72]

The years 1970 to 1984 were to see even more changes at Gales, many of a far-reaching nature. There were important technological developments. Having installed a scientific laboratory in 1962, Gales became, in 1973, one of the first small breweries to introduce its own pure yeast propagation plant. The range of products was increased to include Strong Pale Ale, Super Nut Brown Ale and Nourishing Stout, the last being brewed to German purity laws. While demand grew, increased pressure was placed upon production capacity. In view of the fact that beer consumption nationally had fallen by 12 per cent in the economic recession of 1979–82, the board took the brave decision to expand, no doubt encouraged by the fact that Gales own output had continued its upward trend throughout the recession. Given the Horndean site's cramped nature there was only one possible solution – to build upwards. For 18 months following his retirement as Head Brewer in 1981 Ted Argyle chaired the Development Committee responsible for carrying through what would be the most important expansion of the brewery's productive capacity since its rebuilding following the fire in 1869. A new process floor, costing some £600,000 was erected on top of the existing brewery, providing the company with a potential 40 per cent increase in beer output. In the spirit of nothing succeeding like success, it was increasing output in general, which since 1978 had reached levels higher than before, and demand for HSB in particular, along with increasing outlets and optimism for the future, that occasioned the development. Before an assembled host of invited guests, the new floor was opened on 22 June 1984 by Second World War hero Group Captain Leonard Cheshire, VC, with whom Ted Argyle had long been associated through the Le Court Foundation Cheshire Home at Liss, near Petersfield.

By this time, other changes were also taking place. From a market that concentrated on southern England, Gales' distribution and outlet network began to expand considerably. Deals with Bass Charrington, Courage and Watney's Phoenix Brewery Co. meant that Gales' products would be consumed further afield. Where once the beers had been delivered by horse-drawn drays and new-fangled steam traction-engines, a fleet of modern lorries delivered to an ever-widening band of consumers. For exports to France, Germany and Italy, turbo-charged lorries were hired. Export markets were developed in the USA and Japan while, during the Falklands conflict of 1982, supplies were flown to the South Atlantic theatre of operations aboard Royal Air Force jets.

With all these developments, as well as the substantial growth in output, throughout the 1960s and early 1970s, profits rose steadily. Then, in parallel with the increase in beer production, they climbed to heights never previously achieved. Topping £100,000 in 1975 they rose dramatically to over £500,000 in 1982. (See Table 6.11.)

Table 6.11   George Gale and Co.: net profits, 1959–83 (£)

Year	Profits	Year	Profits
1959	25,122	1972	93,740
1960	27,774	1973	84,574
1961	27,322	1974	82,725
1962	33,349	1975	120,381
1963	38,569	1976	171,699
1964	39,747	1977	199,995
1965	63,128	1978	214,797
1966	76,686	1979	179,693
1967	63,803	1980	412,861
1968	64,274	1981	347,252
1969	57,741	1982	526,706
1970	66,061	1983	425,441
1971	80,889		

Source: Annual Reports and Accounts.

In great part, such developments were the result of key changes at board level. For 44 years, until shortly before his death in 1982, the company was led by Hugh Bowyer. A Gales' director since 1929 and also on the board of Barclay Perkins and Co. in Park Street, Southwark, he had determined Gales' policy through the Second World War and after. Like his father before him, he had taken steps to see that the brewery had been placed in capable hands, having handed over the chairmanship to Noel Chambers, as well as seeing that his son George was appointed to the Board. Noel Chambers was to be Chairman for a six-year period between 1981 and 1987. He had first appeared as an employee of Masons the auditors, at board meetings in March 1960, although his business relationship with Hugh Bowyer was of much longer duration, being an auditor for Gales since 1949. He had a substantial influence on the Chairman's decisions whose respect for the auditor was demonstrated when Chambers was chosen to succeed to the chairmanship of the company. When Masons merged with Whinney Murray and Co. Chambers also became a director of Fuller, Smith and Turner the London brewing company.

During the early 1980s three other key changes took place. In the spring of 1980 Group Captain George Bowyer, the then Chairman's son, joined the board. With the formal permission of the Air Ministry, he had been appointed a non-executive director on 2 June 1972 after returning from a third tour in Malta. He attended periodic board meetings and would spend some of his leave visiting Ted Argyle at the brewery and the licensed houses with Richard Evans Gale in order to familiarise himself with the company. He had first been requested to leave the Royal Air Force to look after the family's interests following the sudden death of the Company Secretary, George Martin, in 1978 and whilst he was serving in the USA. However, by 1980 Hugh Bowyer's health and mobility were failing and his son gained permission to retire prematurely, abandoning his rewarding and successful first career. He worked out his terminal and resettlement leave entitlements at Gales before being put on the payroll in July 1980 when he finally retired from the service. He became a director in charge of production follow-ing Ted Argyle's retirement from the board in 1983.[73]

When George Bowyer joined the company he found that Bowyers and Gales had continued working together. The Managing Director since 13 March 1978 had been Richard Evans Gale, only son of Rich-ard Walter Gale and his wife Thelma May. Trained at a Norwich brewery, he entered the Horndean business in September 1960. At its meeting on 13 March 1961 the board agreed that he should be paid £750 per annum, plus expenses. He would be responsible for calls upon company houses and prepare a weekly journal concerning same, plus his comments, for presentation to each board meeting.[74] In May 1972 he became a director and five years later Managing Director. He was a Director of Horndean Hotels Ltd, past Chairman of the South East Brewers' Association and a director of the Brewers' Society.

The year after George Bowyer joined the board there was an impor-tant change at the head of the production department. In July 1981, Ted Argyle, after many years admirable service, stood down as Head Brewer. His replacement – Derek Lowe – had first joined the company in 1966, working for 11 years as Assistant Brewer in charge of quality control. A break of four years ensued, during which time he served as second brewer with Theakstons, the noted northern brewery at Masham. Under his skilful guidance Gales would continue their long tradition of producing award-winnng beers.

Two years after Derek Lowe's arrival and only a year after Hugh Bowyer's death Richard Walter Gale followed him to the grave, passing away on 3 September 1983 at the age of 76. In an interview some six weeks before his death, he reminisced of his early life, experiences in the company and what he knew of its early history. George Alexander Gale, he considered, was something of a mean individual whose first wife was an invalid. He recounted with relish his five years as a pupil of Peter Marsland in Huddersfield, of working with George Peters in Ports-mouth, of the close association between his family and that of his wife's, the Evans family. His work with the Territorial Army brought him great fun as he 'met so many nice people'. He also remembered chauffeuring H. F. Bowyer each Monday to catch the 8.40 a.m. from Petersfield to London and collecting him at 5.40 p.m. He also noted how George Gale's son, David, had held Manor Farm, Horndean, and thought that he had died in 1981 or 1982.[75] Here was a man who could recall the offspring of the company's founder yet was still present at a time of major technical and economic change in the company. Almost two months later about 200 mourners packed Blendworth church for a thanksgiving service in his memory. To carry out his last wish the mourners then filled the *Ship and Bell* at Horndean. As the officiating clergyman the Reverend John Scott explained 'Dick had a tremendous sense of humour. He asks that everyone present has a drink with him at the *Ship and Bell* – his spirit will be there'.

R. W. Gale's death came at a time of much change. Ted Argyle had retired and long-serving Company Secretary and director, the experienced George Martin, who had been with Gales since May 1956, had died and been replaced by Clive Jones in 1978. But it was Hugh Bowyer's death that brought to an end another chapter in Gales' history. Unlike his father, Herbert, who had seen constant growth in his 40 years of leadership, Hugh Bowyer had experienced a period of considerable fluctutations. A world war, in which new heights of output were reached, had been followed by 15 years of decline in which equally new depths were plumbed. However, his final years had been rewarded with spectacular growth and he left the Brewery not only in good hands, but seemingly in a stronger position than it had ever been.

Notes

1. T. R. Gourvish and R. G. Wilson, *The British Brewing Industry 1830–1980* (Cambridge, 1994), p. 356.
2. Ibid., p. 360.
3. Gale and Co. Minute Book March 1936–November 1965, pp. 132, 133, 138.
4. Ibid., pp. 162, 194.
5. Ibid., p. 138. He requested that his wife might hold the licence in his absence.
6. Gale and Co. Minute Book March 1936–November 1965 (looseleaf), p. 207.
7. Ibid., p. 205; company obituary notice. His rank in the Territorial Army was that of Major, Royal Artillery: *Army List* for October 1940, 484c.
8. Gale and Co. Minute Book March 1936–November 1965, pp. 133, 139.
9. Ibid., pp. 150, 157.
10. Ibid., p. 130.
11. On 8 October the company decided to proceed with Air Raid Insurance

at 35s. per cent payable. Of this sum, 12s. would be found by the employee and 23s. by the company. Some 32 of the staff took advantage of this arrangement; ibid., p. 136.

12. In February 1941 the company increased its Fire Policy coverage by £120,000, divided between Atlas Insurance (£80,000) and the Union Assurance Society (£40,000); ibid., p. 140.

13. Gale and Co. Minute Book March 1936–November 1965, p. 138. The firm was based at 215 Lake Road, Portsmouth; *Kelly's Directory of Hampshire and the Isle of Wight* (1939), p. 408.

14. *Kelly's Directory of Hampshire and the Isle of Wight* (1939), p. 506. Some 55 pockets were placed in store at Havant and another 60 at the brewery itself; Gale and Co. Minute Book March 1936–November 1965, pp. 134, 137.

15. Gale and Co. Minute Book March 1936–November 1965, pp. 141, 142. Settlement of a War Damage claim for £10,000 was noted in September 1941; ibid., p. 145.

16. Ibid., p. 148.

17. Ibid., p. 147. After R. N. Gale's death it is not clear who ran the brewery. Possibly it was Hugh Bowyer on the end of the telephone to Childs. In any case, Hugh Bowyer had rejoined the RAF in February 1939 becoming an Acting Squadron Leader shortly after the outbreak of the Second World War in September 1939, and served until 1 December 1941. He then returned to work at Barclay Perkins. His wife Clare had taken the children to Canada in June 1940, returning to the farm at Scaynes Hill in October 1941. The widowed Elsie Bowyer was always at Horndean and would have played a part as a director. Certainly she signed many of the company's cheques during this period.

18. *HT*, 8287, 28 November 1941.

19. Gale and Co. Minute Book March 1936–November 1965, pp. 147, 156.

20. Ibid., pp. 145, 146, 152–6. The Hawkley contact was Benjamin Taunton Warner, of Lower Green. Stevens and Sons, motor engineers, occupied 177–81, Fleet Road, Fleet (*Kelly's Directory of Hampshire and the Isle of Wight* (1939), pp. 266, 234).

21. Whitbread Archive, 365/4 Brickwood and Co. Ltd, Directors' Minute Books 1929–50, p. 257. We are most grateful to Philip Eley for this reference.

22. Gale and Co. Minute Book March 1936–November 1965, pp. 125, 148.

23. Ibid., pp. 162, 182, 193.

24. Ibid., p. 206.

25. Gourvish and Wilson, *British Brewing*, pp. 359, 361.

26. R. G. Wilson, *Greene King: A Business and Family History* (London, 1983), pp. 208–9.

27. Gourvish and Wilson, *British Brewing*, pp. 366, 630.

28. Summary Book, 1938–57.

29. Chairman's Annual Statement for 1949, dated 8 May 1950.

30. Ibid.

31. Gourvish and Wilson, *British Brewing*, p. 371.

32. Ibid, p. 365; H. Janes, *The Red Barrel: A History of Watney Mann* (London, 1963), pp. 167–73.

33. Gourvish and Wilson, *British Brewing*, pp. 373–91.

34. Summary Book 1938–57; Cash Summary Book 1932–66.

35. Gale and Co. Minute Book March 1936–November 1965, p. 246.
36. Ibid., pp. 246, 104.
37. What follows is derived in part from a company prepared notice about E. T. Argyle prior to his retirement on 7 October 1983, and from the *Army List* for October 1940, 11280.
38. Registered in 1890, Offilers was taken over by Charrington United Breweries in 1965 along with 238 public houses. The brewery was closed 30 September 1966 (N. Barber, *Where Have All the Breweries Gone?* (Swinton, Lancs., 1981), p. 8.
39. Argyle joined the Sherwood Foresters Regiment in Derby and, on 25 May 1940, was commissioned into the Black Watch (Royal Highland Regiment) as a Second Lieutenant. Seeing service in Crete, Syria and the Western Desert, he rose to the rank of Major and was wounded at Tobruk. In 1944 he served as a member of the Military Government, British Army of the Rhine. Registered in June 1931 to acquire three other local brewing firms, Border Breweries (Wrexham) Ltd were taken over by the regional brewery Marston, Thompson and Evershed of Burton upon Trent in 1984 (Gourvish and Wilson, *Brewing Industry*, p. 592).
40. Gale and Co. Minute Book March 1936–November 1965, pp. 249, 253. He was also in attendance for the two other board meetings in 1949 on 23 September and 5 December (ibid., pp. 254, 257).
41. Ibid., pp. 292, 308–9, 323. Mears continued to attend board meetings as a director until December 1958.
42. Ibid., p. 324.
43. Ibid., pp. 333–4. On 30 October 1957 it was resolved that the pension would be payable by purchase of a £4,205 Annuity Contract from the Eagle Star Insurance Co. Ltd (ibid., p. 340).
44. Gale and Co. Minute Book March 1936–November 1965, pp. 253, 288, 336, 338–9. Unfortunately, Childs did not enjoy a long retirement, dying on 5 March 1958 (ibid., p. 346). *HT*, 9136, 14 March 1958. Martin was elected a director on 15 May 1959 (ibid., p. 363).
45. Gourvish and Wilson, *British Brewing*, p. 448.
46. Ibid., pp. 460–74, 623–29.
47. Whitbread Archive, 386/6 Portsmouth and Brighton United Breweries Ltd, Directors' Minute Books 1951–54, 27 August 1952, pp. 109–10.We are most grateful to Philip Eley for drawing our attention to the records relating to this and the followng four footnotes.
48. Ibid., 24 September 1952, p. 114.
49. Ibid., 6 November 1952, p. 124.
50. Ibid., 10 December 1952, p. 131.
51. Ibid., 19 December 1952, pp. 133–4.
52. Gale and Co. Minute Book March 1936–November 1965, pp. 363, 371–2, 386.
53. Ibid., pp. 296, 298, 345, 353, 365, 367, 374, 381.
54. Ibid., pp. 389, 438, 440, 454.
55. Ibid., pp. 234, 239, 241, 261, 309, 319, 352–3, 359, 384, 389, 398, 406, 412, 420–21. Founded in 1883 and registered three years later, Plowman Barrett and Co. were taken over by the Wenlock Brewery Co. in 1951 (Barber, *Breweries Gone*, p. 24).
56. Gale and Co. Minute Book March 1936–November 1965, p. 408.
57. Janes, *Red Barrel*, p. 173; Property Deeds Collection (Gales Archive).

58. Property Deeds Collection (Gales Archive); J. H. Smith, *Grayshott: The Story of a Hampshire Village* (Petersfield, 1978), chap 7.

59. Gale and Co. Minute Book March 1936–November 1965, pp. 293, 315, 320, 377, 411, 392.

60. Ibid., pp. 388, 437, 340–41.

61. Ibid., pp. 406, 372. The 1960 outing took place on 21 May with a trip to the Isle of Wight.

62. Letter from E. T. Argyle to *Yesterday* (October 1988), p. 61. We are obliged to Group Captain R. G. Bowyer for drawing this item to our attention.

63. Gourvish and Wilson, *British Brewing*, p. 448.

64. Ibid., pp. 456–7.

65. Ibid., pp. 581–2.

66. Ibid., pp. 582–3.

67. Information kindly supplied by Derek Lowe.

68. Again information from Derek Lowe.

69. Gourvish and Wilson, *British Brewing*, pp. 449–50.

70. Monthly Returns 1965–84.

71. Gourvish and Wilson, *British Brewing*, p. 578.

72. Monthly Returns 1965–84.

73. Following attendance at Upper Canada College, Toronto and Shrewsbury School, George Bowyer enrolled as a cadet at the RAF College Cranwell in September 1950 for officer and pilot training. After graduating in April 1953 he specialised in the anti-submarine role. Three of his four flying tours on Shackleton squadrons were based in Malta where, from 1969 to 1972 he commanded No. 203 Squadron, overseeing its conversion to the Nimrod four-jet Shackleton replacement. Squadron service was interspersed with two tours on the personal staff of the Commander-in-Chief, Coastal Command at Northwood; first as the ADC starting in February 1959 and then as his Personal Staff Officer after attending the RAF Staff College, Andover in 1965. A tour on the Directing Staff of the College of Air Warfare, Manby and Cranwell was followed by a year at the US Navy War College, Newport, Rhode Island, the only RAF officer ever to enjoy the privilege. This was followed by a two-year assignment on the staff of the Commander, Naval Air Forces, Pacific Fleet based in San Diego. In May 1978 he was promoted to Group Captain on taking command of RAF Newton, Nottinghamshire, and in July 1980 he retired prematurely in order to join the company.

74. Gale and Co. Minute Book March 1936–November 1965, pp. 383–4.

75. Notes from an interview by the authors with Richard (Dick) W. Gale, 22 July 1983.

CHAPTER SEVEN

Towards 2000: the company since 1984

For the British brewing industry the period following the economic recession of 1979–81 became one of stability of output at the level to which it had fallen in 1982. During the rest of the 1980s this meant annual production of between 36 and 37 million bulk barrels (see Table 7.1). Even so, changes in the composition of the market for alcohol, which had already become noticeable before 1984 (see Chapter 6) were enhanced. By 1990 lager represented over half the beer market in Britain when a decade earlier it had been less than a third. The introduction of Australian draught lagers – Fosters and Castlemaine XXXX – and to a lesser extent, Budweiser from America, assisted this trend. At the same time, whilst the decline in the consumption of bottled beer was halted in the late 1980s, draught beer consumption continued its downward trend, although its fall was, in some degree, offset by the increase in the market share of canned beer. From 1988 this had included draught (canned) beer, a Guinness innovation.[1]

Table 7.1 UK beer production and consumption, 1985–94

Year	Production – bulk barrels (million)	Consumption (pints per head)
1985	36.5	192.1
1986	36.6	191.8
1987	37.8	195.2
1988	37.7	200.2
1989	37.4	200.4
1990	37.4	199.3
1991	36.3	191.9
1992	35.2	185.0
1993	34.7	177.7
1994	34.9	180.2

Source: BLRA *Statistical Handbook* (1995), pp. 7, 32. The above figures, revised by HM Customs and Excise, replace those of Gourvish and Wilson (1984) for the years 1985–90.

The structure of the brewing industry, however, remained much the same, although the Big Six major brewers with tied houses plus the two without, Guinness and Carlsberg, together accounted for 81 per cent of total output by 1985. One major change nevertheless, came when Imperial Group, the conglomerate which owned Courage, was taken over by Hanson Trust in 1986. Some seven months later Hanson disposed of Courage to Elders IXL, the Australian producer of Fosters. As demand for beer continued to fall, so the large producers rationalised by closing some of their brewing plants (by 1986 only 117 breweries of the 142 in 1980 survived) and began to diversify into other leisure and related activities.

For the smaller brewers, in the face of the growing importance of national sales of lager and the take-home trade from supermarkets, holding their market share was to be increasingly difficult. Thus, from a total of 81 brewing companies in 1980, there were only 68 in 1986 – eight large nationals, 12 regional and 48 local.[2] Added to the 81 per cent of total national output of the eight large breweries, the 12 per cent of the regional ones left only 7 per cent for the 48 local breweries. In such a structure and with declining demand, some of the regional brewers began to buy local ones in order to acquire their tied estate. But it was the acquisition of Courage by Elders IXL in 1986 that was to influence the Monopolies and Mergers Commission's enquiry into competitiveness in brewing throughout their deliberations between 1986 and 1989. The commission recommended that no brewing company should own more than 2,000 tied houses[3] and anticipated that some 22,000 public houses worth about £7 billion would be sold. A 'guest' ale should also be available in all tied houses. In the event, the government required brewers owning more than 2,000 houses either to sell their brewing business or half the number of houses they owned over 2,000 (some 11,000 properties in all) by 31 October 1992.[4] Economic recession, the collapse of the property market in the late 1980s and the effect of the government's Beer Orders have seen the end of brewing at some regional breweries and the closure of others by the Big Six, further reducing the number of breweries in the early 1990s.

For Gales, in the post 1984 period, there was to be no stability of output.[5] The brewery's peak performance came in 1984, and the next six years were to see their output fall by some 41 per cent. The trough of this decline came in 1990, with some of the lost ground being recovered in the early 1990s when output rose to nearly 29,000 barrels (see Table 7.2).

Gales substantial expansion of output in 1984 was possible because of the construction of the new £600,000 process floor, built in 1983 and expected to increase productive capacity by 40 per cent. The

Table 7.2 Beer sales: Gales Brewery, 1985–97

| Year | Draught beers (barrels) | | | | | | | Total draught | Keg beers | | | Total keg | HSB in cans and bottled | Total own beers | Foreign |
	XXXL	XXXD	BBB	HSB	5X	POA	Other		777	S'down	Other				
1985	475	239	10,210	19,361	591	2		30,878	1,044	851	110	2,005	1,429	34,312	8,923
1986	313	240	9,288	16,652	564	3		27,060	993	1,101	140	2,234	1,242	30,536	10,379
1987	219	243	8,417	14,550	703	3		24,135	866	1,047	304	2,217	1,573	27,925	11,661
1988	229	302	8,123	12,840	405	1		21,900	812	1,282	101	2,195	2,740	26,835	13,287
1989	153	314	7,165	11,804	358	426*		20,220	792	1,284	432	2,508	3,169	25,897	15,109
1990	92	348	6,332	9,461	354	1,542		18,129	933	1,347	182	2,462	2,311	22,902	16,950
1991	106	343	6,466	8,437	403	3,386		19,141	1,354	2,509	117	3,980	1,768	24,889	20,699
1992	62	252	5,382	8,184	453	3,836		18,235	1,077	2,154	142	3,373	1,826	23,434	21,647
1993	0	129	4,270	8,096	412	3,697	7,457**	24,061	848	1,344	700	2,892	1,914	28,867	25,517
1994	0	88	3,765	9,419	338	3,739	7,015	24,364	755	1,341	1,023	3,119	1,182	28,665	26,225
1995	0	11	3,600	8,700	309	4,077	5,694	22,391	656	1,025	1,108	2,789	944	26,124	24,699
1996	0	0	2,958	8,453	345	3,594	3,888	19,238	513	558	1,964	3,035	1,411	23,684	26,082
1997	0	0	2,613	8,281	249	3,436	3,705	18,284	339	85	2,915	3,339	1,722	23,345	27,967

Notes:
* From 1989 Best Bitter replaced Prize Old Ale.
** From 1993 until 1997 other draught beers included contract brewing for Whitbreads.

Source: Monthly Trade Statements.

development was also designed to introduce much needed improvements in the quality and cost-effectiveness of the product; labour-saving automatic in-place cleaning, more use of hygienic stainless steel piping and plant, a new copper, new cast-iron liquor tanks, clearer and cleaner process floor, bulk sugar tanks and malt storage. Even so, in an age of breweries closing and national output falling, the decision to expand was a courageous one. However, probably the major influence on Gales' output figures from the mid-1980s was a trade deal agreed with Watney's Phoenix Brewery Co. in 1983, by which 10,000 barrels of Gales beer, primarily Horndean Special Bitter, would be taken in some of Phoenix's Hampshire houses in exchange for Carlsberg lager. Gales substituted Carlsberg for Harp which had been sold since 1970. The following year the deal was extended to certain Phoenix houses in Sussex in exchange for Fosters lager. Some 4,000 barrels of Carlsberg and 1,000 of Fosters were sold.

No doubt a major consideration in the decision to extend, therefore, was that extra capacity would be needed to ensure the output necessary to fulfil the contract. In the event, the contract was to be short-lived, for Watney Grand Metropolitan (the result of a merger in 1972), bought Ruddles brewery in 1986. Producing their own real ale, they then had no further need for supplies from Gales. Much of the decline in Gales, therefore, can be attributed to this one factor. Not surprisingly sales of Carlsberg in Gales' houses fell each year until 1992, when they were at about one-eighth of the amount initially sold. Clearly, for Gales, the ending of the contract with the Phoenix Brewery Co. created a difficulty and the board had to consider seriously an alternative course of action. The position was not made easier the following year when their experienced Chairman, Noel Chambers, had to resign early in 1987 because of ill health. He had served the company well for 38 years as auditor with Masons and more recently as director and Chairman. He agreed to continue as company President, but the benefit of his wisdom in this capacity was to be short-lived, for his death came only too soon in December 1988. His experience and wise counsel were sadly missed.

In autumn 1987, fellow director and Company Secretary, Clive Jones, emigrated to New Zealand after nine years of dedicated service and constructive hard work. Thus, two directors, including the Chairman, had to be replaced. Although a relative 'new boy' in the industry, George Bowyer, took over the chairmanship at a challenging time in the company's history. Robin Heathcote was appointed Company Secretary. Dependable and hard-working, he joined the board on 1 February 1990. Additionally, in 1984, Gales had recruited, as a non-executive director, chartered accountant Martin Bunting,[6] who had spent all his career in the brewing industry and was the son of that same Colonel T.

B. Bunting who had been brought in as Company Secretary by Barclay Perkins in 1931 (see Chapter 5). The decisions of these board members would be crucial in ensuring that Gales' difficulties were not to become critical. The immediate response was to expand the range of the brewery's products. A prize-winning Italian pale ale was introduced into the home market, a stout was developed for the German market and Horndean Special Bitter in cans was launched for the take-home trade. The development of the continental ferry port at nearby Portsmouth provided excellent transport facilities to assist expansion on the Continent, hence the Italian and German beers' production. Furthermore, in 1986 came exploratory talks with regard to the acquisition of the Schneider Brewery in France. Clearly, with the growth of the European Community, such an undertaking could be both imaginative and profitable. A team led by the Managing Director, visited the French plant. Unfortunately, the location of the brewery in the deep south of France was hardly ideal. A brewery in Normandy, Brittany or surrounding regions with sea links to Portsmouth would clearly have been more economically placed. It was perhaps fortuitous that the project was not proceeded with before finances had been seriously committed to what was, in any case, a brewery with ageing plant. Horndean Special Bitter in cans was a more certain enterprise, and in the event proved most popular. It was followed by the launch of a new low alcohol bitter, Wyvern, a top fermented lager for Canada and a high-gravity dark barley wine for a national brewer. But it was the introduction in 1989 of a new cask conditioned bitter of 1040' gravity marketed as Gales Best Bitter, which was the most significant product, and which halted the decline in the brewery's output in 1990–91. By 1992 nearly 4,000 barrels were produced and it became second only to the stronger Horndean Special Bitter in Gales portfolio of beers. At a time when, generally, the demand for beer was falling and Gales' other brands were experiencing declining demand, their Best Bitter had bucked the trend, indicating that the right beer for the customer, properly marketed, could still compete against the inexorable rise in demand for lager.

As Gales output declined in the late 1980s, one other simultaneous development was the increase in the sale of 'foreign beers', those supplied by other breweries. These had always formed a small part of Gales' annual turnover, being about one-sixth of the brewery's output at the beginning of the 1960s. However, in 1964 Guinness keg was introduced into Gales houses and by 1970 some 1,000 barrels were being sold. In that same year Harp keg, a lager, was added to the list of foreign sales and immediately overtook Guinness in its first year. By 1975 Gales were selling over 4,000 barrels a year. Other significant additions were Bass's Tennents lager in 1981, sales reaching 2,000 barrels in 1982, Fosters keg and Stella Artois in 1982, and Carling Black Label and Castlemaine XXXX in 1987. Of these, apart from the short-lived Carlsberg contract, Tennents proved the most popular until it was overtaken by Carling Black Label, of which 4,000 barrels were sold in 1990. In that year Fosters, Stella Artois, Castlemaine and Heineken, the latter just introduced, were all selling at over 1,000 barrels. All these lagers, apart from Castlemaine, were to double their consumption the following year. But in 1992, after a slow start, Fosters, humorously advertised as the amber nectar, was to increase its sales amazingly to over 5,000 barrels, with Carling Black Label selling at over 4,000 barrels. There was little doubt that Fosters had become the market leader and in 1994 over 6,000 barrels were sold, resulting in some decline in the consumption of other foreign lagers. The effect of all these developments can be seen in the totals of foreign beers sold by Gales (see Table 7.2). In 1985 foreign beers equalled a little over a quarter of home output, but by 1992 they were beginning to reach almost the same sales level as Gales' own beers. Only a substantial increase in the brewery's output in 1993, resulting mainly from contract brewing for Whitbreads prevented foreign beer sales overtaking domestic ones. However, this was short-lived, for as Gales' output fell when the contract brewing declined from 1994–95, so foreign beer sales overtook their own production in 1996. This trend of the late 1980s and early 1990s was not what Gales had wished for when the new production plant was built in 1983, but, without doubt, substantially added to the brewery's turnover and income in a difficult period.

The increase in turnover partly represented the acquisition of new houses, but it was also indicative of an improved performance by the brewery from 1991 onwards. This was assisted by the acquisition of contracts to supply Whitbreads with two cask-conditioned beers which, by 1993, resulted in a total of over 7,000 barrels being supplied. Perhaps it was just as well that these contracts were obtained, as the hoped for guest ales, to be placed in the national breweries' tied houses, never materialised. It seemed that the tenants of these houses either were not interested in guest ales or were reluctant to stock them. It could not have been because Gales' beers lacked quality for they continued to win awards. For example, in the CAMRA 1985 Great British Beer Festival, Gales' Butser Brew Bitter won first place in the Ordinary Bitter Class and Horndean Special Bitter came second in the Strong Ale Class. In the 1986 British Bottlers' Institute Export Beers Competition, Gales' Strong Ale won a Gold Medal. Clearly, Head Brewer Derek Lowe, was continuing the Gales tradition of producing award-winning beers. Even as recently as 1993, Gales 'Gold', a new light-coloured draught beer, was the overall winner at the CAMRA Portsmouth Beer Festival – while still on test! In competition with most brewers, the company also won the opportunity to brew and package a commemorative bottled beer to launch the Parliamentary Beer Club at the Palace of Westminster. In addition, at the 1993 British Bottlers' Institute Beer Competition, Wyvern Low Alcohol won a gold medal and the championship trophy in the 1994 Brewing Industry International Awards, while Horndean Special Bitter won a silver medal and Prize Old Ale the Championship at the 1993 Great British Beer Festival. More recently, following the gold medal in the 1997 Brewing Industry International Awards, canned HSB was awarded the Silver Medal in 1998.

Despite the evidence that a number of Gales' ales were well received, the bottled beer demand continued to fall in parallel with national trends. Also in line with national demand, Gales' canned beer sales rose. One result of the decline in consumption of bottled beer was that, in 1990, the ageing bottling plant, being less than cost-effective, was closed and bottling contracted out. Contracting out also applied to deliveries on the Isle of Wight from 1992, reducing the need for one vehicle. In fact, a major reorganisation of delivery routes, which took place in 1987–88, had reduced costs and the vehicle fleet by one-third. Similarly, the change to diesel fuel for higher mileage company cars led to significant cost and fuel economies.

One further factor of assistance to the company at this time was the sales of wines, spirits and cider. As in the British brewing industry as a whole, these remained buoyant enough for them to be commented on favourably in most of the Chairman's annual reports in the mid-1980s and the early 1990s, with Gales' Old Country Wines 'performing exceptionally well'.[7] By 1994 almost 70,000 gallons of wines and spirits were being sold.

Further assisting Gales out of the difficulties of the late 1980s was a change in the proportions of tied and free trade. Whereas the free trade had virtually disappeared in the early 1970s (see Chapter 5), the growth of the take-home trade and the company's determined efforts to sell more in it by employing more representatives, helped to see its revival. The Chairman commented on its increase throughout the late 1980s.[8] By 1985 the free trade was responsible for 14 per cent of beer sales, rising to 20 per cent at the beginning of the 1990s. In 1994 the proportion had almost doubled, being just over 39 per cent (see Table 7.3), and represented both the growth in consumption of real ale as well as the increase of free trade representatives. Within the tied trade sector there came a shift in emphasis with increased importance being placed on managed houses. In 1992 the sister company, Horndean Hotels, running the managed houses was absorbed by Gales creating a more economic administration and a closer relationship between the managed

Table 7.3   Tied and free trade: Gales Brewery, 1985–96 (barrels)

Year	Tied	HH	Cols 2 and 3 total tied	Free	Export total	Cols 4, 5, 6 beers	Foreign
1985	25,177	4,549	29,726	4,735	109	34,570	8,810
1986	24,213	4,920	29,133	5,403	199	34,735	6,555
1987	21,494	6,059	27,553	5,968	534	34,055	5,598
1988	20,976	6,402	27,378	7,012	341	34,731	5,635
1989	20,633	7,373	28,006	7,382	491	35,879	5,369
1990	21,078	7,519	28,597	7,637	257	36,491	8,257
1991	26,782	8,117	34,899	8,796		43,695	6,302
1992	23,372	8,371	31,743	10,962		42,705	7,727
1993	18,674	8,581	27,255	11,491	Contract	38,746	9,778
1994	17,628	9,783	27,411	17,603	brewing	45,014	15,306
1995	17,483	10,956	28,439	18,195	4,278	50,912	
1996	15,424	11,244	26,668	21,581	1,540	49,789	

Note: The above figures include sales of beers from other breweries (Foreign) in Gales' tied houses, and hence do not represent Gales' output alone.
HH = Horndean Hotels

Source: Monthly Sales Figures.

houses and the company. Some 28 inns, all providing meals, were managed in 1995 and were responsible for over 35 per cent of tied trade sales, a rise of 12 per cent since 1991.

The number of licensed houses controlled by the company during the decade 1985–95 was always changing partly as a result of the policy of disposing of low barrelage houses and also expanding the number of managed houses. However, in August 1989 Gales had over 90 houses, of which 68 were freehold and at least 23 leasehold.[9] The established strategy of providing houses with a comfortable and pleasant environment for their customers was continued, with constant improvements being undertaken. Between 1984 and 1996 over £10 million were spent on upgrading licensed properties, approximately £100,000 on each house (see Table 7.4).

The decline in brewery output in the late 1980s highlighted the need to improve efficiency and cut costs. Thus, when a new boiler was installed in 1985 it was fitted with a dual-fuel burner, achieving significant economies in fuel consumption by taking advantage of changes in oil and gas prices. In 1987 a new energy management system improved the control of electricity consumption. In the same year, the introduction of an ICL computer brought much change to traditional methods of

Table 7.4   Expenditure on estate, 1984–96 (excl. brewery) (£000)

1984	704	1991	383
1985	664	1992	567
1986	855	1993	567
1987	940	1994	609
1988	1,400	1995	617
1989	1,300	1996	618
1990	812		

Source: Chairman's Annual Reports.

recording information in the brewery as well as a more flexible and customer-orientated service for ordering. Telephone sales and orders replaced postal ordering, linking all customers' accounts to the computer. Simultaneously, an executive committee under the chairmanship of Martin Bunting was formed, meeting monthly to make recommendations to the board. Not only were the directors members, but also the Head Brewer, Derek Lowe, the Financial Controller, Joanna Hockley, the head of the Trade Department, George Turner, the head of Distribution and Technical Services, Tony Cartledge, Company Surveyor, Roy Scott and the general manager of Horndean Hotels, Jeremy Horton. By 1990 the internal organisation of the company had been streamlined, with a revamped computer in every department.

Even so, the late 1980s were to be overshadowed for the whole of the British brewing industry, by the reference to the Monopolies and Mergers Commission in 1986 of 'the supply of beer for retail sale'. Its long period of deliberation created uncertainty and when, finally, it reported in March 1989, the uncertainty did not come to an end. Its recommendations appeared to favour local brewery companies such as Gales. As a consequence of the report in December 1989, the government issued its two Supply of Beer Orders, requiring national brewers to dispose of some of their tied houses and, therefore, forcing them to assess their future strategy. Gales anticipated two potential developments that could be to their advantage. First, there would be a flood of licensed houses on to the property market, generally low barrelage houses unsuitable for management, but possibly including a few potentially better ones to encourage brewers like Gales to buy. Secondly, in May 1990, the 'guest' ale rule was to be introduced, allowing tenants of tied houses to sell at least one beer produced by a different brewery from that owning the tie. Gales intended to bid for any appropriate houses which became available in their trading area, with a preference for those suited to management. They also proposed to seek outlets for their own beers through the guest ale rule.

However, these developments were paralleled by economic recession, but one with a difference. Not only did it have the usual unemployment effect, although at a higher level than at any time since 1932 and high in Gales' trading area in the south, but it also saw the collapse of property prices. For many, especially in the south of England where property prices had risen most, this created the nightmare of negative equity. Their houses were now worth substantially less than the mortgages owed upon them. Government economic policy, based on keeping inflation at a low level, simply exacerbated this problem, since the only solution, in the absence of any other government initiative, was for property prices to rise again. Those caught in the negative equity trap, as well as the unemployed, clearly had less disposable income for purchasing alcohol, thus providing a further explanation for the decline in sales of beer and the trough in which Gales found themselves in 1990.

Depressed property prices, however, are advantageous for those wishing to buy. Gales could not afford to lose any opportunity presented through the Monopolies and Mergers Commission's recommendations. Thus, when a large quantity of licensed houses from national brewers came on to the market in 1990, they acquired 42 for £9.3 million from Allied-Lyons (Friary-Meux) PLC. The number of their houses was increased by almost 50 per cent at a cost of just over £220,000 per house. Significantly increasing Gales' asset value, the acquisition also increased their borrowing substantially. But, a recession, when prices are lower, is the right time to buy, thus helping to safeguard the longer-term future prosperity of the company. As it happens, about half the acquired houses were sold, ensuring that the cost of borrowing was reduced.

The following year, 1991, Gales leased a package of 20 licensed houses on the Isle of Wight from Whitbreads, on a 20-year lease at a rent of £310,000 per annum. With hindsight this can only be described as a major error of judgement. Clearly the Isle of Wight, as Gales would have known from earlier acquisitions there, was not a major beer-consuming region. This deal, therefore, was to prove to be a millstone around the company's neck, for it produced only about £200,000 per year in income. Fortunately, in 1995, Gales were able to purchase the freehold of these properties, thus disposing of the 20-year millstone as well as some of the houses. By 1998, out of a total of 116 houses, only eight were owned on the Isle of Wight.

Simultaneous with these developments, came further changes at board level. In February, 1990, the recently appointed Company Secretary, Robin Heathcote, became a director, and in November, Nigel Atkinson from Courage, joined as Assistant Managing Director,[10] whilst Richard Gale was appointed Deputy Chairman. Shortly after, early in the new year, Sir Charles Tidbury, with a wealth of directorial experience at national brewers Whitbreads, became a non-executive director until his retirement in 1996 when he was replaced by Charles Brims. On 1 November 1994, Nigel Atkinson took over as Managing Director. Richard Gale became a non-executive Deputy Chairman, but only for some 14 months, for he stepped down on 30 January 1993, after more than 32 years' service. First joining the company on 1 September 1960, he became a director on 2 May 1972 and six years later Managing Director on 13 March 1978. He had the distinction of being a direct descendant, great-grandson of the Richard Rogers Gale who had been George Alexander Gale's nephew, working in the brewery when he sold it in 1896. After more than three decades of solid service Richard Gale agreed to remain a trustee of both the company's Pension Scheme and the Gales Youth Trust. With his departure in 1993 came the end of the Gale family's continuous and direct involvement with the day-to-day work of the brewery. It had lasted 146 years, the time which had elapsed since Richard Gale had founded the business in 1847. Even so, it has to be remembered that control had passed to the Bowyer family almost a century earlier. However, another major link with the past had come to an end.

Gales' board of directors now had no long-serving member. Only the Chairman, George Bowyer, who joined the company in 1980 and Martin Bunting, who had arrived in 1984, had board experience before 1990, the three other members being recent appointments. Although short in years of service at Gales, they were not lacking in experience and, in their so far brief period at the helm, the exponential growth of turnover and profits from 1991 to 1994 (see Tables 7.5 and 7.6), rather suggests that the new board had got both their priorities and their decision-making right, and were the appropriate team to take the company towards 2000.

Table 7.5 Annual turnover, 1983–96 (£)

1983	6,468,838	1990	10,965,371
1984	7,471,770	1991	13,305,196
1985	7,605,991	1992	15,277,522
1986	7,631,436	1993	17,741,673*
1987	7,862,649	1994	20,882,408
1988	8,651,479	1995	22,124,855
1989	9,514,201	1996	23,694,967

Note: *Horndean Hotels absorbed by Gales, 5 September 1992.

Source: Chairman's Annual Reports.

Table 7.6   Annual profit, 1983–96 (£000)

Year	Before tax	After tax		Before tax	After tax
1983	592	474	1990	880	697
1984	676	387	1991	1,652	1,293
1985	701	414	1992	1,621	1,318
1986	502	275	1993	1,242	946
1987	598	378	1994	1,370	929
1988	1,120	829	1995	1,623	1,036
1989	1,434	1,082	1996	1,953	1,282

Source: Six Year Financial Reviews.

The future thus looked rather more secure in the mid-1990s than it did at the beginning of the decade and there are currently some interesting developments. Although it has long been possible to visit the brewery in small groups by appointment, the company has decided to exploit its history and use its building as a traditional nineteenth-century brewery for organised heritage tours, having established an entrance through the original *Ship and Bell* where the brewery began. These tours began in 1995. At the same time, the last steam-engine formerly used by the brewery, and which was loaned to Portsmouth Museums, had been restored and installed to power the brewery in its original location. Thus the reintroduction of steam brewing will bring Gales full circle. By developing its own history the company is tapping into another aspect of the leisure market – the heritage sector – which has been so successfully exploited in Portsmouth.

Thus, despite the disadvantages of the UK beer duty which is almost 30 per cent of the price of a pint, and six times higher than that of our neighbour France (see graph), resulting in large quantities of cheap alcohol being imported through ferry ports such as nearby Portsmouth to the disadvantage of both sales in Gales' houses and output at the brewery, the board at Gales have developed a number of strategies to fight back. Not the least of these have been the maintenance of beer quality as well as the introduction of new brands such as GB in 1998, plus enhancements in the quality of management. In the process, in line with changes in the industry generally, the company has evolved from being solely a brewing concern to become a broader retailing enterprise with a stronger base for future development.

Even so, with the brewing industry seemingly in a state of continual flux, Gales will also need to retain the ability to change in order to keep abreast of developing market trends. The national decline in the on

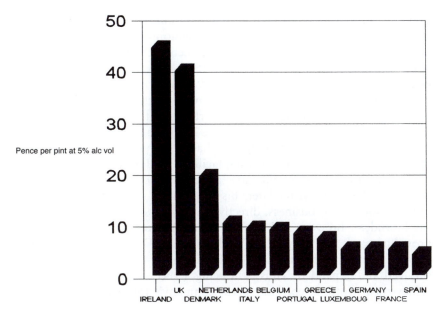

Graph   EU beer duty rates

trade of something like 30 per cent since 1979 is likely to continue presenting problems of over capacity in brewing and a surplus of public houses throughout the country. Gales have responded by disposing of those houses that it regarded as unlikely to expand sales and continued to develop and acquire those which could offer good quality food as well as accommodation. This is a recognition of the rising demand from more couples and families for eating out and having more short-break holidays. For the latter, many of Gales' houses are in locations attractive to short-term visitors. Thus focusing its activities on economic trends, the company has successfully competed in the market-place.

   However, the backbone of any company is its workforce and no business history would be complete without some words being written about them. At the brewery in Horndean, some 90 or so are employed supporting many more managers and bar staff in the licensed houses. What has been notable in the twentieth century is the successful teamwork at the company – an indication of a generally contented workforce. Yet the workforce has had growing demands placed upon it both by the increasingly rapid changes in the brewing industry generally and, in particular, by changing technology. Thus, information technology is continually developed as is training in the multi-skilling of all employees with rewards for excellence. As a result, in 1994, Gales became Hampshire Company of the Year by showing its achievements in the previous three years and looking forward to future developments. It did so with confidence and enthusiasm as demonstrated in its recent accounts. Turnover rose by some 116 per cent between 1990 and 1996 while profits, which as recently as 1987 were just over £500,000, consistently topped £1 million after 1991. Few companies in the industry can have matched this rate of growth in the early 1990s and it augurs well for the future, being important for the local economy and for future generations of workers at the Horndean Brewery.

When, a century and a half ago, Richard Gale purchased the *Ship and Bell* licensed house with its brewing facilities in Horndean to ensure that one of his four sons would have an inheritance, he could not have envisaged that, 150 years later, his acquisition would have become a multimillion pound business, directly employing around 100 workers at the Horndean Brewery and owning over 120 houses (see Appendix 3) providing work for many more. Whilst, since 1847, the number of breweries in Britain has fallen from 45,000 to only a few dozen, Gales both survived and expanded. Thus, still being a successful enterprise was an achievement worth celebrating on the company's 150th anniversary.

Notes

1. T. R. Gourvish and R. G. Wilson, *The British Brewing Industry 1830–1980* (Cambridge, 1994), pp. 585–86. This was achieved by the use of the widget in each can.
2. Ibid., p. 590.
3. *Monopolies and Mergers Commission, Supply of Beer*, Cmnd. 651 (1989).
4. The Supply of Beer (Tied Estate) Order 1989, S.I. 1989 No. 2390, 19 December 1989.
5. Most of what follows is taken from the Chairman's Annual Statements and the Monthly Trade Statements.
6. Martin Bunting also became a Trustee of the Bowyer Trusts and, after Noel Chambers's retirement, Senior Trustee.
7. Chairman's Annual Statement 17 May 1993.
8. Chairman's Annual Statements, 20 May 1986; 26 May 1987; 1990.
9. Managed and Tenanted House List August 1989.
10. Nigel Atkinson has been the key outside appointment of the late twentieth century. Educated at Haileybury and attending Sandhurst, he was an adjutant in the Royal Green Jackets, seeing service in Northern Ireland, and became a director of Courage.

Family trees:
Gale and Bowyer

The Gale Family

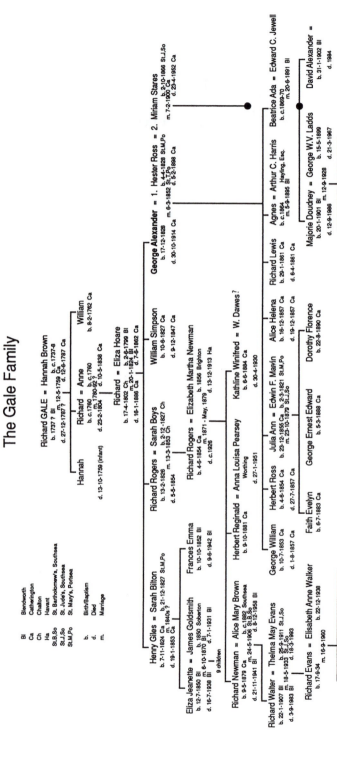

BI	Blendworth
Ca	Catherington
Ch	Chalton
Ha	Havant
St.B.So	St. Bartholomew's, Southsea
St.J.So	St. Jude's, Southsea
St.M.Po	St. Mary's, Portsea
b.	Birth/Baptism
d.	Died
m.	Marriage

Note: Bold represents Chairman of Company.

The Bowyer Family

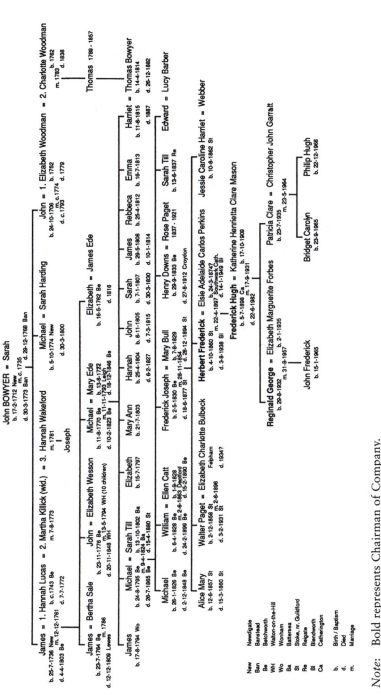

Note: Bold represents Chairman of Company.

Company officers

Company Chairmen

1888–97	George Alexander Gale
1897–1938	Herbert Frederick Bowyer
1938–81	Frederick Hugh Bowyer
1981–87	Owen Leonard Noel Chambers
1987–	Reginald George Bowyer

Company Secretaries

1888–93	Jeremiah Samuel Stubington
1893–97	John Le Feaver
1897–1927	Ernest H. Taylor
1927–41	Richard Newman Gale
1941–57	Frederick Ammon Childs
1957–78	Cecil George Martin
1978–87	Clive Maurice Jones
1987–	Robin Alexander Bridges Heathcote

Head Brewers

1900–22	Sidney Steel
1922–54	William Barton Mears
1954–81	Edward Thomas Argyle
1981–	Derek James Lowe

George Gale and Co.: house list as at 20 April 1998

House	Address			
Alice Lisle	Rockford Green		Ringwood	Hants
Ark	127 Meggeson Avenue	Townhill	Southampton	Hants
Basketmakers	12 Gloucester Road		Brighton	E. Sussex
Bat and Ball	Broad Halfpenny Down		Hambledon	Hants
Beehive	34 Middle Hill	Englefield Green	Egham	Surrey
Berkley Arms	Delling Lane	Old Bosham	Chichester	W. Sussex
Brewers Arms	170 Milton Road		Portsmouth	Hants
Bridge	87 High Street		Shoreham by Sea	Sussex
Bridge Tavern	54 East Street		Old Portsmouth	Hants
Bull's Head	11 South Street		Dorking	Surrey
Bull's Head	Fishbourne Road	Fishbourne	Chichester	Sussex
Bull Inn	High Street		Sonning	Berks
Calleva Arms		Silchester	Nr. Reading	Berks
Castle	1 Finchdean Road		Rowlands Castle	Hants
Castle	164 High Street		Ryde	Isle of Wight
Cedars	2 Station Road	Wootton	Ryde	Isle of Wight
Chairmakers	Worlds End	Denmead	Portsmouth	Hants

House	Address		
Coal Exchange	21 South Street		Emsworth	Hants
Crabtree	6 Buckingham Road		Shoreham by Sea	Sussex
Cricketers	Commonside		Emsworth	Hants
Curlew	Petersfield Road	Westbourne	Havant	Hants
Dewdrop	96 Wick Street	Wick	Littlehampton	W. Sussex
Dolphin	7 Park Road South		Havant	Hants
Druids Arms	11–13 Binsteed Road	Buckland	Portsmouth	Hants
Eastgate	4 The Hornet		Chichester	W. Sussex
Elmer	89 Elmer Road	Elmer Sands	Middleton on Sea	Sussex
Falcon	17 Swanmore Road		Ryde	Isle of Wight
Farmer	Catherington Lane	Catherington	Portsmouth	Hants
Fisherman's Haunt		Winkton	Christchurch	Dorset
Four Horseshoes		Long Sutton	Nr. Basingstoke	Hants
Fox		Cane End	Nr. Reading	Berks
Fox	Andover Road	Newfound	Nr. Basingstoke	Hants
Fox and Pelican	Headley Road	Grayshott	Hindhead	Surrey
George Inn	Eartham		Chichester	W. Sussex
Golden Eagle	1 Delamere Road	Southsea	Portsmouth	Hants
Golden Lion	High Street		Fareham	Hants
Good Intent	College Street		Petersfield	Hants
Graduate	10 New Road	St Mary's	Southampton	Hants
Harvest Home	Southwick Road	Denmead	Portsmouth	Hants
Heroes	125 London Road	Waterlooville	Portsmouth	Hants
Hogs Lodge	London Road	Clanfield	Portsmouth	Hants

Horse and Jockey	Botley Road	Curbridge	Nr. Botley	Hants
King Charles	6 Lovedon Lane	Kings Worthy	Winchester	Hants
Kings Arms	19 Havant Road		Emsworth	Hants
Kings Beach Hotel	The Parade	Sea Lane	Pagham	W. Sussex
Kings Head	The Square	Wickham	Fareham	Hants
Kittiwake	1 Sandy Point Road	Sandy Point	Hayling Island	Hants
Limeburners		Newbridge	Billingshurst	E.Sussex
Lord Raglan	35 Queen Street		Emsworth	Hants
Maypole	9 Havant Road		Hayling Island	Hants
Milkmans Arms	55 North Street		Emsworth	Hants
Miners	112 Funtley Road	Funtley	Fareham	Hants
Murrell Arms	Yapton Road	Barnham	Nr. Bognor Regis	W. Sussex
New Inn	16 Bevois Valley Road		Southampton	Hants
Newport Arms		Braishfield	Romsey	Hants
Off Licence	2 Ludlow Road	Paulsgrove	Portsmouth	Hants
Old House at Home	2 South Street		Havant	Hants
Old House at Home	62 Love Lane		Romsey	Hants
Old Ship	261 Bridge Road		Lower Swanwick	Hants
Original Twyford Arms	67 Twyford Avenue	Stamshaw	Portsmouth	Hants
Pack Horse	Woodcote Road	Mapledurham	Reading	Berks
Park Tavern	11 Priory Road		Chichester	W. Sussex
Pointer	High Street	Newchurch	Sandown	Isle of Wight
Prestonville	64 Hamilton Road		Brighton	Sussex
Prince of Wales		Hammervale	Haslemere	Surrey
Queens Head			Farnham	Surrey
Red Lion	9 The Borough	Chalton	Portsmouth	Hants

House	Address		
Red Lion	High Street	Southwick	Fareham	Hants
Red Lion	Old Portsmouth Road	Milford	Nr. Godalming	Surrey
Red White and Blue	150 Fawcett Road		Southsea	Hants
Rising Sun		Milland	Nr. Liphook	Hants
Robin Hood	6 Homewell		Havant	Hants
Roebuck	Kingsmead	Wickham	Fareham	Hants
Royal Albert Hotel	123 Albert Road South		Southampton	Hants
Royal Oak	Pagham Road	Lagness	Chichester	W. Sussex
Royal Oak	Pook Lane	East Lavant	Chichester	W. Sussex
RMA Tavern	58 Cromwell Road	Eastney	Southsea	Hants
Ship	24 High Street		Emsworth	Hants
Ship	Langstone Road	Langstone	Havant	Hants
Ship and Bell Hotel	London Road	Horndean	Portsmouth	Hants
Ship and Castle	90 Rudmore Road		Portsmouth	Hants
Sir Charles Napier	50 Southover Street		Brighton	E.Sussex
Sociable Plover	2 Ludlow Road	Paulsgrove	Portsmouth	Hants
Spotted Cow	131 London Road	Cowplain	Portsmouth	Hants
Spotted Cow	Selsey Road	Hunston	Chichester	W. Sussex
Square Brewery	The Square		Petersfield	Hants
Stag	183 New Road	Copnor	Portsmouth	Hants
Still and West	2 Bath Square		Old Portsmouth	Hants
Temple	82 Forest Road	Liss Forest	Liss	Hants
Thatched House	8 Limmer Lane	Felpham	Bognor Regis	W. Sussex
Thomas à Becket	146 Rectory Road		Worthing	W. Sussex

Name	Address	Town	County
Three Horseshoes		Bighton	Nr. Alresford	Hants
Three Horseshoes		East Worldham	Nr. Alton	Hants
Travellers Joy	325 Main Road	Southbourne	Emsworth	Hants
Trax	59 North Street		Havant	Hants
Uncle Tom's Cabin	38 Havant Road	Cosham	Portsmouth	Hants
Unicorn	High Street		Bognor Regis	W. Sussex
Union	Watch House Lane		Cowes	Isle of Wight
Vine	School Green Road		Freshwater	Isle of Wight
Vine			Hannington	Isle of Wight
Vintage Inn	Winchester Road	Shedfield	Nr. Fareham	Hants
Vth Hants Volunteer Arms	74 Albert Road		Southsea	Hants
White Buck Inn	Bisterne Close		Burley	Hants
White Hart	Dover Road		East Cowes	Isle of Wight
White Horse	39 Chichester Road	South Bersted	Bognor Regis	Sussex
White Horse	High Street	Whitwell	Ventnor	Isle of Wight
White Horse	The Square	Westbourne	Emsworth	Hants
White Horse	Priors Dean		Nr. Petersfield	Hants
Whyte Harte	High Street	Hamble	Southampton	Hants
Wickham Arms	102 Bognor Road		Chichester	W. Sussex
Windsor Castle	33 St Thomas' Road		Gosport	Hants
Woodcock	Church Road	Beacon Hill	Hindhead	Surrey
Woodman	18 London Road	Purbrook	Portsmouth	Hants
Woodman	Hammerpot	Angmering	Littlehampton	Sussex
Wykeham Arms	75 Kingsgate Street		Winchester	Hants
Wyvern	Common Barn Lane		Lee-on-Solent	Hants

Select bibliography

Manuscript sources

Barclay's Bank, Commercial Road, Portsmouth

George Gale and Co. Property Deeds.

East Sussex Record Office, Lewes

Richard Rogers Gale to Elizabeth Newman, May 1879.

George Gale and Co., Horndean

Balance Sheets and Annual Accounts 1907–39.
H. F. Bowyer's Pocket Book 1896–1935.
Cash Summary Book 1932–66.
Chairman's Annual Statements.
Collection of Property Deeds.
Gale and Co. Minute Books 1888–1927; 1927–78; 1936–65 (loose leaf); 1966–78.
List of Properties and Consumption 1930–34.
Managed and Tenanted House List August 1989.
Monthly Returns 1959–64; 1965–84.
Ordinary Share Certificates 1888–1927.
Preference Share Certificates 1888–1955.
Private Ledger Nos 2, 3, 4, 6, 7, 1895–1902; 1903–11; 1912–19; 1929–35; 1936–44.
Schedule of Properties 26 September 1898.
Summary Book 1938–57.
Typescript notes by E. T. Argyle, n.d.

Guildford Muniment Room

RB 670 Bowyer MS.
Stoke Parish Register 1877.

Guildhall Library, London

MS 14989/7–17 Royal Farmers Insurance Company, Minute Books 1845–69.

Hampshire Record Office, Winchester

B/2/A Episcopal Visitation Returns, 1725.
20 M81/A/PX1 Horndean Parish Council Minutes 1894–1944.
43M75/E/B2/1 Clarke-Jervoise Estate papers.
57M92/4 Clarke-Jervoise Estate papers.
Horndean Tithe Map, 1842.

Portsmouth City Records Office

CHU 2/1C/16 St Thomas Portsmouth Marriage Register 1851–55.
CHU 3/1B/14, 15 St Mary's Portsea Parish Baptism Register 1827; 1828.
CHU 36/1B/2 St Jude's Southsea Marriage Register 1870–89.
CHU 39/1A/3 Chalton Parish Register 1747–1807.
CHU 39/1A/5 Chalton Parish Register 1813–92.
CHU 39/1B/2 Chalton Parish Marriage Register 1838–1938.
CHU 40/1B/1 Blendworth Parish Baptism Register 1813–1914.
CHU 40/1C/2 Blendworth Parish Marriage Register 1837–1929.
CHU 40/2/2, 3 Blendworth Churchwardens' Accounts and Vestry Minute Book 1706–83; 1785–1862; 1865–96.
CHU 40/3/1 Blendworth Free School Account Book 1702–1827.
CHU 40/3/7 Blendworth Transcripts and Monumental Inscriptions.
CHU 40/4/3 Papers *re* building of Blendworth Church 1849–52.
CHU 40/4/4 Papers *re* Appleford's charity.
CHU 41/1A/7 Catherington Parish Baptism Register 1868–94.
CHU 41/1B/1–3 Catherington Parish Baptism Register 1813–42; 1842–68; 1868–94.
CHU41/1D/1, 2 Catherington Parish Burial Register 1813–56; 1856–1900.
CHU41/13/14 Catherington Parish Magazines 1919–26.
Parish of Portsea Rate Books 1861; 1868–85; 1891; 1896.
PR/H7/2/1/3–8 Annual Reports, Royal Hospital, Portsmouth 1879–1914.
S3/56, 98, 114 Borough Sessions Papers, Depositions 1711, 1732, 1741.

Public Record Office

HO107/396 Census of Great Britain 1841.
HO107/1677 Census of Great Britain 1851.
RG9/699 Census of Great Britain 1861.
Prob 11/1667 Will of Michael Bowyer dated 30 March 1822.
WO 30/48. War Office, Miscellanea, Survey of Inns 1686.

Private Ownership

George A. Gale, Private Ledger 1888–1914. In the possession of Major W. R. N. Ladds.

Whitbread Archive, London

365/1–4 Brickwood and Co. Ltd, Directors' Minute Books.
386/6 Portsmouth and Brighton United Breweries Ltd, Directors' Minute Books.

Printed primary sources

Calender of Home Office Papers 1760–1765; 1773–1775.
Calendar of Treasury Books 1710.
Minutes of the Meetings of the Town Council of Portsmouth 1919.
Poll Books for Hampshire 1705; 1736; 1780; 1790.

Oral interview

Major R. W. Gale, 22 July 1983.

Contemporary magazines and newspapers

Magazines

Annual Register, 1758–1918.
Gentleman's Magazine, 1731–1800.
Nautical Magazine, 1834–38.
The Hampshire Repository, 1799.

Newspapers

Hampshire Telegraph, 1799–1942.
Hampshire Post, 1875–76.
London Gazette, 1709–11.
Portsmouth Evening News, 1883–1914.
Portsmouth Times, 1887–1903.
Southsea Observer, 1874–75.
Sussex Advertiser, 1863.

The Times, 1787–1914.

Directories and Gazetteers

Dring and Fage's *Almanac and Brewers' Directory* (1876)
The Hants and Dorset Court Guide (1897).
Kelly's Directory of Hampshire and the Isle of Wight (1939).
Kelly's Directory of Portsmouth (1853); (1880); (1895); (1898); (1903); (1910); (1913–14); (1920); (1939).
Kelly's Directory of Wiltshire and Dorsetshire (1895).
The Manual for British and Foreign Brewing Companies for 1936–37.
Post Office Directory of Hampshire (1855).
Post Office Directory of Hampshire (1859).
Post Office Directory of Wiltshire (1875).
White's Directory of Hampshire (1859); (1878).

Official publications

Air Force Retired List 1984.
Army List January 1927; January 1930; October 1940.
BPP: *Reports from Select Committee on the Telephone Service, 1895–98* (Dublin, 1971)
Monopolies and Mergers Commission, *Supply of Beer*, Cmnd. 651 (1989).
Royal Flying Corps: Casualties and Honours during the War of 1914–17 (comp. G. L. Campbell) (1987 reprint).
Royal Air Force List April 1918; 1955–80.

Printed secondary Sources

Albert, W. and Harvey, P. D. A. (eds), *Portsmouth and Sheet Turnpike Commissioners' Minute Book 1711–54* (Portsmouth Record Series, 2, 1973).
Barber, N., *Where Have All the Breweries Gone?* (Swinton, Lancs., 1981).
Brewers and Licensed Retailers Association (BLRA) (formerly Brewers' Society) *Statistical Handbook* (London, 1997).
Brown, J., *Steeped in Tradition: The Malting Industry in England Since the Railway Age* (Reading, 1983).
Bruce, G., *Kimberley Ale: The Story of Hardys and Hansons 1832–1982* (London, 1982).

Carus-Wilson, E. M., (ed.), *Essays in Economic History*, vol. 2 (London, 1962).

Childers, S. (ed.), *A Mariner of England* (London, 1970 edn).

Cloake, M. M., (ed.), *A Persian at the Court of King George 1809–10* (London, 1988).

Curwen, E. C., *The Journal of Gideon Mantell* (Oxford, 1940).

Dunn, M., *Local Brew: Traditional Breweries and their Ales* (London, 1986).

Fryde, E. B., Greenway, D. E., Porter, S. and Roy, I. (eds), *Handbook of British Chronology* (London, 1986).

Gourvish, T. R., *Norfolk Beers from English Barley: A History of Steward and Patteson, 1793–1963* (Norwich, 1987).

Gourvish, T. R. and Wilson, R.G., *The British Brewing Industry 1830–1980* (Cambridge, 1994).

Gutzke, D. W., *Protecting the Pub: Brewers and Publicans against Temperance* (Woodbridge, 1989).

Harrison, B., *Drink and the Victorians: The Temperance Question in England, 1815–1872* (London, 1971).

Hawkins, K. H. and Pass, C. L., *The Brewing Industry: A Study in Industrial Organisation and Public Policy* (London, 1979).

Janes, H., *The Red Barrel: A History of Watney Mann* (London, 1963).

Lewis, S., *A Topographical Dictionary of England* (4 vols, London, 1842 edn).

Low, D. M. (ed.), *Gibbon's Journal to January 28th, 1763* (London, 1929).

Luttrell, N., *A Brief Historical Relation of State Affairs from September 1678 to April 1714* (6 vols, Oxford, 1857).

Mathias, P., *The Brewing Industry in England, 1700–1830* (Cambridge, 1959).

Mathias, P., *The First Industrial Nation* (2nd edn, London, 1983).

Mitchell, B. R. and Deane, P., *Abstract of British Historical Statistics* (Cambridge, 1962).

Monckton, H. A., *A History of the English Public House* (London, 1969).

Parsons, R. J., *Catherington: The Church and Village* (Catherington, 1986).

Pinkerton, J., (ed.), *A General Collection of the Best and Most Interesting Voyages and Travels in all Parts of the World* (17 vols, London, 1808–14).

Potter, J., *The Traveller's Pocket-Book* (17th edn, London, 1775).

Quennell, P. (ed.), *Memoirs of William Hickey* (London, 1960).

Serocold, W. P., *The Story of Watneys* (St Albans, 1949).

Smith, J. H., *Grayshott: The Story of a Hampshire Village* (Petersfield, 1978).

Stapleton, B., *Waterlooville: A Pictorial History* (Chichester, 1996).

Stapleton, B. and Thomas, J. H. (eds), *The Portsmouth Region* (Gloucester, 1989).

Stratton, J. M., *Agricultural Records 220–1977* (2nd edn, London, 1978).

Vaizey, J., *The Brewing Industry 1886–1951: An Economic Study* (London, 1960).

Webb, J., *Portsmouth Free Mart Fair: The Last Phase 1800–1847* (The Portsmouth Papers, no. 35, 1982).

Wilson, G. B., *Alcohol and the Nation: A Contribution to the Study of the Liquor Problem in the United Kingdom from 1800 to 1935* (London, 1940).

Wilson, R. G., *Greene King: A Business and Family History* (London, 1983).

Wolf, L. (ed.), *Essays in Jewish History* (London, 1934).

Wrigley, E. A. and Schofield, R. S., *The Population History of England, 1541–1871: A Reconstruction* (London, 1981).

Journal articles

Dingle, A. R., 'Drink and Working-Class Living Standards in Britain 1870–1914', *Economic History Review*, 2nd series, **25**, no. 4 (1972), pp. 608–22.

Macdonagh, O., 'The Origins of Porter', *Economic History Review*, 2nd series, **16**, no. 3 (1964), pp. 530–35.

Pelham, R. A., 'The Agricultural Revolution in Hampshire, with special reference to the Acreage Returns of 1801', *Proceedings of the Hampshire Field Club*, **18** (1951–53), pp. 139–53.

Sigsworth, E. M., 'Science and the Brewing Industry, 1850–1900', *Economic History Review*, 2nd series, **17**, no. 3 (1965), pp. 536–50.

Unpublished studies

Anon., 'Records of the Manor of Chalton' (typescript study, 1959, copy in Portsmouth Central Library).

Griffiths, J. M., 'The Rev. Charles Joseph, Leader of the Portsmouth Sound Purity Organisation' (unpublished dissertation, Portsmouth Polytechnic 1984).

McIntyre, J., 'Rowlands Castle, Hampshire, 1790s to 1860s' (unpublished dissertation, Portsmouth Polytechnic, 1986).

Thomas, J. H., 'Dirty but Necessary: The Coal Trade of Portsmouth and the Solent Ports 1700–1830' (unpublished paper, 1988).

Thomas, S. L., 'Living off the Land: A Study of Portsea Island Agriculture, 1793–1851' (unpublished dissertation, Portsmouth Polytechnic, 1985).

Worton, B., 'The Parish of Blendworth, Hampshire, 1700 to 1851' (unpublished dissertation, Portsmouth Polytechnic, 1982).

Index